WRENCHED FROM THE LAND

WRENCHED FROM THE LAND

ACTIVISTS INSPIRED BY EDWARD ABBEY

INTERVIEWS WITH **ML LINCOLN**

EDITED BY **ML LINCOLN** AND **DIANE SWARD RAPAPORT**

FOREWORD BY **BILL McKIBBEN**

University of New Mexico Press | Albuquerque

ISBN 978-0-8263-6152-3 (paperback)
ISBN 978-0-8263-6153-0 (electronic)

Library of Congress Control Number: 2019955126

Cover illustration: *The Needles* by John De Puy
Frontispiece: Dave Foreman, cofounder of Earth First!, and Tim DeChristopher, climate activist, 2014. Photographer Merrick Chase.
Designed by Felicia Cedillos
Composed in Sabon LT Std 10/14

To Cynthia, my sister,
who truly loved everything about the Southwest and
to Diane Rapaport, my longtime friend and camping buddy.

Contents

Foreword

BILL MCKIBBEN

I was unprepared for how much I was going to like this book—I inhaled it in the course of a day, and then went back to re-read many of the interviews. Each on its own is powerful, but together they paint a group portrait of a time, a place, and a way of looking at the world that offers some nostalgic solace, but also some astute counsel for moving ahead into our current mess. The moral seriousness—and the articulate eloquence—of the people in these pages puts most American intellectual and activist communities I know to shame. The steadfastness and endurance that has clearly animated their lives is testament to the power of the landscape. And yet there is a good deal of mischief, too, and that is where Ed Abbey perhaps comes in.

Abbey had a great many important ideas about the world, and he was also one of the funniest writers America ever produced. No author that I can think of produced two books as disparately great as *Desert Solitaire* and *The Monkey Wrench Gang*. The first is a twentieth-century Walden, but where is Thoreau's comic novel? The second is latter-day Twain, but where are Sam Clemens's great essays? And above and around all that, Abbey was a character of the first order, the kind of character that has mostly died out in our cultural life. I met him but twice, once for an excursion into Arches (which required, in an effort to avoid paying the federal government a ten-dollar entrance fee, that we take down a fence and drive my rental Buick through a sandy wash), and once in Tucson, not far from the bungalow where Dave Foreman and others were producing the *Earth First! Journal*. He left an impression on me, of course, but then he left an impression on all his readers. I remember Wendell Berry once saying that the rule in his house was he couldn't read Abbey at bedtime, because he would cackle and giggle half the night. Me too.

But as this volume makes abundantly clear, he was also, in his particular way, a great activist. Not of the organizing variety, but of the creative variety: he knew what stories would work to make people mad and inspired. And since stories are how we understand and act on the world, that made him crucial. It is no wonder that Earth First!'s first action was unrolling a crack down Glen Canyon Dam—that's a touch straight out of Abbey, and I think it might not have occurred to anyone otherwise. He knew that people respond to charts and graphs, yes, but that we mainly respond to romance, to bravery, to humor—he knew that we pull over to look at a crash.

I should say that I'm not really a member of the same club as these interviewees, though a number of them are friends and a couple of them dear ones. Mostly, that's because I'm from the East—those "fuzzy hills" that Abbey wanted to escape but that draw me in even more than the stark vistas of the West. Our wilderness is no less powerful than the red rock and the pinon country (meet me in the center of the Adirondacks someday or on the wintry slopes of the Presidentials), but its outlines are more or less settled: we've known for a good long time what is protected and what isn't. So the fights over land are less wrenching.

Which is good because it's given us mental room to take on some other battles, maybe most important, the fight against climate chaos. Those are the key battles of our time, sometimes engaged in the landscape of the West—Tim DeChristopher's noble bid for drilling leases is the perfect example—but often engaged in landscapes more emotionally arid and literally moist, Washington, DC, for instance. And I can say that as I've tried to balance writing with activism, I've found myself drawing on the Abbey tool kit again and again. It's true that a few of the conceits haven't aged that well: it's not as much fun to attack the Sahara Club anymore, because the actual Sierra Club has reformed itself and become a crack fighting force against the coal plants Abbey hated. It turned out that educating girls and empowering women were the best weapons in the population fight—that's how we've gone from the average woman having 6 kids apiece to 2.3. He was pushing the boundaries of political correctness when he wrote, and those borders have grown much tighter; I worry that there are some young people today who can't read past the provocations, but I trust there are many more who can.

His spirit—grounded in a particular place, defiant, fierce, and full of laughter at his own good jokes—lives very much on in the people he reached. Many of them are in these pages, and it is necessary and enriching to have their memories. But far, far more are people who simply read, and never forgot, his words.

Introduction

The story behind the publication of this book and the making of my two documentary films *Drowning River* (2007) and *Wrenched* (2014) began when I met Charles "Chuck" Bowden.

His book *Blue Desert* struck me for its descriptions of how growth had ravaged the lands of the West and the people who lived there. I had just moved to Tucson in 1989 to finish a degree in photography. Chuck and I agreed to have supper in a south Tucson restaurant, where he introduced me to his favorite Mexican soup, menudo, of tripe and pigs feet. I remember pretending to love it as much as he did. This was the year author Edward Abbey died, and Tucson was feeling the loss of one of America's most uncompromising, irascible, and humorous defenders of Southwest lands.

At dinner, Chuck talked about the loss of his friend Ed. In our conversation, and in many to follow, the force of what Chuck believed, the way he spoke about his love of birdwatching, and his passion for a place or person riveted my attention.

Years later, in his interview for *Wrenched*, Chuck said,

> An odd thing happened in my life. As long as Ed Abbey was alive, I thought I could just drink, fornicate, and do whatever I wanted—because he was tending the shop. When he died, I suddenly realized I had this crushing burden. I got far more involved in practical land issues than I had before. Over about a ten-year period, I worked with people to lock up about a million acres.

Wrenched from the Land

In March 2017, I was fuming over the reckless and regressive politics of the new administration, which placed the environment and Native American lands under siege. In front of me was a bookcase with twenty-five large notebooks of thousands of pages of transcripts of interviews that I had amassed during the making of *Wrenched*. Here were the heroes that carried the legacy of Edward Abbey's ideas into the twenty-first century. They represent a potent counter to anti-conservation politicians and climate deniers. Suddenly something clicked. I remembered Kieran Suckling, cofounder of the Center for Biological Diversity, saying to me, "Activism is not waiting for your opponent to retire." That's when I decided to publish this book.

Out of forty interviews, my editor, Diane Sward Rapaport, and I chose to feature sixteen. Some were Abbey's closest friends and staunchest allies who tell stories about hiking or monkeywrenching with Abbey. They are not an idol worshipper's crowd. None put him on a pedestal.

Four reveal how they became the inspiration for Abbey's most memorable characters in his comic masterpiece, *The Monkey Wrench Gang*. Although they admit to likenesses, they also say that the characters most resembled Abbey himself.

Many talk about the impact of Abbey's words. As climate activist Tim DeChristopher said in his interview,

> The really powerful thing I learned from Edward Abbey is this. It really does take action to make us whole again, to put us in that right place, and to fix our soul. So I really feel like I owe Abbey a debt of gratitude. He planted seeds in my head a long time ago, and my thoughts grew and grew until finally I couldn't hold them in anymore.

Beyond Abbey's influence are the mesmerizing stories activists tell about what motivated them to become passionately committed to their causes. Many started formidable movements and gathered impressive followings of their own. They lit the flame of environmental activism and changed the course of contemporary conservation history. They turned their rage into lifelong commitments and gave the movement its soul.

None considered what they were doing as a job or career. To them it was what Dave Foreman, cofounder of Earth First!, calls "holy work."

The Lure of Wild Places

Wilderness is not a luxury but a necessity of the human spirit, and as vital to our lives as water and good bread. A civilization which destroys what little remains of the wild, the spare, the original, is cutting itself off from its origins and betraying the principle of civilization itself.

—EDWARD ABBEY, *Desert Solitaire*, 1968, p. 211

My first connection with wilderness began when I was a child. We were living in rural Connecticut, which had its own special geology. When the Ice Age glaciers receded, they revealed spectacular rock formations, rolling hills, and lakes. My brother and I were explorers as we ventured out all day long with our collie Texas as our babysitter.

In the 1960s, I lived a very simple life in the Vermont woods in a cabin with no electricity or running water. I grew a garden and bathed in the cold stream out back. I fell in love with the expansive silence and beauty.

From then on I understood what connection means to wild places and sought them out. They nourished my curiosity and kept me sane. I hiked the canyons of the Colorado Plateau, visited remote ruins in the Yucatan, and trekked in the western Himalayas in Nepal, naïvely hoping to enter Tibet.

In the early 1990s, my feisty activist friend, seventy-five-year-old Katie Lee, invited me to be her tentmate on a twenty-one-day trek in the Pamir Mountains of central Asia's Tajikistan (formerly of the Soviet Union) and the Silk Road cities of Uzbekistan. It wasn't just the untrammeled wilderness of these remote high mountain ranges and wild rivers that awed me but also my encounters with its nomadic people. As natural healers and ecologists, they taught me much about their deeply rooted connection to the earth and the plants and animals on which their health and spiritual lives depended.

One day I came down with flu-like symptoms. I was dizzy and heard helicopters when there were none. Along the trail we stopped at an isolated yurt, and a young Tajik woman served tea, bread, and yogurt. As we left to continue on our fifteen-mile trek to camp, the woman suddenly rushed out to hand me her baby daughter. As I held her, I understood that the mother wanted me to take her out of the Soviet Union. Strange as it seems, though, I had previously considered adopting. But in this encounter I knew it was impossible.

A Call to Action

The world has changed since Edward Abbey died. So much of what he predicted has come to pass. The Southwest lands he fought to save are overwhelmed by millions of visitors and industrialists bent on pillaging its natural resources.

Ed would likely not have foreseen hundreds of thousands of teenagers from all over the world skipping school so they could protest a planet wounded and imperiled by climate change. Ed would have applauded the courage and noncomplacency of sixteen-year-old Swedish student Greta Thunberg, who, in April 2019, challenged members of the English Houses of Parliament with her words: "You lied to us. You gave us false hope. You told us that the future was something to look forward to . . . We children are doing this because we want our hopes and dreams back."

The importance of our collective call to action is summed up by the statement made by Tim DeChristopher at his sentencing hearing on August 4, 2011, for bidding on oil and gas leases, which months later were termed an illegal Utah BLM auction:

> Those who are inspired to follow my actions are those who understand that we are on a path toward catastrophic climate change. They know their future is on the line. Given the destruction of our democratic institutions that once gave citizens access to power, my future will likely involve civil disobedience. Nothing that happens here today will change that. You have authority over my life but not my principles . . . I want you to join me in valuing this country's rich history of nonviolent civil disobedience . . . The choice you are making today is: What side are you on?

The strong alliances forged between early conservationists like John Muir and Rachel Carson, the activist leaders in this book, and legions of new protestors give us hope that the increasingly disastrous effects of climate change can yet be mitigated. We can no longer be passive against mass extinction, nihilism, and greed. We are being wrenched from the lands that sustain us.

Edward Abbey in Turkey Pens Ruins, Grand Gulch, Utah, 1988. Photographer Mark Klett.

WRENCHED FROM THE LAND

1 | CHARLES "CHUCK" BOWDEN

Biography

Charles "Chuck" Bowden's activism bears out the old adage: "The pen is mightier than the sword." His writing is renowned for its passionate defense of wilderness; relentless condemnation of the hypocrisy of corrupt politicians, border police, drug dealers, and criminals; and his eloquence on behalf of the Mexican poor.

He has written more than twenty-five books including *Killing the Hidden Waters* (1977), *Blue Desert* (1986), *Frog Mountain Blues* (1987), and *Red Line* (1989).

Bowden was the first American to write about the anarchy that resulted from the drug wars in Mexico and border violence in such books as *Down by the River: Drugs, Money, Murder and Family* (2002), *Murder City: Ciudad Juárez and the Global Economy's New Killing Fields* (2010), and *Some of the Dead Are Still Breathing: Living in the Future* (2009). He once walked across the desert with the *immigrados* in the heat of June just to be able to report with firsthand veracity on its brutality. When he came out, he laid on the floor of a Basque Bar in Tacna, Arizona, and told the bartender to keep bringing him water: "I drank for eight hours before I could urinate. That's how far gone I was."

Chuck was introduced to Ed Abbey by conservationist Dave Foreman in the early 1980s in Tucson, Arizona, and they became friends. Bowden said, "Ed Abbey made us understand that we were killing the last good place."

Charles Bowden meets Edward Abbey. Chuck had an interview with Dave
Foreman so I came along to make a few images for the *Tucson Daily Citizen*
newspaper, and when we arrived Abbey said no photos. So I slung the camera
around my neck and, using a wide angle lens, grabbed a few images without
looking through the camera. I was not fooling anyone, but they really didn't care
just so I wasn't posing folks, and I grabbed a few spontaneous moments like the
introduction and a pensive Abbey. (Mid-1980s.) Photographer P. K. Weis.

When Bowden died in 2014, all those who knew of his work felt they
had lost a most powerful voice for the Southwest.

Bowden partnered with many photographers to capture these "last
good places"—among them, *The Sierra Pinacate* (1998; with Julia D.
Hayden), *Stone Canyons of the Colorado Plateau* (1996; with Jack W.
Dykinga), and *Inferno* (2006; with Bill and Alice Wright).

My interview with Chuck took place at a historic inn, in Mesilla, New
Mexico, and on the banks of the Rio Grande. Chuck commented, "This
is the second-greatest river in the American West. The Colorado is the
greatest. Now they're both tombs of their ecosystems."

ML Lincoln: To read any of your work is to understand that you have a deep love of the natural world. Can you talk about this?

Chuck Bowden: When people ask me what "love of the land" means, I say if you ask the question, you'll never understand the answer. Love of the land is just a bunch of little noises you make in a language. I was born feeling closer to the earth than I felt to my government or human beings. It just is. I've never had any interest in nature as other people talk about it. I love life. I hate national parks—even though I helped create a few—because, in a sense, they say, "Well, this is the part of nature that's special."

My favorite part of the desert isn't Monument Valley or some cretinous place where people go with their goddamn cameras. It's to stop the car, get out, walk a couple of miles into a creosote flat where there's no topography, but just these carefully spaced creosote bushes.

If you do a 360-degree turn you can't find a center to it. You just sleep, lie down there, and spend days. The key to the desert is that it has no center. There's such a diminution of water that it gives you this sense of limitless place.

When you're in the desert, God—if there is a God—is everywhere. It's not: you go to the desert to find the Holy Mountain. The desert is a Zen state. It's a very sparse biomass that hasn't got a Jerusalem. That's what I like. I like being in a place where I cease to exist. I once spent ten days in June fifty miles from a road in the Cabeza Prieta, which gets maybe one to three inches of water a year. I was alone. I plopped down in this totally uninhabited place that is thousands of square miles.

What I noticed as the days went on is that I lost consciousness of where my body ended and the world began. It's called the oceanic experience in Freudian psychology. I lost all boundaries. I also noticed the wildlife lost all boundaries. Every night I'd lay down on my tarp with my sheet—Christ, it was 110 degrees out there—and just doze off. And at the same time every night, a coyote would crawl up near my head and howl and then run away. It would wake me up.

I was camped with twelve vultures. There was a dead coyote about twenty yards from where I threw down my bag. The vultures spent a

Charles Bowden hiking Paria Canyon. Photographer Jack Dykinga.

whole week disassembling a coyote, and we just lived together. I'd walk a half a mile up to the water hole and there were hundreds of bighorn sheep grouped there because it was the heart of June, and there was hardly any water left.

I would sit on a rock, and they'd walk around me. And every day, I think it was at noon, a golden eagle landed and took a bath. And he would leave. As soon as he left, a red-tailed hawk would land and take a bath. And the vultures would come up once a day and they'd all line up like penguins, based on their pecking order. And they would each drink, each in turn. This went on for days.

I lost my identity. You go out there and think you'll write and be profound. I couldn't even write words. I became a very happy idiot. And I regretted coming back. I've always regretted that I returned from that trip.

When I came back, I started a magazine. It was like entering hell. I had employees, advertisers, all the things you never want to meet in life.

ML: I was living in Tucson then and remember one of your first articles in *City Magazine* was about the Colorado River.

Bowden: The history of the Colorado River is progressive murder.

The Colorado Compact in 1922 divided the water in the river among seven states. It said the flow was sixteen million acre-feet. Big lie. Then came the dams. Hoover Dam cut off the flow to the Colorado Delta, which was one of the richest biological zones in North America. Aldo Leopold said it was the greatest wilderness he'd ever seen on Earth. It was the nursery of a lot of species in the Pacific. The Delta died. Never got another drop of water. It was a kind of genocide of species. The most endangered porpoise on Earth, the vaquita, is virtually gone from there.

Finally, the Bureau of Reclamation tried to put a dam at the confluence of the Yampa and Green Rivers at Echo Park, Utah, in Dinosaur National Monument and got beaten back. During the late fifties and early sixties, the Bureau built Glen Canyon Dam on the Colorado River between Arizona and Utah. Now we're dealing with a manmade disaster. What was the greatest river in the American West is now one big pipe full of chemicals, sewage, and spillover from agriculture. It's a tomb of an ecosystem. And it gets worse as you go down the stream.

That's it in a nutshell. The short version: human greed destroyed life.

ML: I read that someone once asked Floyd Dominy, who was the former head of the Bureau of Reclamation and helped push Glen Canyon Dam through Congress in the 1950s, "What about the silting? What are you going to do about that?" And he said, "Well, I'm going to let the next generation think about it."

Bowden: That's right. Look, there are two things that have time stamps on them, and then they expire. One is irrigated land. No one has ever irrigated on Earth without eventually having a problem when silt builds up. And the second thing is a dam. No matter what you do, it fills in behind with silt.

All you have to do is go up in the Rocky Mountains in Colorado.

Walk up any stream and you get these little benches of meadows, and they're almost invariably from beaver dams. Beavers build a dam, it silts in, becomes meadow stream, and cuts other channels—that's just life.

They tried to stabilize the Mississippi River and destroyed the wetlands and the Delta of the Mississippi in Louisiana. But the river is still going to move. Eventually, New Orleans will not be on the river. The river will swing further west, and New Orleans will be stranded. In the meantime, we've spent billions channelizing it.

Building dams is always temporary. Now, in the United States, we literally—except for a few places—ran out of dam sites. Between the Corps of Engineers and the Bureau of Reclamation, two organizations dominated by cement heads, they put the goddamn things everywhere and created natural disasters.

Now we're in a circumstance where the Colorado River is dying and silting is occurring behind Glen Canyon Dam. Someday there might not be a dam. It may just be a wall with no water behind it.

ML: What was *The Monkey Wrench Gang* influence on dam building?

Bowden: What Ed Abbey did in *The Monkey Wrench Gang* was make a shift in people's heads from moaning about the canyon they lost to deconstructing the dam. He made us realize we've gone down a road that's fatal to us, to the ground around us, and to what we call our civilization. Ed made us recognize that we'd done something terrible, and we're not going to do it anymore. We need to fix and restore. He made that almost a national idea.

What the book says is that the salvation of the United States and of the planet is blowing up the property that's killing it—in this case, Glen Canyon Dam. And the reason the book has never been made into a movie, in my opinion, is for one simple reason: the boys who sign the checks get frightened when you want to make a movie about destroying the infrastructure of the country to save it.

The Monkey Wrench Gang is an incendiary device bound as a book, but it's a ribald, comic novel so the reader will accept it. If it were a serious novel, nobody would ever be able to make it through it. I never could get through *Walden Pond*. As far as I'm concerned, Thoreau is a goddamn bore. But there are millions of people, literally, who read *The Monkey Wrench Gang*—and considered it a great contribution—and laughed as they read it and remembered every scene.

And it really worked. I talked to Senator Barry Goldwater a couple of years before he died up at his house in Phoenix, and he said, "There'll never be another Glen Canyon Dam built in this country. That's over." I knew Stewart Udall, who served as US secretary of the interior from 1961 to 1969, and he said that creating the dam was the tragedy of his generation.

STEWART UDALL

Throughout Stewart Udall's distinguished career (1920–2010), he fought, wrote, and lectured about the preservation of wilderness treasures and the importance of clean air and water. Among Udall's accomplishments as secretary of the interior from 1961 to 1969 was overseeing the addition of four national parks, six national monuments, eight national seashores and lakeshores, nine national recreation areas, twenty national historic sites, and fifty-six national wildlife refuges, among them Canyonlands National Park in Utah, North Cascades National Park in Washington, and Redwood National Park in California, according to a March 28, 2010, article written by Kurt Repanshek, "Stewart Udall: A Model of a Conservationist," in NationalParksTraveler.org.

A pioneer of the environmental movement, Udall warned of the dangers of pollution, overuse of natural resources, and dwindling open spaces in the United States in his best-selling book *The Quiet Crisis* (1963), revised in 1988 with the addition of nine new chapters, including "The Myth of Superabundance."

The book isn't even a novel of imaginary characters. Anybody that actually knows Ed's world knows he just copied people he knew for the novel. I told him once, "You know, I really think you're a pretty good novelist, except I know your friends." Abbey's imagination gave a plot to their lives. Everybody around Ed, including me, wanted to blow up the goddamn dam. He invented a sort of comic scenario and he implanted the idea. The real idea about blowing up Glen Canyon Dam was that Abbey was talking about a real tragedy that had to be undone so that the Colorado River would run free again.

But that was part of the joy of Abbey, at least to me, because I find life ridiculous. Once you know life's a tragedy, which it is, you have to laugh or you're not going to make it. It's a kind of strange movie God created, that nobody gets out of life alive. Even when you start this movie, you know how it's going to end. You die. That's why humor is essential—and red wine.

ML: Disaster to the Dam almost happened in 1983? What did you do?

Bowden: In the spring of 1983, there was such massive flow in the Colorado River that Glen Canyon Dam started to shake, and the engineers thought it might go. You know, I almost went back to church. I thought: There is a God, if he gets rid of this bastard.

What I wanted was to see the effect of the flows on the Delta at the Sea of Cortez. I had a friend, Bill Broyles, and we consulted the tide charts. We wanted to be there when we could get the highest tides in the Sea of Cortez that year, which I think was late February or early March. We rented a canoe, drove to Yuma, threw it in the river, and rode the river all the way to the sea. For the first time since Hoover Dam was built, the river made it to the Sea of Cortez.

We got down to the Delta, which had been dead for, what, fifty years, and it was exploding with life: plants, animals, everything. It was magnificent.

At the Gulf, you get one of the highest tides in the world. When the tide comes in, it is so high that it rides on top of the river and races north. And if you're on the river when this happens, you die. It took out steamboats in the nineteenth century. So we rolled the goddamn canoe down there, pulled it way up on shore—we had a tide chart—and waited. The moon came out. And this huge wall of water raced up the

Colorado River. Thousands of birds started screaming, because it was a freak occurrence.

Now, that has never happened again in my lifetime, and it won't happen again until we blow up Hoover and Glen Canyon. So I have a feeling for the Delta that's not just based on Aldo Leopold saying it was a great wilderness. I've been carrying that with me. I was there for this brief moment when it came back to life before it got murdered again by the US government and my fellow citizens.

ML: You devoted some part of your life to creating national monuments. Could you talk about why?

Bowden: An odd thing happened in my life. As long as Ed Abbey was alive, I thought I could just drink, fornicate, and do whatever I wanted—because he was tending the shop. When he died, I suddenly realized I had this crushing burden. I got far more involved in practical land issues than I had before. Over about a ten-year period, I worked with people to lock up about a million acres.

During that period I asked Doug Peacock, whom I've known for years, "Well, how did you decide what to do?" He said, "When I'm out there and I see something that doesn't belong there, I fuck with it." I said, "Okay. Now I know the ground rules!"

What I did was help create the Sonoran Desert National Monument in south-central Arizona. I also had a hand in establishing the Escalante Grand Staircase National Monument in Utah. I didn't do it by myself. Nobody can do it alone. I contributed everything I could at the time.

I knew when I was doing this that refuges would never be permanent solutions, they're stopgaps. I helped create these monuments to save species—kind of like Noah's Ark—until this firestorm of destruction and greed passes, so that when the war of human beings against other life forms had passed, these other life forms could repopulate.

I never would have done that if Ed hadn't died. So in that sense, Edward Abbey fucked up my life. It's the best I could do in my lifetime. When I come back in my next life, and I'm God, I'll do a fuller job.

SONORAN DESERT NATIONAL MONUMENT

The 496,400-acre Sonoran Desert National Monument is located east of Gila Bend, Arizona, and is but a portion of the 120,000-square-mile Sonoran Desert, which extends into California and Mexico. The monument contains some of the most biologically diverse species of plants in that desert, as well as an extensive Saguaro cactus forest. The monument contains three congressionally designated wilderness areas, which include three distinct mountain ranges, separated by wide valleys, many significant archaeological and historic sites, and remnants of several important historic trails. The monument was established by Bill Clinton's Presidential Proclamation in 2001 and is administered by the Bureau of Land Management (BLM).

Bowden's lyrical book *Inferno* (2006) describes the stark and lonesome beauty to be found in the monument. It was written while he was lobbying the government to create it. Accompanied by the stunning black-and-white photographs of Michael Berman, Bowden writes, "We need these places not to remember our better selves or our natural self or our spiritual self. We need these places to taste what we fear and devour what we are. We need these places to be animals because unless we are animals we are nothing at all."

ML: What happened when Ed Abbey died?

Bowden: When Ed Abbey died [March 14, 1989], his wife Clarke called me that morning. A bunch of people were packing Ed's body with ice and were going to haul ass out to a place I knew to bury him. Ed wrote his own epitaph: "No comment." Writerly control, you know! That's what they scratched on his headboard!

I stayed behind and wound up manning the phones. I started getting calls from media around the country asking, would I write an obit. I wrote a couple of obits and was paid a lot of money, $1,500, $2,000 per piece. I've forgotten how much. I didn't want the money. I wasn't raised to make money off the body of a friend. So I cashed all the checks, put all the cash in a grocery bag, and went down to the house where Earth First! had an office, and said, "Here. This is your problem. I don't want anything to do with this goddamn money."

ML: How would you describe Earth First!?

Bowden: I didn't even know Earth First! existed until I saw the 1982 film *The Cracking of Glen Canyon Damn* with Edward Abbey and Earth First! [produced by Christopher "Toby" McLeod, Glenn Switkes, and Randy Hayes]. That's where I saw Earth First! activists unfurl a 300-foot-long plastic banner that simulated a "crack" down the 710-foot concrete face of the dam.

You can't understand Earth First! unless you realize it was guerilla theater, street theater. They found a theatrical way to protest power. And Dave had a genius for it. I know he's a great guy and loves nature, but basically he's a snake oil guy. He could sell ice to an Eskimo. You need a guy like that. He's a great public speaker. He's fun to listen to. You don't think you're hearing a lecture. He's basically the guy you want to have a cup of coffee with or a beer.

Once I knew about the plastic crack, I didn't feel alone. I was like a lot of people who went to environmental meetings and groups—it was like going to church. There's some guy that's even holier than God in front, or a woman, talking about how they talk to a tree or some dribble. And then there's the audience, the communicants. I was tired of loving the natural world and watching the goddamn environmental movement become a sort of dull religion.

Earth First! brought fun back into what we call *environmentalism*. They also moved it past conservation, which is a kind of hobbyhorse of the rich: we'll rape the country and create a deer park somewhere. Earth First! and Edward Abbey had an outlook on the world that was ecological. It wasn't, "Let's save a viewpoint."

Dave Foreman and Earth First! created a mass movement. They made you feel you weren't crazy, that other people also thought the world was going toward Armageddon. And now it's here. People were attracted to Earth First! because it said, "Let's save the United States. We've turned our country into a natural charnel house." The most brilliant bumper sticker the boys ever cranked out was "Rednecks for Wilderness," because it was inclusive for a change. I know plenty of people that hunt and fish, etc., and love nature who can't stand being near environmentalists or the Sierra Club because they think these people look down at them, because these people have a list of who can be pious and who can't.

Earth First! didn't have any list. You were in or out. You were either going to save the natural world or you were an enemy of it. That's it. You can drink anything you want, smoke a cigar—Earth First! didn't give a damn. Actually, they had no organization. The charm was you couldn't join Earth First!; you could only belong to it. They didn't want a structure, because if there was one, some scum would show up and take it over. The only indication of membership was a subscription to the *Earth First! Journal*. When Dave and the boys started it, they wanted a sunset law—they thought Earth First! should run no more than ten years. What they wanted to accomplish was very damn simple. They wanted to take the environmental movement and all these conservation groups, and let's say their position was more toward center/right; Earth First! wanted to be so damn crazy that groups would get more radical and still look like they were moderates compared to them.

One thing that Foreman and these guys knew was you can't survive this movement unless you have a good time. I mean, Jesus Christ, we've raised a couple generations of environmentalists who define themselves by what they won't eat. This is a preposterous stance. Dave Foreman used to hand out this card that said when you die you wanted your body moved to grizzly country and left on a hillside to be recycled by a grizzly bear. I used to have one. I always liked that.

ML: Some people connect Abbey's death in 1989 and the timing of the arrest of Dave Foreman whom the FBI had been watching for years. What was your take on this?

Bowden: I never asked Dave Foreman or anybody involved what really happened that led to the FBI bust. Ed died on March 14, and the bust was on May 31. But here's what I do know. When Dave was arrested, he calls me from federal jail, because he needs bond. So I went down and said, "Here's the mortgage on my house." I owned it free and clear. Whatever people think of Dave Foreman, I knew this guy would never run. I never gave it a thought. That's not who he is. I've known him for years. He's sort of like me—he's never going to live someplace where they don't have ketchup on the table.

Then a remarkable thing happened. The court said, "Well, we don't need the bond now." They just released him on his signature.

ML: During the bust, the newspapers referred to Dave Foreman and Earth First! as terrorists.

Bowden: The people that own countries use the word *terrorism* to denounce the people who don't own countries. Now, the Earth Firsters! weren't terrorists. They were basically theatrical comedians pulling stunts. Dave Foreman and members of Earth First! had done a fair amount of monkeywrenching. They spiked trees, put sand down the fuel tanks of bulldozers. But they didn't hurt people. They didn't advocate violence. I mean, nobody in Earth First! seriously thought that because of their actions the republic would shut down.

See, Ed had a point. People get confused. They think anarchy means you're going to throw a brick through a window. But what Abbey means is an absolute—in his sense, he was a classical anarchist, meaning he didn't trust centralized power and considered any concentration of power as dangerous. But he wasn't a terrorist. That's why he was a lifelong member of the National Rifle Association—because he thought if everybody had a gun, the government would be a little more careful how it talked to us.

ML: There's a lot of fear and tension . . .

Bowden: The biggest drug in my country isn't alcohol. It isn't marijuana. It isn't heroin. It isn't cocaine. It's fear. We have a country

Portrait of writer Charles Bowden in Anapra, northwest Juárez, on the border between Mexico and the United States. Photographer Julian Cardona.

dominated by fear. I've never been afraid in my life in any real sense. People here are being raised with fear, with apprehension. Apparently, nobody ever told them they're going to die anyway. They might as well at least get laid and have a good time. They're all terrified.

Our politicians feed it. Our politicians now run for office on fear. I'm supposed to stand here on the banks of the Rio Grande and be afraid of somebody in the Middle East. I'm supposed to stand here and be afraid of some poor Mexican that just wants to get a job. You either make their world better or they'll move to a better world. If you don't want Mexicans in the neighborhood, stop creating slaves in Mexico.

This is nonsense. There's nothing to be afraid of except this, what's up there, the sky. Hoover Dam is being murdered by the sky. The rains don't come. All the Southwest forests that I've spent my life in are damaged, and not simply because of fire but because of heat and changing moisture patterns. We've got bristlecone pines on Mt. Whitney that have been there thousands of years that are dying.

I have a Hackberry tree in my yard in Tucson. All the leaves fell off around the third week in November. Now they fall off around New Year's Day. The warming is real. If you're a birdwatcher, and I am, I go through 100, 150 pounds of bird seed a month. Wherever I am, I've noticed the migrations have changed because of global warming.

Go out and talk to Arizona ranchers who basically are pretty conservative guys who live out on the land and raise beef. I never met one that didn't believe in global warming, because they have seen the species change on the ranch, and it's been in the family for five generations. They've seen springs that they've used since 1880 go dry and never come back, things that had never happened before. They know things are changing.

It's an interesting country, to live in a place where every beast in the field knows the climate's changing, but the people running the political parties don't seem to believe it. I'm sure there are goddamn animals out there with an IQ of 2 that know more about global warming than my government!

Thirty or forty years ago, global warming could have been forestalled. Now the world has changed because of it. The only thing that seems to impress my fellow citizens and get them to stop slaughtering the land is out of their hands. Global warming will lead to the collapse of the American economy and become the greatest boons to the ground we've ever seen.

Phoenix and Tucson will be dead in their tracks. Both cities are untenable. There's no way these cities can survive through time. There is no resource base for them. They're colonial outposts of an American empire, subsidized from the outside, and the sooner they die, the sooner I'll be happy.

Look, we may have to tighten our belts. But I'm not afraid, because, you know, tightening your belt doesn't end life. I've been broke a lot of times in my life, and the wine still tastes good and the girls still look pretty. I mean, it ain't the fucking end of the world to not be rich.

So we'll get through this. But we'll never get through it if we approach the changes with fear in our hearts. We have to approach it with appetite, love—lust helps too. We need to acknowledge that change is happening and say we have to share the pain. You can't be in the house on the hill when people are starving on the street. We have to share. We're like a herd of gazelles—we either hang together or die separately.

Human communities are like ecosystems. They have to have a lot of things at the table, a lot of different opinions. The late senator Daniel Moynihan said, "Every person is entitled to their own opinion but they're not entitled to their own facts." I haven't any problem with people being on the right or the left. I have a problem with them not talking to each other.

I'm patient. I believe in the future. Look, I get tired of people afraid of the future. It's the only goddamn place we're going. That's all that's left to you and the rest of your life. And if you're afraid of it, go to hell. Okay.

2 | DAVE FOREMAN

Biography

Dave Foreman is renowned for his lifelong activism to protect American wilderness. He cofounded Earth First! (1980) and the Wildlands Network (1991) and founded the Rewilding Institute (2002). Foreman is the author of seven books, including *Ecodefense: A Field Guide to Monkeywrenching* (1985), *Man Swarm and the Killing of Wildlife* (2011), and *Rewilding North America: A Vision for Conservation in the 21st Century* (2004). For more than a quarter of a century, Foreman has written a column called "Around the Campfire" to educate, provoke, and inspire conservationists. The column first appeared in the *Earth First! Journal* during the early 1980s; current and archived copies are currently found on the web pages of the Rewilding Institute. The website also offers podcasts from people involved in rewilding projects for saving nature's building blocks.

I interviewed Dave in his home in Albuquerque, New Mexico, and in the neighboring Sandia Mountains. He had returned a few months back from a twenty-two-day canoeing trip on the wild Noatak River in Alaska. He told me this story:

> The most fun I had, the great excitement, was meeting up with a musk ox. When we saw each other, the bull started snorting and pawing its feet and started chasing me. And here I am, this old crippled guy with a bad back and arthritis, running across the tundra. The other boats coming along got a great show. One of my friends

said, "You know, I can't think of a better place or way for Dave to die." I took that as a real compliment, because it's the biggest wilderness in the country, and getting stomped to death by a musk ox, you'd just be really—really Pleistocene.

Dave lives with his wife in Albuquerque, New Mexico. (www.rewilding.org)

————

ML Lincoln: How were you influenced by Ed Abbey?

Dave Foreman: Ed Abbey was a very early influence on me before I even knew who he was. When I was in the fifth grade in Albuquerque, New Mexico, smoke started coming out of one of the volcanoes on the west side of town. I was just thrilled to death: our volcano's erupting! It turned out that some college students had dumped tires and set them on fire. It wasn't until I moved back to Albuquerque after my Earth First! trial and was talking about the volcano to John De Puy—the famous Southwest artist and close friend of Abbey—who said, "Well, you know who did that?" I said no. He said, "That was Ed Abbey."

Back in 1971, a bartender friend gave me a copy of *Desert Solitaire*. There was something about Abbey's style, and what he said that really spoke to me when I read it. It was the first book that I fully agreed with. It was how I thought. I asked the bartender, "Where did you get it?" He said, "I got it from Debbie, the other bartender." In this way, Abbey was responsible for my first marriage, to Debbie Sease.

Ed's book *Desert Solitaire* captured the way a lot of us felt, particularly in the Southwest, about the land and getting out into the wilderness. The book taught me to love deserts in a way that nobody else had. For such a long time I had a medieval alpine aesthetic of what wilderness should be—high country, snow-capped mountains, and jewel-like lakes. I learned that dry lands, grasslands, and sagebrush flats were beautiful and worthy of protection.

So even before I met Ed, he was having a big influence on me.

ML: How did you develop such an all-encompassing love of nature and wilderness?

Foreman: I've always wondered why I became such a nature lover. It seemed to have been something inherent in growing up in Albuquerque and seeing the Sandia Mountains every day. To me, they were a great wilderness. We lived near the edge of town and I loved going into the desert to catch horny toads and watch prairie dogs. I've always felt connected. They were my neighbors and friends. Because my dad was in the Air Force, we frequently moved. When I was two years old, we went to the Philippines. There was something about the jungle and the snakes that really got to me.

When I was seven, we went to Bermuda for two years, and I started snorkeling and seeing coral reefs. One day, right after a hurricane hit, when you were not supposed to swim out past the reefs, I was standing on the beach when suddenly there was a commotion out on the reef. A shark had taken off the legs of a lieutenant in the British Navy who had swum out there. When they brought him on shore, there was blood everywhere. He died a couple of days later.

It's awful to say it, but there was something that absolutely fascinated and thrilled me about being there when a shark attacked somebody. It sealed my fascination with wild things. And though I didn't know the word at the time, *wildeor*—from Beowulf and Old English, which means self-willed beast, self-willed animal—defines that fascination. The idea of animals with big teeth has stuck with me forever. It's what I was interested in.

When I was in junior high and high school, being a Boy Scout was really important, because my family didn't go outside except for picnics. The Scouts gave me a way to camp, hike, and get out into the wilderness. I just ate it up.

I became an Eagle Scout at thirteen. Those of us who were Eagle Scouts seemed to go one of two ways: either we become very strong establishment types or we become radicals against the system. I guess I went toward the radicals.

ML: When did you become interested in activism?

Foreman: I joined Young Americans for Freedom [YAF] in college. In the 1960s, conservatism had a lot more variety to it, and there was tolerance for different approaches. I was in the part that was very libertarian, or even anarchist. For example, at the University of New Mexico, YAF and Students for a Democratic Society [SDS] had joint tables to legalize marijuana and to do away with the draft.

ML: What was your first conservation job?

Foreman: When I got out of college in 1972, I was a mainstream conservationist. I was hired in 1973 by the Wilderness Society as the regional representative based in Albuquerque. They were a family of nature lovers. I loved sitting around the society's council meetings then, where Bob Marshall's brothers talked about him, Aldo Leopold, and other conservationists. Mardy Murie, who helped in the passage of the Wilderness Act and was instrumental in creating the Arctic National Wildlife Refuge, often talked about her husband, Olaus Murie, a renowned biologist and one of the country's great champions of wildlife and wilderness.

They were my mentors, along with those in the generation older than mine, like Ken Sleight, Katie Lee, and David Brower—and many more. I've learned so much from them, the elders of my tribe, my parents and grandparents in the conservation family.

The year I was hired the US Forest Service was beginning to evaluate roadless areas. A lot of people, including me, proposed that a forty-thousand-acre roadless area in the Sandias be designated as wilderness. The Forest Service opposed it because they said you could see the sights and sounds of Albuquerque. We said that didn't matter. Once you were inside the area, it was really wild. With the help of two Republican senators, this area, along with nine others in the United States, were designated as part of the 1978 Endangered American Wilderness Bill. We established the precedent that wilderness areas depended on what was inside it, and not what was outside and around it.

ML: What were your frustrations at the Wilderness Society and how did they lead to the founding of Earth First!?

Foreman: Eventually, the society wanted me to work full-time in Washington, DC, and I was really reluctant to do that. Debbie Sease, my wife at the time, agreed to go back only if she could get a job, too. That was the deal we made.

In 1978, we moved. The society hired her as the Wild Rivers and BLM wilderness review coordinator. I had the wonderful title of coordinator of wilderness affairs, which you can read into in various ways. I basically acted as conservation director.

When I was in DC, I played that game. I think I did it quite well, but it also made me realize that while I was trying to be a moderate, to work within the system, to play by the rules, I found out that didn't work all the time.

The Forest Service's Second Roadless Area Inventory [RARE II] inventoried sixty-two million roadless acres on the National Forest. We consciously asked for half of it. We ended up with fifteen million acres, which was a real loss. We thought we had gone out of the way to be reasonable and fair. I felt we got screwed. The mining industry, the oil industry, the ranchers, didn't play fair and got their way. These frustrations and disappointments led to starting Earth First!.

But at the end of 1977, the Wilderness Society was in a state of turmoil and some of the old guard people had retired. Our executive director was Celia Hunter, the first woman bush pilot in Alaska, an outfitter, just a fabulous conservationist and person. In 1978, she was replaced with a businessman, Bill Turnage, who proceeded to completely change its personality. Like other conservation groups, it became focused on organizational effectiveness and raising money. Although these are important, they aren't as important as needing to go back to the traditional roots of conservation and remember that we are a family of nature lovers.

ML: What was Earth First!'s role in the old growth issue?

Foreman: The first thing Howie Wolke and I did at the start of Earth First! in 1980 was to say that all US Forest Service roadless areas should be protected.

The Sierra Club, the Wilderness Society, and other conservation groups didn't support that. They thought we were being extreme.

In 1983, Earth First! held a road show in southwestern Oregon. There we discovered that the Sierra Club and other conservation groups had essentially decided they had lost on the old-growth forest issue and weren't going to fight it anymore; in particular, they weren't going to fight the construction of the Bald Mountain Road into the Kalmiopsis roadless area, which was the largest roadless area left on the Pacific Coast and the biggest chunk of old-growth forest as well.

We decided we weren't going to let that happen. That was the beginning of real civil disobedience for Earth First!. The Kalmiopsis was where I got run over by a truck. I was blocking the narrow mountain road leading to the road-building site, when a pickup full of bulldozer operators pushed me, and I fell down underneath the truck. I held on to the bumper so I wouldn't get crushed by the tire and got dragged awhile. The truck finally stopped and a guy named Les got out and said, "Why don't you go back to Moscow, you dirty communist?" And I said, "But, Les, I'm a registered Republican!" And I'm lying under his truck!

ML: Did Ed Abbey influence Earth First!?

Foreman: I've always felt that my generation of Western wilderness folks, who came into conservation in the 1970s and early 1980s, were probably more influenced by Abbey than anybody else. He was a voice for us, a folk hero, and a cultural model. He was a terrific inspiration. His ideas shaped us into a fairly distinct cohort of conservationists.

Earth First! decided to take Abbey's message and really inject it into the politics of the nation and try to transform the conservation movement. I think we did.

What Ed Abbey brought to conservation was a very good sense of humor, particularly the ability to laugh at oneself.

And we had that, very much so, in the early part of Earth First!. Ed helped us take a more irreverent look at our actions and allowed us to really think outside the box. We did not take ourselves too seriously, even though we were involved in pretty serious things. I see today that the humor has slipped away.

Dave Foreman at Round River Rendezvous, Idaho, July 4, 1986.
Photographer David J. Cross.

ML: Was humor the idea behind the Buckaroos of Earth First!?

Foreman: In the early 1980s, there was a more emotional side to conservation. This was right when the so-called Sagebrush Rebellion was springing up. The impression those folks were trying to put out is that they were real people and conservationists were a bunch of effete wimps. We thought, okay, we can play redneck too.

THE SAGEBRUSH REBELLION

The Sagebrush Rebellion, which began in the 1970s, sought more state and local control over federal lands, primarily those managed by the Bureau of Land Management (BLM) and, in some cases, demanded outright transfer of lands to state and local authorities and/or privatization. (In thirteen Western states, federal lands include between 20 percent and 85 percent of a state's area.) The "rebels" not only included miners, loggers, and ranchers who used these lands but also local politicians, state legislators, and US congressmen. One leader included San Juan County, Utah, commissioner and uranium miner Cal Black, the model for Edward Abbey's antagonist Bishop Love in his novel *The Monkey Wrench Gang.* The rebels were against environmental regulations imposed by the Wilderness Act (1963), Endangered Species Act (1973), and the Federal Land Policy Management Act (1976), which required federal lands to be made available for "multiple use," including recreation.

Today, the Sagebrush Rebellion has strengthened due to the growth of private militia groups, such as the Oath Keepers, and the court's inability to prosecute such events as Cliven Bundy's refusal to pay grazing fees and remove his cows from BLM lands in Nevada. The latter resulted in an armed standoff between his followers and the BLM, and led to Ammon Bundy's takeover of the Malheur Refuge in southwestern Oregon, claiming that the refuge and other public lands belonged to the public. Some state legislatures have proposed bills asking that BLM lands be returned to the states; to date none have passed. The US Department of the Interior, under the direction of President Donald Trump, has shrunk wilderness lands previously designated as national monuments and lessened existing environmental regulations by curtailing federal funds in favor of increasing such extractive industries as oil/gas and mining.

The idea behind the Buckaroos was that we were bigger rednecks than the antiwilderness rednecks. If they wanted to tangle, we were there. I remember sitting in Woody's Tavern in Moab. In the early eighties, it was not a mountain-bike Mecca. It was a uranium mining town. A bunch of us Buckaroos were talking about nuclear waste being dumped next to Canyonlands National Park. The redneck miners couldn't help but overhear us, so one of the guys came over and said, "Well, where do you think we ought to put the nuclear waste?" I said, "I think we ought to stuff it up Ronald Reagan's ass." He went back to his table and said, "Come on! We're gonna fight these guys!" And they said, "Who are we gonna fight?" He said, "Those big cowboys over there." They decided they didn't want to fight us after all, so we bought them beers and they bought us beers. I guess we got the impression across that we were rough guys, too, and not a bunch of urban wimps. The Buckaroo image was another way of saying that you could be a patriotic, redneck conservationist.

In those early days, what we really wanted to do with Earth First! was to make it very clearly an American patriotic thing—like the Boston Tea Party—so we used the Don't Tread on Me flag [designed during the American Revolution].

We played that up with the Sagebrush Patriot Rally [on July 5, 1981, Moab, Utah]—our counterpoint to the Sagebrush Rebellion. One of the key things that broke up Earth First! was the left-wingers not wanting to have those American symbolisms.

We felt that Earth First! needed to use arts and music to create a culture and more of a sense of belonging. During the antiwar movement and the civil rights movement in the sixties, music was used to inspire.

We wanted to do that, too. So we published *The Earth First! Li'L Green Songbook* by Johnny Sagebrush [a.k.a. Bart Koehler] in 1986. Then various troubadours started doing tapes, which were sold through the *Earth First! Journal*. And nights at the Round River Rendezvous, our annual gathering, turned into people doing music together.

The funny thing was when I worked for the Wilderness Society in the 1970s, I received a number of death threats. After Earth First! I didn't get any death threats. The other side respected us for being tough.

ML: What was Earth First!'s initial public action?

Foreman: We were looking for some way to announce that Earth First! was on the scene and show our humor. In 1981, we decided to fake a crack in Glen Canyon Dam. Thanks to people like Ed Abbey, Katie Lee, and Ken Sleight, the whole idea of the dam as a symbol of the industrial destruction of the West took hold for my generation of conservationists.

We spent some time walking around the dam and looking at it from the bridge and trying to figure out what to do. One of the ideas we had was, mounting a 55-gallon drum of black paint in a pickup truck and putting it on some kind of structure so we could pour it over the side. Then somebody in Flagstaff came up with the idea of making a large crack out of black plastic. That idea clicked. We went into the hardware store and bought three 100-foot rolls of black plastic, a thousand feet of duct tape, and all this other stuff. When we were checking out, the guy at the counter said, "Now, what are you all doing with this?" I said, "Oh, we're graduate art students at Northern Arizona University and this is our master's thesis." He said, "Oh, I'd like to see it" and I said, "Well, look at the newspaper in a couple of days." That's how we created this 300-foot-long tapered strip of black plastic in the city park in Flagstaff.

Our idea worked perfectly. The roll of black plastic just unfurled and went down and looked like a big crack had happened on the dam's concrete face.

That's where I first met Ed Abbey. We had been in contact before then and I sent him an invitation to come. He did and spoke to the group.

After I got to know Ed, we'd go for walks, and I'd want to sit down and talk to him about strategy. He said his job was inspiration and to get people worked up, but not to deal directly with strategy. He told me that was my job.

The crack in the dam was a fun thing to do. Even the sheriff's deputy who came to deal with the problem was amused by it and was very happy to get to meet Ed Abbey. People working for the Park Service thought so too.

We were later told by a law enforcement person for the Park Service—a friend of ours—that the FBI had confiscated the crack and dusted it for fingerprints. Not that they needed to, because it was obvious who had their fingerprints on it, so that was pretty hilarious. And supposedly, it's still somewhere in a basement in Washington, DC.

I have often felt that they can't beat you up too much if you keep them laughing. It's a way to live. Having a sense of humor is a way to survive.

ML: What did the early actions of Earth First! accomplish?

Foreman: The actions on behalf of the old growth forests and dam building drew a lot of media attention to Earth First!. More importantly, it expanded the terms of the debate and led to long-term changes. Our motto was "No Compromise in Defense of Mother Earth."

Before we put the crack on Glen Canyon Dam, taking down dams wasn't part of the conversation. Afterward, people were not so afraid to talk about removing them or even doing it. Eventually their efforts led to a number of dams being taken down. Today, there is a serious effort to decommission Glen Canyon Dam by various organizations, such as the Glen Canyon Institute in Salt Lake City.

The ancient forest issue is a very good example of cooperation between Earth First! folks and the mainstream conservation movement, and also between people in the Forest Service who were giving us a lot of support. Hydrologists, botanists, and others that were down there on the Siskiyou National Forest in southwest Oregon were giving us information.

Andy Kerr of the Oregon Wilderness Coalition [now Oregon Natural Resources Council] was able to use some of that information to raise money and file a lawsuit against the old-growth logging in roadless areas—based on California's successful lawsuit over deficiencies in the RARE II Environmental Impact Statement. They won and stopped the building of roads. He helped to create a national old-growth protection campaign, or [what became known as] the Ancient Forest Alliance.

In 2000, President Clinton and the Chief of the Forest Service came out with the Roadless Rule, which proposed that all roadless areas on the National Forest be protected. If Earth First! had not been agitating to protect them, the rule would never have happened. To me, that's the best single example of expanding the parameters of any debate, by asking for what you really want.

These are good examples of how taking what may seem to be an extreme position at one time actually can become very mainstream later on.

ML: The crack in the dam and tree spiking were types of monkey-wrenching. What is your understanding of Abbey's term *monkey-wrenching*?

Foreman: One of the myths is that Ed Abbey's book, *The Monkey Wrench Gang*, really created the idea of monkeywrenching or eco-sabotage. But he was really writing about stuff that had been going on for a long time. I knew people who were cutting down billboards in the 1950s. So in some ways, Ed was just reporting on what had been going on.

Abbey talked about how the word *sabotage* comes from the French word for a wooden shoe, *sabot*, sort of the French version of Ned Ludd types who used to toss their wooden shoes into the gears of machinery. The British call this action a spanner in the works, and *spanner* is the English word for a monkey wrench. So the idea of monkeywrenching comes from a worker taking a monkey wrench and putting it into the gears of industrial machinery.

Then I came along and made *monkeywrench* one word. Ed was still using it as two words, *monkey wrench*. But I saw it as *monkeywrench*.

Ed's approach to monkeywrenching was pretty modest, the way it should be. You make it not worth the while of folks in the extraction industry to go into a certain wilderness. You slow something down.

Ed made it very clear in *The Monkey Wrench Gang*. Number one rule, Doc Sarvis says: nobody gets hurt. That's the difference between monkeywrenching and arson and sabotage. In *Hayduke Lives!*, Abbey deals with the dangers of going farther than that. And that's why a person who's going to be a monkeywrencher, either back in the 1980s or today, has to really be mature, wise, and strategic. And I think that's what Ed was showing in both books, that: "Hey, this is serious stuff. There are a lot of funny things about it, but it's still serious stuff, and you have to be careful."

ML: And paper monkeywrenching?

Foreman: Paper monkeywrenching is a matter of stopping agencies or others from doing bad things by using the system against them. It's been going on for a long, long time. Even the Wilderness Act in 1964 was a form of paper monkeywrenching. It said, "We can't trust you, Forest Service or Park Service, not to trash your land, so we're just taking that control away from you in these specific areas and we, Congress, are going to decide what to set aside."

Earth First! started out doing paper monkeywrenching before we did any civil disobedience. I was on the mailing list of every national forest in the country. I'd get a mailing announcing a timber sale in a roadless area or road building. I would fill in the blanks in a form letter and send it in. I stopped hundreds of timber sales in roadless areas.

Today *paper monkeywrenching* has come to mean using the law against illegalities in the system. That's why the kind of actions the Center for Biological Diversity does are valuable. It is really an extraordinary group. They are hardcore. They are philosophical. They are committed. They're ethical. They're also very effective. They have real expertise, both as scientists and lawyers. Kieran Suckling, Peter Galvin, and Todd Schulke, the people who started it, understand the system and know that they have to be tough in dealing with it.

ML: Why did you retire from Earth First!?

Foreman: At the Grand Canyon Rendezvous that we held in Flagstaff, Arizona, in the summer of 1987, I realized that our members were beginning to split on many fronts.

It began with the more left-wing politically correct side and the Buckaroo side who disagreed on the question of overpopulation. Our original members were very much a population stabilization group, and I have always been there. I remember distributing over a hundred copies of *The Population Bomb* by Paul Ehrlich at the University of New Mexico after it came out in 1968. One of the issues I work mostly on today is reducing population growth.

Abbey spoke at that Rendezvous, but by then, many newcomers were embarrassed by him. Some East Coast anarchists accosted him, and that's when I began to realize that Earth First! was going in other directions. One of the reasons that Ed was so savaged by left-wingers—and Ed was a left-winger himself in many ways—was that he was politically incorrect, and his stance on overpopulation was one of those issues.

The more countercultural left-wing bunch also rejected the whole Buckaroo approach. I always wondered why were they attracted to Earth First! in the first place, if they didn't like the personality and style of it, and the tougher and more humorous roles we took because we felt they were needed.

There was also a split between the people who felt that Edward Abbey was for them, like the Buckaroos, and the people who were not.

There were people there who leaned toward the Earth Liberation Front [ELF] international anarchist movement, or the Animal Liberation Group [ALF], a radical animal rights movement. Neither group had a real foot in conservation. One of the problems with their approaches was that their tactics go way beyond monkeywrenching. When you start dealing with arson, which is what some people in the animal rights movement went for, you're in a whole other ball game. You end up with really bad prison sentences. Somebody threw their life away for no good reason, for no accomplishment. I've been very sorry to see that kind of thing happen. As I've always counseled, I don't care what you're doing;

you have to have good strategy, whether you're the Nature Conservancy or direct action–type folks. You have to think it through. People haven't done that very well.

I noticed also that there was a big shift in the way law enforcement dealt with the environmental movement. When Earth First! started up, law enforcement was much more relaxed and friendly, not so heavy-handed.

When I was arrested up at Yellowstone National Park in 1985 for chaining myself to the door of Grant Village, the Park Service cops that arrested us were on our side, and we were laughing and joking the whole time. About a dozen Earth First! protestors were dressed up as grizzly bears to complain about the hotel being built on grizzly habitat.

Then the Feds started coming down hard to discourage any kind of direct action. Even people who were doing nonviolent civil disobedience started getting hard sentences and getting pretty beat up on during the arrest process.

The 1987 Rendezvous was also interesting because that was the first time that some of the FBI snitches came into Earth First!, like Ron Frazier. That's when we first met. And as it came out when I was on trial, Ron was on LSD during the whole Rendezvous. I then started moving on to other things and that was before the FBI ever arrested me in May of 1989.

ML: I know this was a very hard time in your life, but could you tell us why the FBI targeted and arrested you in 1989?

Foreman: I didn't know why I was arrested when it happened—it could have been half-a-dozen things, I thought. Hmm. Which one? The Prescott action wasn't on my list of possibilities. I was told that one of the things that the US Attorney's Office charged me with was conspiracy to damage government property along with four others in Prescott, Arizona, in part, because of my book, *Ecodefense: A Field Guide to Monkeywrenching.* I had autographed two copies of the book, saying "Happy Wrenching" and gave them to FBI informants. The government pointed to that act as proof of my part in the conspiracy.

Ed died in March of '89, and the FBI arrested four folks in Prescott and me at the end of May. Some people have thought that perhaps it was Ed's death that caused them to do that, but if we really look at it, the FBI already had been doing this investigation for a year and a half. The undercover FBI agent had just been working on the people in Prescott to try to get them to do something, and it took him a lot of work to get them to do anything.

I think that's what really drove the timing of the arrest. But the thing I missed through all of it was Ed not being there, because Ed could have so well excoriated the government spooks and undercover agents and the whole repression of Earth First!. We didn't have that voice, which I really missed. And the irony was that my wife, Nancy, and I had already basically left Earth First!.

I know that in the last few years before Ed died, he sent off for his FBI file and was upset because it didn't have much in it. But there were some pretty funny things, like how they were following him around when he was a school-bus driver in Death Valley National Monument.

But my lawyers—Gerry Spence and Sam Guiberson—recognized that for two years the FBI had been manipulating these poor people in Prescott as a means to try to get me and wreck the Earth First! movement.

The undercover agent ended up taping himself talking to other FBI agents. This was right after he had talked to me, and he said something like, "Now, Foreman's not the guy we want to bust because he's a per-petrator. We want to bust him because we're sending a message, and that's all we're doing." And then he says, "Oh, shit. We don't need that on tape."

Up until that time, the Feds had told the folks from Prescott that if they would testify against me, they would let them walk. They showed the character not to do that, which took a heck of a lot of courage. I understand why people plead guilty to something that they don't do. After six weeks of trial, their attorneys asked the Feds about plea bar-gains. The Feds said, "Sure, but Foreman has to plead, too." Spence was sure I'd be found not guilty, but my feeling was that I couldn't let the others down. They were looking at long sentences if found guilty but much shorter if they pled. So I agreed to a plea bargain as did the others. Mine was to plead guilty to a felony of damaging unspecified government property. After five years of probation, the US attorney would move to dismiss the felony charge, and I would then plead guilty to a misdemeanor of damaging unspecified government property worth less than $100 and pay a $250 fine. And that's how it came down.

The FBI had spent $3 million trying to frame me.

The charges were officially dropped against me five years later (1997), and that turned out to coincide with my fiftieth birthday. I had a "Fifty and Free" birthday party, and some friends—one of them an attorney—put together this little certificate, declaring me a nonfelon, with the fake signatures from Janet Reno, appointed attorney general of the United States in 1993, and Louis Freeh, who was the director of the FBI from 1993 to 2001, on it. I like to joke that I'm one of the few people around that's been certified by the US Department of Justice not to be a felon.

Ever since that trial, Nancy only allows me to sign copies of *Eco-defense* if I include the following disclaimer: "To so-and-so. *Ecodefense: A Field Guide to Monkeywrenching* is for entertainment purposes only. No one involved with the production of this book—editors, contributors, artists, printers, or anyone else—encourages anyone to do any of the stupid, illegal things contained herein." This way, I can't be charged with conspiracy.

ML: Didn't that produce a sea change in your life?

Foreman: In *Confessions of an Eco-Warrior*, I joked that it was time to hang up my pearl-handled monkey wrenches. I'm not the person I was in 1980 when I started Earth First! with Howie and Mike and Bart and all. We were quite thoughtful in our approach, and I think we largely accomplished what we wanted to. But then things changed, and we needed to move on.

There's no way I'm going to go out and do civil disobedience today, with my bad back and arthritis and everything else. I don't want to get beat up that way. I got run over by the pickup truck in 1983; if that happened now, it'd kill me. I was fine back then!

ML: An example of how you moved on was that in 1991, you co-founded the Wildlands Project, and in 2002 you founded the Rewilding Institute. What were they about?

Foreman: In the early 1990s I began to talk to conservation biologists like Michael Soule and Reed Noss, and we realized that we needed to marry traditional wilderness and wildlife conservation with the new science of conservation biology, to both give the science of ecology more of an activist role and to put more science into conservation.

The Wildlands Project was the result. We wanted to look at the big picture. We felt it was not enough to just protect an isolated wilderness area here and a national park there. We took Reed's idea about wildlife corridors, which I like to call *wildways*, and doing it on a larger scale. Our idea was to establish a network of protected core wilderness reserves and national parks and provide linkages between them.

There's a whole range of things that we can do to restore the amount of Earth that is given over to wild things, as opposed to which is given over to us. So if we can restore big wilderness, close roads, restore the native species to it, such as wolves in Yellowstone or cougars back East, black-footed ferrets, Bolson tortoises—and then protect wildlife movement linkages between the protected places—then we are doing something to restore on a continental scale. That is the essence of wilderness restoration, putting all the natural pieces back in place, and the basic idea of the Wildlands Project.

A wonderful example is the California condor, which had not been in the Grand Canyon for thousands of years. The US Fish and Wildlife Service began reintroducing captive-bred condors into the Grand Canyon in 1992. Today there are as many as five hundred wild condors. That's the best example I can think of, from the standpoint of restoration, of thinking deep in time.

When we do ecological or wilderness restoration, we have to think deeply. We're so shortsighted, as human beings. We only can think back maybe a hundred years and forward twenty years, but we have to do much more than that.

That, in turn, led to my founding of the Rewilding Institute in 2002

Dave Foreman in the Arctic National Wildlife Refuge, September 2014.
Courtesy of the Collection of Dave Foreman and Nancy Morton.

and set a new standard for conservation. What the Institute is trying to do is see the conservation movement as our constituency. Our job is to talk about vision. It's to talk about values. It's to talk about what conservation should be and what we should be trying to work on. It's a very small group and it will stay that way.

Right now I'm at about the best place in my life because I have my own organization, the Rewilding Institute, where I don't have to worry about what other people want. In my previous conservation life—whether the Wilderness Society or Earth First! or the Wildlands Project—while I was always myself, there was always an organization with a bunch of other people in it requiring a lot of give-and-take.

I'm just not an organizational person. I'm a lot better on my own. I think most people who have worked with me in the past would agree—I'm an awful board member; I can be a bully and an asshole. I want my way.

Abbey had that wonderful luxury of just being Ed Abbey and not representing anybody else. Right now, I can pretty much do that.

ML: Can you talk about the giveaway of our public lands? Of course, that's a huge controversy.

Foreman: Since the beginning of the United States, there's been this notion that there's always land over the next ridge, out to the West, that's ours to go in and grub out whatever kind of resources we can and without responsibility.

We saw that with the way the early lumbermen just cleared off the great Eastern forests and the pineries of the Great Lakes states. We saw it with the coming of the cattle and the sheep here in the West. They just graze the place down to bare dirt and then blame it on drought and not take responsibility themselves for the fix.

A second aspect is getting people to understand that the public lands in the United States really sets us apart from all other countries and the world. In many ways, our public lands are the essence of our character and our conservation history; they're not just the private property of miners and ranchers and oil men who lease them. These lands belong to all of us.

A problem we are facing today is that so many conservationists want win-win solutions. They want to be able to sit down in a local café and have coffee with their rancher or miner or oil-men neighbors. But sometimes conservation is just a fight. It's who's got the power. We have got to flex our muscles better as conservationists, because we do have public support for what we want to do. Instead of thinking we can negotiate everything, let's figure out when we can negotiate. But other times, let's organize and let's fight and let's protect the land like we used to do.

ML: What do you mean when you say, "One must know a place in order to save it"?

Foreman: At the very beginning of my conservation career, Clif Merritt with the Wilderness Society taught me that you have to know the land. You're much more effective if you know the place you're trying to save. If you don't know the places you're proposing for wilderness, you're going to lose.

Whether you're a lobbyist in Washington, DC, working for the Sierra Club or Wilderness Society, who never goes backpacking or river-running, or an activist that just doesn't get out in wild places, you aren't going to be as effective as somebody who does. You could make a compromise that may be deadly to the integrity of the place. It becomes an abstract lobbying game that they're playing.

I think people need to be encouraged to take a more ecological view of wilderness—to go slow, to wander, to mosey around, poke around, to look at the plants, to birdwatch, to just sit quietly and let the place seep into them.

The same holds true for outdoor recreation and wilderness. Abbey taught me that wilderness was more than a recreational place to be used for the challenge of adventure. He talked about how the more stuff you have between you and the wild, the less you're tied to it. You can only experience so much nature on a mountain bike. The more equipment you have, the faster you go, the less you experience the wild. That's why the thrill culture worries me. There's nothing wrong with thrills, but you need the other side of wilderness, the more contemplative side, the quiet approach. When we are able to do that, we have a much richer experience.

One of the things that really bothers me when I'm up here in the Sandia Mountains in Albuquerque is, where are the little kids? If I'd been raised in this neighborhood, with a place like this around me, I would have been out there all the time. I would have been making forts in the rocks and chasing lizards.

Although part of the reason is they're plugged into video games, there's also a phenomenon I call "Rottweiler mommies," who don't want their kids to go out and be away and get hurt. Kids are supposed to fall down and skin their legs. They're supposed to get up and explore the world. They aren't.

It scares me. The one thing I've noticed about people who become conservationists is their experiences as little kids playing in the wilderness and watching their private wonderland be destroyed. They're natural monkeywrenchers. I've talked to many people who pulled up survey stakes when they were young because some development was going into their backyard wilderness. And if kids aren't getting out and seeing places like this, even though they live right next door to them, what's going to happen?

I've often found that showing the movie *Lonely Are the Brave* [1962], based on Ed's novel *The Brave Cowboy* [1956], is a good way to get people talking about knowing a place you are trying to save. Here's the hero of the film, Jack Burns, on the west side of Albuquerque, where Rio Rancho now is. It's all built up but when the movie was shot, it was completely open space. And you get to this scene—here's the Sandias, here's Albuquerque, and here's this barbwire fence. Burns gets down off his horse, clips the fence, and rides through. That scene was very symbolic of Jack Burns being a throwback to the time when the West was unfenced.

That scene says something about wilderness. In the Wilderness Act, the word used is *untrammeled*. And a *trammel* in French is a net or a hobble, so wilderness means untrammeled or unhobbled.

Jack Burns was completely unfenced. Jack is the spirit of wilderness, or the spirit of wild. As he breaks away up into the Sandia Mountains, he crosses Highway 66 and gets nailed by a semi-truck carrying toilet parts. It's quite the ultimate comeuppance for a self-willed beast that is trying to escape the impress of the state, to be nailed by a truck hauling toilet parts.

ML: You have the strong belief that we need wilderness for our survival. Why?

Foreman: There are two questions there. Why do we, as human beings, need wilderness, and why does everything else need wilderness, too? It comes to, we evolved in the wilderness. Wilderness is our natural home. I think that we're unhealthy if we aren't surrounded by wild country and by big wild animals.

A deeper answer is that we need wilderness for its own sake and for all the other species that depend on it. To me, the essence of wilderness is unhindered evolution, that life goes back 3.5 billion years, complex life half a billion years—all this was going on before us, and it was wild.

That was also the force behind deep ecology that the Norwegian philosopher Arne Naess developed back in the 1970s. And Arne just died at the age of ninety-four. He was a great, great person, really a funny guy to be around. Strains of Arne's ideas also go back to John Muir and Thoreau, and contemporary writers such as Ed Abbey and Aldo Leopold. It has been said that Earth First! was a blend of Ed Abbey and deep ecology.

DEEP ECOLOGY

The deep ecology movement was catalyzed by the publication of a paper by Norwegian philosopher and mountaineer Arne Naess called *The Shallow and the Deep, Long-Range Ecology Movement: A Summary* (1973). The core principle of this movement is that life is interdependent: loss of plant and animal organisms negatively impacts and threatens life on Earth.

In 1984, Naess, along with George Sessions, codified eight guidelines to help people understand the ramifications of this principle. These are summarized on the website www.deepecology.org:

1. The well-being and flourishing of human and nonhuman life on Earth have value in themselves (synonyms: inherent worth, intrinsic value, inherent value). These values are independent of the usefulness of the nonhuman world.
2. Richness and diversity of life forms contribute to the realization of these values and are also values.
3. Humans have no right to reduce this richness and diversity except to satisfy vital needs.
4. Present human interference with the nonhuman world is excessive, and the situation is rapidly worsening.
5. The flourishing of human life and cultures is compatible with a substantial decrease of the human population. The flourishing of nonhuman life requires such a decrease.
6. Policies must therefore be changed. The changes in policies affect basic economic, technological, and ideological

structures. The resulting state of affairs will be deeply different from the present.

7. The ideological change is mainly that of appreciating life quality (dwelling in situations of inherent worth) rather than adhering to an increasingly higher standard of living. There will be a profound awareness of the difference between big and great.

8. Those who subscribe to the foregoing points have an obligation directly or indirectly to participate in the attempt to implement the necessary changes.

Naess is widely considered as the father of the deep ecology movement. A compendium of Naess's prolific writings is found in *The Selected Works of Arne Naess, Volumes 1–10* [2005].

People ask a lot, "Well, why are you a conservationist? Why do you work on wilderness and wildlife?" There's only one real answer, and it's the first line in Aldo Leopold's *Sand County Almanac*: "There are some who can live without wild things and some who cannot." We're cannots. The effective conservationists are cannots. They have to be out with wild things.

That's why when I got halfway crippled with my back trouble, and at times haven't been able to walk a hundred yards, I set up my yard for birds so I can sit in my recliner chair, look out the window and see the wild things. I have to have that. That's what motivates me. That's what I care about.

ML: What is the most important issue for you today?

Foreman: The one thing that is wrong with what everybody does in conservation today is that they have forgotten about overpopulation. In the seventies, all conservation and environmental groups had overpopulation at the top of their list. Here we are thirty or forty years later and everybody is afraid of dealing with it. Suddenly the subject became politically incorrect. That's why I wrote *Man Swarm and the Killing of Wildlife*, published in 2011, because I wanted to try to re-create a population control movement within the conservation movement. I want to show how our overpopulation is the main driver behind the extinction crisis, behind greenhouse gas pollution, behind all the other things we're doing to the wild earth.

In some ways I am more radical than those who say we have to stop the industrial state. I don't think there's any way possible we can do that. I think we have pushed things so far that there is no way that there's not going to be a complete collapse. Industrial civilization is going to break down. There is going to be a big die-off of people. I don't know what will come after that.

Folks are fooling themselves if they think changing light bulbs is going to change the world. It's far more important not to have children. Ed was a hypocrite, too, about overpopulation. He said, "Overbreeders like me, with five kids, ought to be heavily penalized." And it was funny. David Brower had five kids, too. At one of my talks, I caught hell when I brought up overpopulation. The person called me a hypocrite because I had five kids. I said, "Well, thanks a lot for the great honor of confusing me with Dave Brower, but I've got no kids. I've got three cats."

I'm eager for people to use all kinds of effective tactics that will save any building block of evolution, so the world can begin to heal itself once we aren't consuming everything.

Aldo Leopold famously wrote that land is a community, and we need to realize that we aren't lords and conquerors but are plain members and citizens of this land community with everything else. And I think in many ways that's the essence of the conservation consciousness, is that we are part of this natural community—along with the mountain [mahogany] and everything else.

I think we really have to challenge people to take the long view and urge them to use self-restraint, to voluntarily hold back. People have to learn how to be better neighbors, to have the generosity of spirit and the greatness of heart to share Earth with the many other species who are our family and our neighbors, members of the same community.

I don't expect people to be perfect. I don't expect everyone to be as brave as Paul Watson, founder of the Sea Shepherd Conservation Society. I don't expect everybody to be as committed as I am. To me conservation is life. It's what I do. It's what my calling is. It's not a job; it's never been a job. It's holy work.

3 | PAUL WATSON

Biography

Paul Watson is a Canadian American marine activist who founded the Sea Shepherd Conservation Society in 1977, an international organization that uses direct action to end the destruction of ocean wildlife. A reasonable mission. But what has made Watson feared are his tactics. His ships are the only ones to have been used as battering rams against fishing trawlers and whaling ships that are illegally poaching.

Watson's fleet of twelve ships has saved six thousand whales from Japanese whalers. Only ten endangered Fin whales were killed in a decade where five hundred were slated to die. Not one endangered Humpback whale has been killed. Their efforts have cost the Japanese whalers tens of millions of dollars. Unfortunately, the Japanese are now using satellite imagery to track Sea Shepherd vessels in order to protect what is an extremely lucrative industry.

Not all of their tactics invite controversy. The Sea Shepherd Conservation Society has helped design a method for sinking driftnets without ecological damage; coordinate wildlife rescue efforts after pipeline ruptures and spills; and protect the Canadian harp seal.

Sea Shepherd's activities were the focus of a reality TV series, *Whale Wars*, airing on the Animal Planet network. Watson was involved with the series from 2007 to 2013.

Watson has written four books, including *Earthforce! An Earth Warrior's Guide to Strategy* (1993), which endorses the monkeywrenching tactics of Edward Abbey. The foreword was written by Dave Foreman.

43

In 2008, the *Guardian* [United Kingdom] newspaper designated Watson as one of "50 People Who Can Save the Planet." In 2010, he received the Asociación de Amigos del Museo de Anclas Philippe Cousteau Defense of Marine Life Award in recognition of his work. In 2012, Watson was the second person after Captain Jacques Cousteau to be honored with a Jules Verne Award dedicated to environmentalists and adventurers.

I interviewed Paul at a hotel in Santa Monica, California, and a second time on a yacht in Marina Del Rey, California. (https://seashepherd.org)

———

ML Lincoln: When did you begin being an activist?

Paul Watson: My evolution as an activist began when I was ten years old. I was raised in a fishing village in Eastern Canada, right on Maine's New Brunswick border, and spent a summer swimming with a family of beavers. We had a lot of wildlife there, and it was a lot of fun. The next summer, I couldn't find the beavers. When I began asking questions, I found out that trappers had taken them during the winter. I got so angry that I began to walk the traplines, free the trapped animals, and destroy the traps.

In June 1975, when I was twenty-four, the Greenpeace Foundation came up with an idea to protect whales. Three of us went out in a rubber boat—Rex Weyler, foundation cofounder, and Bob Hunter, Greenpeace cofounder, and myself. We placed it in front of a 150-foot Soviet harpoon vessel that was bearing down on us. We were about sixty miles off the coast of Eureka, California; this was before the 200-mile coastal zone [exclusive economic zone] was established in 1982 by the United Nations, which enabled member countries to limit fishing from foreign vessels within this zone. The Russians were pursuing eight sperm whales that were fleeing for their lives, and every time that the harpooner tried to get a shot, I would maneuver the boat and block his harpoon. We were reading a lot of Gandhi at the time, so we thought all we had to do was get between the harpoon and the whales, and we'd be able to protect them. This worked for about twenty-five minutes, until the captain on the Soviet vessel came out and came down the catwalk, screamed into the ear of the harpooner, and then looked at us, smiled, and went like this [*makes throat-slitting motion*]. That's when I realized Gandhi wasn't going to work for us that day.

A few moments later, there was this incredible explosion. The harpoon flew right over our head and slammed into the backside of one of the whales in front of us. It was a female, and she screamed. It was like a woman screaming. It absolutely took us by surprise. Then she rolled over on her side in a fountain of blood. Suddenly the largest whale in that pod slapped the water with his tail, disappeared, swam right underneath the vessel, and threw himself out of the water straight at the harpooner on the Soviet vessel to protect his pod. But they were waiting for him with an unattached harpoon, and a harpooner pulled the trigger and hit the whale in the head point blank, and he fell back screaming and rolling in agony.

He looked straight at us and dove back down into the water, and then I saw a trail of bloody bubbles. He came up and out of the water at an angle so that his next move was to fall straight down on top of us. As I saw his head rise out of the water, I looked into this eye, an eye the size of my fist, and what I saw there changed my life forever. I saw understanding. The whale understood what we were trying to do. And I could see the effort he made, and as he pulled back, his muscles flinched, and he began to sink back into the sea. I saw his eye disappear beneath the surface, and then he died. He could have killed us and he chose not to do so. So I'm personally indebted to that whale for the fact that I'm still alive.

As I was sitting there with the sun about to go down, and the water was full of blood from the dead whales, I thought, why are we doing this? The Russians aren't eating these whales. They are killing them for sperm oil, which is used for lubricating high-heat-resistant equipment and the construction and manufacture of intercontinental ballistic missiles. They are destroying this incredible, socially complex, intelligent, magnificent creature for the purpose of making a weapon meant for the mass extermination of human beings. That's when it struck me. We are insane.

Paul Watson aboard the Sea Shepherd, 2010. Photographer Jo-Anne McArthur.

And from that moment on, I said, I'm not doing this for people. I'm doing it for the whales, for the sharks, for the fish—that's who my clients are. I don't care what people think about what we're doing because we don't represent them. We represent the victims of humanity. So that was pretty much the life-changing moment for me.

ML: Edward Abbey said nature needs no defense, only defenders. As a defender, you said in your book *The Whale Warriors* [2007], "I plead responsibility," not "I plead guilty." Can you explain that?

Watson: We all have a responsibility to protect the ecosystem that supports us. And we're really not doing this for the earth, because the earth will survive, always has, always will. No species can live on this planet outside of the laws of ecology. So if we don't conform to those laws, we will simply go extinct. What we're trying to do is protect humanity from ourselves. If we're going to have any future at all, then we have to make sure that we have a viable ecosystem to support future generations.

ML: What do you know about Edward Abbey?

Watson: Edward Abbey was one of three early advisors when I set up the Sea Shepherd Conservation Society. The other two were Margaret Mead and Buckminster Fuller. I never met Ed, just corresponded with him, and had a pretty good relationship. He'd tell me what he thought—especially when I was doing the wolf campaigns up in the Yukon. He was very, very helpful to me at that time.

I read *The Monkey Wrench Gang* in 1975, when I was in Hawaii. I remember that it was a captivating book. I think you can really identify with the characters. They had the courage to go out and do what they believed in.

In Abbey's last chapter of *Hayduke Lives!*, "End of the Trail, White Man," George Hayduke, fleeing from his enemies, reaches the Gulf of Mexico. He jumps into the sea, followed by gunfire, and swims to a ship named Sea Shepherd. I'll read you that portion: "'That you, George?' a voice called down from the rail above. 'It's me, Paul' . . . Had us worried, buddy, all that vulgar gunfire. You all right?' 'I'm all right, Captain.' Hayduke wrapped a hand around the ladder's bottom rung and rested for a moment. He stared back at the Coast of Sonora in Mexico, the dark unpeopled desert, the rising brightening and triumphant moon. . . . The captain hollered . . . 'Run up the black flag . . . with the red monkey wrench. Party time: George Hayduke's here.'"

I still remember the day Ed Abbey died. I was in Santa Monica, sitting in a car waiting for somebody, and I bought the *Los Angeles Examiner*. I never ever buy a newspaper. The first page I opened had a big picture of Ed and a story that he had died. That was March 14, 1989. To this day, I find it really strange that I would actually pick up that newspaper.

Abbey's books romanticize what a lot of what people were trying to do to take action against the destruction of the environment. *The Monkey Wrench Gang* was a very romantic book, and his characters were very colorful. And that really helped motivate people.

Abbey certainly was inspirational to the Earth First! movement, which got a lot of individuals involved in activism.

ML: One of the nonviolent activities advocated by Earth First! is tree spiking. Tell me what you Canadians did about tree spiking?

Watson: What isn't commonly known is that some friends and I practically invented tree spiking. In 1982, we set up a group called the North Vancouver Garden and Arbor Club, and went up and spiked two thousand trees on Grouse Mountain and prevented the destruction of that forest. It's still there because of what we did.

Because there was no law then against tree spiking, it wasn't illegal, so we could come out and say that we had done this. The laws were passed after the fact, but I call it the inoculation of a forest against a disease called *clear-cutting*.

ML: How did you think up the name Sea Shepherd?

Watson: When I was in Greenpeace, I led the campaigns to protect the seals off the coast of Labrador. And I wrote an article back then called "The Shepherds of the Labrador Front," because the baby Harp seals were actually described by the missionaries to the Inuit people as *kotik*, or the Lamb of God. So we were like shepherds protecting the seal pups. It's a good analogy for us, protecting our clients, our flocks—the whales and seals and dolphins and sharks. I try to be a good shepherd and to defend as much of my flock as I can.

ML: You have been at loggerheads with Greenpeace for a long time. What do you think about Greenpeace and other environmental and conservation organizations?

Watson: First, I do not consider organizations like Greenpeace, the Sierra Club, and National Wildlife Fund as part of the environmental movement. They're feel-good corporations. They're around to make everybody who joins them feel like they're part of the solution and not part of the problem.

They absolutely hate us for what we do. I can't think of one of these big organizations that would endorse, support, or give us the time of day. I actually call ourselves "The Ladies of the Night of the Conservation Movement." People may agree with us, but they don't want to be seen with us in the daylight.

In 2011, Greenpeace had a $40 million budget to spend on preventing illegal whaling. What was their big campaign? To send origami whales to Obama. I don't know what he's got to do with Japanese whaling, but Greenpeace figured if they sent enough origami whales, he would help end whaling. He didn't.

Another year, Greenpeace spent $70 million a year on direct mail—sending out paper that will only get a 1 to 2 percent return. That's an incredible waste of resources, and it all comes down to bringing in money.

They've forgotten where they came from. I find it really funny when I hear Greenpeacers saying, "You know, we were blocking ships way back in the seventies. We were doing that." No. Not one of them was there when we were out facing the harpoons. Some of them weren't even born. And yet they want to capitalize on what happened in the early days and disavow contributions of some of the early founders and members, most of whom have sailed with me on Sea Shepherd vessels—Bob Hunter, Rod Marining, Al Johnson, and John Cormack.

In my opinion, the best way of judging the value of an environmental organization is to say that if they spend more money on making money than they actually spend in the field on the causes they espouse, then I would think that they can be dismissed.

What the environmental movement needs is more individuals and small community-based organizations or grassroots groups with passion, imagination, and courage. People like Dian Fossey, Farley Mowat, Jane Goodall, Steve Irwin, Dave Foreman, and Ed Abbey have made a huge difference.

What defines people like them is that they are not worried about how they're going to be perceived or what people are going to think about them. I think that's really, really important.

What is sad is that many environmental organizations only pretend to support these people. Take, for example, Dian Fossey. Here's a woman who had to beg for every penny she could get from the National Geographic Society and from the World Wildlife Fund, and they threw her peanuts in exchange for the money they raised off of her. And when she got heavy with the gorilla poachers and started talking really strongly against them, they cut her off. She ended up getting murdered for her views. The environmental organizations weren't there to protect her. They're still making millions of dollars off of that woman's name. To me, they're just exploiting her passions.

One of the most successful activists of all time was the Fox. Do you know who he is? Very few people to this day knows who he is. In Illinois, he blocked up smokestacks, painted the office of the president of Standard Oil with oil and dead birds and animals, dumped a jar of polluted slime from U.S. Steel's drain on their new carpeting. He did all of these things, and he was never caught. Why? Because he was one person, acting by himself, without the knowledge of any single other person. That was the key to his success. That is the ultimate way to act. You've got to be Zorro, which also means the "fox"—that's the absolute guaranteed way of not getting caught. Don't bring anybody in on it.

ML: Didn't you once call the Sierra Club the Avon ladies?

Watson: No, I call Greenpeace the Avon ladies. I call the Sierra Club the Siesta Club Conversation Society—they're always sleeping and just talking. What's interesting is why I accused Greenpeace of being the Avon ladies.

In 1986, we had just sunk half of the Icelandic whaling fleet. I was doing a talk show in Vancouver when somebody called in a bomb threat to protest my actions, which I thought was a little bizarre, and we had to evacuate the building. While we were outside, a reporter says, "Greenpeace has just called you an eco-terrorist. What's your response?" I didn't want to get into a big thing with Greenpeace, so I just said, "What do you expect from the Avon ladies of the environmental movement anyway?" That was in reference to their knocking on doors, always asking for money. So, they called me an eco-terrorist and then got upset when I called them a bunch of Avon ladies. They've never forgiven me for that.

ML: Didn't Greenpeace accuse Sea Shepherd of acts of violence?

Watson: When I was with the Green Party in Canada, Greenpeace tried to kick me out for sinking those whaling ships in Iceland, saying that that was an act of violence. I said, "Well, Sea Shepherd has never done anything violent. Sinking a piece of metal is not violent. Martin Luther King once said you can't commit a violent act against a nonsentient object." Greenpeace and the Green Party said, "Well, we consider it violence."

To people who say, "I've never supported an act of violence in my life," I say, "You pay taxes?"

"Yeah."

"Well, then you're supporting the war in Iraq, so don't give me any crap about not supporting violence. You do it every day."

ML: Dave Foreman, Earth First! cofounder, calls you the premier eco-warrior. How is an eco-warrior different than an eco-terrorist?

Watson: I don't really know. Officially, I'm an eco-terrorist as defined by Japan. That's why I am on the Interpol Red List, which is for serial killers and war criminals. I'm the only person in the history of the Red List to be placed on the list for "conspiracy to board a whaling ship." As you know, the Dalai Lama is a terrorist as defined by China. So in a world where the Dalai Lama is a terrorist, I don't really mind being one.

I don't have a criminal record. I'm not wanted for a real crime.

The eco-terrorists are those who are terrorizing the environment. That is, to me, the definition of eco-terrorism. Exxon is an eco-terrorist company. British Petroleum [BP] is an eco-terrorist company. Monsanto is an eco-terrorist company.

The word *terrorism* gets thrown around so much, it doesn't even mean anything. If you throw a Molotov cocktail at a tank in Israel, then you're a terrorist. But if you drop napalm onto a school bus full of Palestinian children, then that's a military act. It doesn't make any sense at all.

People who are trying to protect our planet should be rightfully called eco-warriors. I don't really go for the titles very much, but I think when you are defending the natural world, of course you're going to bring a lot of anger and hostility toward you, because there's so much money being made from destroying this planet.

The fact is no conservationist or environmentalist has ever killed anybody, to my knowledge. So, calling us terrorists doesn't make any sense.

ML: Does Sea Shepherd Conservation Society commit illegal acts?

Watson: When we interfere with illegal whaling, illegal seal hunting, and illegal fishing, we're called criminals. In fact, we're are actually interfering with people who are breaking the law.

Sea Shepherd is not even a protest organization. We're not protesting anything. We're intervening against illegal activities. The reason why we've never been convicted of a crime is because our opponents are criminals. A lot of them are governments, but they're still criminals.

We use direct action as a strategy for accomplishing a number of things, one of them, direct intervention to interfere with the profits of our opposition and, two, to dramatize things and make people aware of what we're doing. According to the old saying, "Action speaks louder than words," and, you know, it's true. It's how you get people's attention.

For instance, in 1986, we sank half of the Icelandic whaling fleet and destroyed the whale processing plant, costing them $10 million worth of damage. We shut down their operations for seventeen years. That sounds illegal. I flew to Reykjavik to demand that they arrest me. They brought me in and interrogated me. "Are you admitting to sinking these ships?" I said, "Well, yeah. You know we sunk 'em. We're going to sink the other two at the first opportunity." The next morning, the police took me to the airport, put me on a plane, and sent me home. The minister of justice said, "Who the hell does he think he is? He comes into our country and demands to be arrested. Get him out of here." They knew that to put me on trial would be to put Iceland on trial. So this is where we throw their contradictions and their hypocrisies right in their face. And so everything we do is overt because, again, we're going against people who are acting illegally.

The Japanese whaling fleet has no legal reason to be in the Southern Ocean Whale Sanctuary. I keep saying, "What is it about the word *sanctuary* you don't understand?" And yet, they keep trying to throw all these loopholes and everything like that in. But, you know, Australia is taking them to court. The United States condemns them. But still nobody does anything about it.

SOUTHERN OCEAN WHALE SANCTUARY

In a near-unanimous vote, the International Whaling Commission established the Southern Ocean Sanctuary in 1994, primarily to protect whales in the Southern Hemisphere as they migrate through and feed in the region. Only Japan dissented. Because the sanctuary applies only to commercial whaling, Japan has continued to hunt whales inside sanctuary boundaries for purposes of scientific research. Many antiwhaling activists, however, believe that much of the catch within the sanctuary is actually used for commercial purposes. The Southern Ocean Sanctuary also plans to contribute to the restoration and protection of the unique and fragile Antarctic marine ecosystem.

ML: Sea Shepherd protects oceans, just as Abbey and Earth First! protected the lands of the Southwest . . .

Watson: We have an advantage over people trying to protect forests or stopping mine sites, because we're operating in a no-man's land where there is no law. The reason we can get away with what we're doing is that we are operating in a legal limbo, which is like the modern-day equivalent of the Wild West.

Seventy-one percent of the world's surface is ocean. And it's virtually unprotected. Yes, we have the rules, the regulations, the treaties, and the laws to protect the ocean, but there's no enforcement. There's a lack of economic and political motivation on the part of governments to do anything about it. The oceans are there to be exploited, but there's no money to be made from protecting them.

So it's a big free-for-all out there—anarchy out on the oceans. Anybody can do whatever they want. There's more illegal fishing going on than there's legal fishing, and the oceans are being destroyed.

And there's this other thing that I call "the tragedy of the commons." For instance, a Portuguese fisherman comes to the Grand Banks. He knows that the Northern Cod is going extinct. But he knows that if he doesn't catch them, the Canadians or the Cubans or the Spanish will. So he says to himself, "Well, I might as well catch them."

The bottom line is that if we wipe out the fish and destroy the plankton, the oceans will die. And if the oceans die, humanity dies. We cannot live on this planet with a dead ocean.

ML: How do you handle the risks you take out there?

Watson: The two best sources for understanding strategy are Sun Tzu, who wrote *The Art of War*, and Miyamoto Musashi, who wrote *The Book of Five Rings*. Both said that the way of the warrior is a resolute acceptance of death, that you go into a conflict accepting the fact that you're going to die and, therefore, no longer worry about the consequences. You go ahead and achieve your objectives. It removes that moment's hesitation of fear, which can get you killed. You go into these conflicts knowing that you're prepared to make that ultimate sacrifice.

In 1979, when I tracked down the pirate whaler, *The Sierra*, I had twenty crew members on board. When it was in the harbor, I said to the crew, "Here's my strategy. We're just going to go out, and we're going to ram it. We're going to disable it. I can't guarantee that you're not going to get hurt, but I can guarantee you one thing: you're going to jail in Portugal. You've got ten minutes to decide whether you're with us or not. And if you're not, then pack your bags and get off and onto the dock." And seventeen got off.

Fortunately, the two that stayed were engineers. We went out, we rammed *The Sierra* twice, disabled it, and finished its career. We were apprehended by the Portuguese Navy. I was brought before the Port Captain and charged with gross criminal negligence. I pointed out that there wasn't anything negligent about what I did, since I hit them exactly where I intended to hit them. He sort of laughed and said, "Well, that's true." Then he said, "But more importantly, I don't know who owned that boat, *The Sierra*, because it was a pirate boat. Until I do, you're free to go." So I walked out the door. Later, one of my crew members said, "Well, if I knew you were going to get away with it I would have been there too."

Sometimes you have to go ahead and do these things knowing there's no way to get away with it. What is amazing is how many times you can actually walk through the fire and come through unscathed. Courage can be its own reward. So that kind of attitude does make a difference.

Equally, you have to be on the alert for sabotage. The ship's constantly under surveillance. We've had sabotage attempts, and you just have to accept that sabotage is always a possibility and that you're going to suffer some sort of damage because of it.

We have to be very vigilant about the people who come on board our ships. For instance, none of the crew is allowed in the engine room. If you're not an engineer, you don't go into my engine room on my ship. We keep a good watch on that. We also have twenty-four-hour gangplank watches.

For the most part, we've been pretty lucky. And as I said in my book *Earthforce*, you don't do those kinds of activities with anybody you haven't known for seven years.

ML: What are your ecological principles?

Watson: There are three basic laws of ecology. The first is the law of diversity: the strength of an ecosystem is dependent upon diversity within it. The stronger the diversity, the stronger the ecosystem.

The second is the law of interdependence: all species, plants, animals, and humans are interdependent with each other. When explaining the basic laws of nature, I like to paraphrase distinguished naturalist and writer John Muir's famous quote ["When one tugs at a single thing in nature, he finds it attached to the rest of the world."] by saying, "If you pull on any part of the earth, you'll find it intimately attached to every other part of the earth."

The third is the law of finite resources: limit to growth, limit to carrying capacity. Right now, in order for our human population to grow, we're literally stealing the carrying capacity of other species. And as our population increases, other species simply disappear. And that pulls us back into the laws of diversity and interdependence, because we're only going to remove so many species before the whole system begins to collapse.

I like to compare the earth to a spaceship that is traveling through an incredible, never-ending voyage around the galaxy. It has a life-support system, which is our biosphere, that provides us with the food we eat, the air we breathe, and a built-in climate control. That system is maintained by a crew: worms, bacteria, insects, fish, and all the creatures that make it possible for humans to be here. We're not the crew; we're passengers with a crew that labors to keep this life-support system going. We're killing that crew. We can only kill off so many before the life-support system begins to fail. And if it does, then humans also will be victims.

People get outraged when I say that worms are more important than people. They say, "How can you say something so insensitive and outrageous?" And I say worms are more important than people because worms can live on planet Earth without us; we can't live without them. Bees and fish and insects are more important than people because we need them; they don't need us.

It's that kind of understanding that people need to learn if we're going to survive. We are not as important as these creatures. But when you become alienated from the laws of nature, you become victims of a dying planet because you just don't even see the signs, and if you don't see them, then you're probably going to die.

Too many of us have lost that feeling of harmony with the natural world and live outside the boundaries of the basic laws of ecology.

Many people live in an anthropocentric culture where all the values are human oriented. Everything revolves around humanity. And we haven't even been here very long. We think it's all created for us. We have constructed this antinature fantasy that we live in so that we're no longer a part of the natural world.

You know, twenty-one million subscribers are paying fifteen dollars a month to play the video game Warcraft. That's much more than the number of active environmentalists on the entire planet. If you can't make the connection between the billions of dollars spent on video games and the pennies that environmentalists are struggling and competing for every day, you're not going to understand that the life of the planet is at stake.

Biocentric people feel that they are part of the natural world and that all of these plants and animals are part of us and that we are connected to them. This ideology was once dominant upon the planet. That is still the ideology of indigenous people who today are a very, very small minority.

As a good example, when the 2004 tsunami hit in the Indian Ocean near Sumatra, the native people, who were close to the earth, elephants, and other animals, headed for higher ground. As the water receded, others went out and started kicking and stomping fish and crabs and were busy doing that when the wave came in. They were so busy destroying nature that they didn't see the signs that nature was about to destroy them.

ML: That brings up a question here, when you say people have lost awareness of the natural history of the planet. There's a process that I call forgetting. People are forgetting what a wilderness feels like. They are forgetting what it is to see large fish in the ocean, forgetting what it means to be awed by nature. And you've said that making history fit into our present history creates that type of forgetting. Can you explain that?

Watson: I find it appalling how many people don't know anything about the history of their own country, let alone the history of the planet. History to me is one of the most important things to study, because if you don't know where you came from, how do you know where you are? And if you don't know where you are, how do you know where you're going?

History teaches us the lessons, where we got it wrong in the past, and hopefully we can correct those and not make the same mistakes again. But history does illustrate that, in fact, we do make those mistakes over and over and over again because we just never seem to learn.

Human beings have this incredible ability to adapt to diminishment. So as things are diminished, they just simply accept that and move on. They forget where they've been and have very little vision as to where they're going into the future. For example, if you compare the oceanic ecosystems today compared to what they were even thirty or forty years ago, you would know they have been vastly diminished.

If people go diving in, say, Cocos Island off of Costa Rica or the Galapagos, they say, "Oh, my God, it's incredible, the wildlife under there and everything." But what they're seeing is only about 20 percent of what it was only forty years ago. So they forget how even more magnificent it was before. And then ten years from now it'll be more diminished, and people will say it's still looking good, but that's only because that's what they're used to. Either they don't have the memory, or they refuse to understand or see what it used to be.

ML: What do you see for the future of the planet?

Watson: One hundred years from now, I would envision a world that looks like 1818. We'll be back to sailing ships, riding horses, and like that, because, at some point, we're going to reach peak oil.

We have had the advantage in the last couple of hundred years of being able to plunder entire continents. And that has led to many generations of people on this planet living in absolute total affluence, like kings and queens. And that's just not going to happen in the future. Nobody will ever live like that again.

I think it was Albert Einstein who said if the honeybee disappears, he'd give humanity four years. But I think plankton is more crucial.

Plankton provides 80 percent of the oxygen that we breathe. Plankton sustains us. They're probably the most important organisms in our oceans. Since 1950, we've already seen a 20 percent decrease in plankton. If we cause too much damage, our earth ship will literally sink. And still, the Japanese and Norwegians are mass harvesting plankton to make a protein paste to feed the livestock without any environmental impacts being done on it at all.

I don't believe that it's too late for the planet. The planet will always survive. The planet will be here. We're in the midst of another major extinction event—the homeless scene, as some call it—where we'll lose more species of plants and animals between 2000 and 2065 than the planet has lost in the last 65.2 million years. As an environmentalist and conservationist, all you can really do is try to buy time. You try to buy territory for species to survive and to ride out what we're doing here until one of two things happens: we either come to our senses, which seems highly unlikely, and learn to live in harmony with the natural world, or we go plunder so far until the laws of ecology kick in and just brush us away.

ML: Is there any way to harness public support?

Watson: You will never get public support on any revolutionary agenda. Never has happened, never will. Anybody who thinks that they're going to get a majority of people on their side for any significant social change is living in some dreamland. People are, for the most part, apathetic sheep. They just go along with whatever is going on.

All you need is 7 percent support, like what happened in the American and French Revolutions. But if you can get that, now you've got a wave going, now you've got a movement going, and things can change. We're still a long ways from that 7 percent, but that's what we have to look for. But it won't be easy.

ML: The seal hunt is a patriotic symbol of the true North. Whaling is a patriotic symbol for the Japanese. Domestic oil drilling is a patriotic symbol for the Americans. How can you change what happens under the parameters of cultural territorialism based on destruction?

Watson: The destruction of the planet is hewn under patriotism, whether it's the Japanese whalers or the American oil drillers. Everything is said to be for a patriotic cause.

And, yes, persistence is important for overcoming this patriotism toward destruction, but equally, you have to partner it with a focus on the economics. That is what is effective. You can't appeal to people's morality or ethics because I don't think many people have them. By constantly harassing, intervening, and obstructing them, we cut down their kills, which then impacts their profits.

The Japanese whaling industry has not made a profit since we began going after them. In 2012, they were devastated. I mean, they only took 17 percent of their quota before they had to retreat from the area where we attacked them. They've lost literally about $200 million. This is the language they understand. It's the same with the seal hunt. Ultimately, seal pelts had to be banned in Europe and other places, and once they were, the price dropped from $110 down to $8 to where it now is practically nonexistent.

Nobody can cite me one example of where a whale in the Southern Ocean has been saved by any other means than what we do. And when people say, "Well, you should be educating the Japanese people," I say, "No. I'm not a missionary. I'm not going into Japan and tell them what to do. I'm going to the Southern Ocean and take action against what they do because it's illegal. It's not my place to go and teach the Japanese morality. It's my place to stop their illegal activities."

Back in 1975, after that experience with looking into the eye of the dying whale, I came to the conclusion that humanity is insane. And from an ecological point of view, we're absolutely, totally insane. So, you know, having accepted that, then you're really not too surprised or shocked at anything else that happens.

Ever since I was young I've been very much concerned with protecting wilderness, especially the ocean. I've just been doing this, all my life. I really haven't done anything else. I feel very much alive on the ocean. A lot of people are afraid of the sea, but I feel much more comfortable on the deep sea than I do on land. It's a feeling of belonging in the right place and knowing that you're a part of that wilderness of life.

I don't get worried, I don't get stressed, because I realize that in the long run, it's all just folly. And you control that folly by working within the context of it. But in the end, does it really matter? Because we tend to think of ourselves as being far more powerful and influential than we ever really are.

Our hope lies in the fact that the laws of ecology will address this wrong and make it right. I'm extremely optimistic for the fate of the earth, but not too optimistic for the fate of humanity.

4 | KATIE LEE

Biography

Katie Lee is venerated as the most flamboyant of the eco-warriors that took up the torch that conservationists Edward Abbey and David Brower left burning after they died—to sing, write, and lecture about the destruction of Glen Canyon and the importance of restoring the Colorado River. She often said that the only thing that prevented her from blowing up Glen Canyon Dam was that she did not know how.

Katie wrote three books about her canyon experiences, *Glen Canyon Betrayed* (2006), *Sandstone Seduction: Rivers and Lovers, Canyons and Friends* (2004), and *The Ghosts of Dandy Crossing* (2014), and she recorded many albums and videos celebrating the Colorado River and the beauty of Glen Canyon.

The documentary film *Drowning River* honors the spirit of her struggles. Katie's passion was taking down the damn dam at "Loch Latrine" (her words for Reservoir Powell). Not many could be aware of the power and beauty that Glen Canyon held for her and others until they read her words, or had the opportunity to see her extraordinary archives of original prints and slides and heard her powerful protest songs. One could not help but make the excruciating comparisons between pre-dam and now.

During its filming, Katie shared stories about her tomboy adventures in Tucson, Arizona, roaming the canyons and shooting rabbits for the family stew pot during the Depression.

She began her kaleidoscopic career as a Hollywood stage and screen actress and a svelte folk singer. In the 1960s, she wrote a history of cowboy songwriters that became a classic, *Ten Thousand Goddam Cattle: A History of the American Cowboy in Song, Story and Verse*, and a two-album set by the same name. She made an award-winning video, *The Last Wagon* (1972), which celebrated the lives of Gail Gardner and Billy Simon, two Arizona cowboy legends.

Katie was inducted into the Arizona Music & Entertainment Hall of Fame in 2011 and the River Runners Hall of Fame in 2016.

We both moved to the mountain community of Jerome, Arizona, in the early 1980s and became friends. I interviewed Katie at her home in Jerome, Arizona, surrounded by maps of Baja, California, and artwork of the Southwest canyons she loved to roam, especially the paintings of Serena Supplee. I also interviewed her on the banks of the San Juan River in Bluff, Utah, because I wanted to film her by the river and canyon country that she called home. She always told me that she felt she was born with sandstone in her veins. (https://nau.edu/special-collections/order-from-the-archives/)

———

ML Lincoln: How did your friendship with Abbey begin?

Katie Lee: During my honeymoon with my third husband, Brandy, we camped by the Colorado River, near Fisher Towers outside of Moab, Utah. I lay on the sand and read Edward Abbey's *Desert Solitaire*. I hadn't heard of him. I thought, "Wow, this guy is something else. He really knows this country and loves it. I'd really like to know him."

Then Brandy and I took off up the La Sal Mountains on a dirt road that starts near Castle Creek and ends up on the other side of Moab—a gorgeous ride. As we drove, we saw all these survey stakes tied with beautiful little Day-Glo ribbons. With a few choice cusswords, I said, "Oh, no, they're gonna pave this road." Then I started pulling the stakes up and throwing them down in the canyon, maybe thirty, forty of them. "Even though it wouldn't stop the road builders, it'll slow them down."

When I got home, I taped one of the stakes to my album, *Folk Songs of the Colorado River*, wrapped it up, and sent it to Ed in Organ Pipe National Monument. I asked about his book *The Brave Cowboy*.

About a week later I got a postcard.

September 25, 1969. Dear Miss Lee: Thanks very much for the Songs of the Colaradie [*sic*]. It's a great record and I've been playing it about three times a day, wallowing in nostalgia. I'll probably be working at Organ Pipe again this winter [as a seasonal park ranger], west of Tucson. Come and visit if you have a chance. I'd like to meet you and, better yet, hear you sing those songs live, in person. So don't forget to bring your guitar. Best regards, Ed Abbey, Box 38, Ajo, Arizona.

Then a couple of days later I got another postcard. "September 27, 1969. Dear Miss Lee: *Muchas gracias* for the surveyor stakes. Keep up the Lord's work. I'm sorry, but that book, *The Brave Cowboy*, has been out of print for several years. Only own one myself. Try the libraries. *Fire on the Mountain* is still in print, though, Dial Press, New York. Best, Ed Abbey, RD1, Home, Pennsylvania." This card's from Pennsylvania, and it's a Grand Canyon card.

That's how our friendship began.

ML: Do you think music communicates ideas better than words?

Lee: One thing Abbey used to say to me was, "Katie, why don't you shut up and sing?" Not too different from what my river companion and photographer Tad Nichols told me, "Katie, sometimes you get so mad when you talk, you do more harm than you do good."

Music is a great carrier of messages. You sing a lyric to someone and it'll reach down and grab places that do not ever get touched by a conversation or by words. When I sing, I'm not forcing anything on them. The songs carry a belief with them, and I don't think there's any doubt about that. But when I sing, they're going to hear the message, whether they like it or not, whether they get it or not. They can turn it off. But they do get it and remember it. That is why my music has helped so much with what I have done or tried to do about Glen Canyon.

In 1988, a year before he died, Ed sent me this postcard about my CD *Colorado River Songs*: "Dear Katie: Quote me if you wish. 'Anyone who loved the living Colorado River pre-damnation—[before it was ruined] by the swine who run America—will love these songs by a pioneer Glen Canyoneer, Katie Lee. Love and luck, Ed Abbey.'"

ML: What was your initial reaction when you first got hold of *The Monkey Wrench Gang* and started reading it?

Lee: Ed sent me his book right off the bat: "Be one of the first people who get to read it." After I read it, I wrote back, "It's like Glen Canyon Dam's encounter with *The Monkey Wrench Gang*. Shit, oh dear, Ed, you'll have every river runner, strip mine hater, power plant despiser, and sign detester groveling at your feet. Better go hide somewhere—that is, all save from me."

As I read his book, I was just like many of my activist friends—I threw it up in the air about fifteen times, laughing my head off. It was fantastically funny. We were all thinking: wouldn't it be great if the dam was blown up? By that time we all knew that it was built in porous sandstone and that one day the river would get pissed off and work itself around that dam and just blow it apart. But Abbey's idea buoyed our spirits. We got to laugh about that dam, maybe for the first time.

That book turned a lot of people's heads, and I knew when I was reading it that it was going to do just that. It brought people's attention to issues that they had no idea existed at all—how the water tables were dropping in the Navajo Nation because of the Peabody Coal Mine. It's a true art to take something as serious as the destruction of Glen Canyon and make people aware through humor that it was a big mistake. To me, that is the real value of that book.

It also connected people with a wider circle of activists. It helped readers think that maybe environmentalists were not all the crafty, evil, destructive people that some of the right-wingers wanted you to believe. Abbey's book embodied that tradition of do-no-harm-to-people monkeywrenching by folks who got upset with all the roads that were going through the beautiful places where they'd hiked for years. They then found themselves defending those lands by standing in front of bulldozers, or using a jar of peanut butter here and a little sand down a gas tank there. You know, I never wanted to kill anything really, except meat for dinner, until those bastards built that dam.

I can remember some of my friends in Southern Utah just going bananas. "Don't they understand that these machines cost millions of dollars?" And I'd say, "Yes, they do. But it doesn't take a million dollars to repair a gas tank, so don't get so excited."

ML: Many readers associate the character Hayduke in *The Monkey Wrench Gang* with Doug Peacock and Seldom Seen with Ken Sleight.

Lee: I've known Ken Sleight for many, many years. I've known Doug Peacock for almost as many, but not quite. They are friends of mine. Doug is very intense, and Ken is la-di-dah, laid back and sweet. Even though they're so different, both are serious men who love the country. They love where they go and what they do.

Craig Childs, ML Lincoln, Ken Sleight, Katie Lee, Ken Sanders, Jack Loeffler, and Kim Crumbo at the Flagstaff Mountain Film Festival screening of select scenes of *Wrenched*, October 2012. Photographer James Q Martin.

I think that Doug Peacock had more trouble trying to live down Hayduke, because people who read Abbey's book just sort of looked and talked to Doug like he was Hayduke, regardless of whether he did or did not do those things that were mentioned in the book. And in most instances, he did not.

So I was really thrilled when I read Doug's book *Walking It Off* [2005], because I felt that he had finally gotten Ed off of his back. Now, that may sound harsh but you must realize that when a man is suddenly thought to be another man, not himself, where is the man's personality itself? It made Doug angry, because nobody knew Doug Peacock. He may have had similarities to Hayduke, but so what?

As a character, Hayduke was stronger than Seldom Seen. So I can see why it just didn't affect Ken Sleight the way it did Doug. Ken is such a water-roll-off-of-the-back, just like it rolls down the river. It didn't bother Ken at all to be associated with Seldom Seen. You could talk up, down, inside out, whatever, and Ken would just always be Ken. But when he's pissed, he'll stand in front of bulldozers, just like the rest of us. When we believe in something, we believe in it. But knowing Ken as I do, I have to say that Ed just drew him the way he might have drawn a portrait.

ML: Some people even say you were Bonnie. Can you talk about this?

Lee: I don't see how Ed might have patterned Bonnie after me. I myself can't see that.

Some said to me, "Well, you want to blow up the dam." I said, "I'd like to have somebody else blow the dam. I don't want to blow it up and go to prison. But I'd be very happy if somebody else did it."

A lot of people have speculated about who Bonnie might have been, maybe one of his girlfriends, but I didn't know who it might have been.

But there was one character in the book whose real name was used: Calvin Black. I have always called him Calvin Blacktop, because he wanted every road in Utah paved. Calvin lived in Blanding, Utah, and owned the old Elk's Café, I think it was called. I would see him in there now and then whenever I came up to run the river, and I'd say, "Calvin, why do you have to pave everything?" "Well, I've got to be able to get there in a hurry." I said, "Why is everybody in such a hurry?"

The man was so brilliant that in order to prove that uranium was safe he wore a piece of yellow cake around his neck and died of throat cancer. Brilliant, right?

ML: What makes Abbey a great writer?

Lee: He didn't waste words. He could say it all in a few words, whereas I have to take ten pages to get a similar idea out.

When we read Ed today, he's as present in our lives as he was thirty years ago. The art of a true writer is somebody who can bridge the generation gap and can lay it out there on the plate and be eaten up and help make another activist. I think he knew in his heart that his words were going to keep on going.

Ed once said to me, "Great writers steal. Mediocre ones merely borrow." And I pondered that for a long time, before I knew what he was talking about. I once accused him from stealing a scene from one of my books where I can't get out of this pothole of water, and I'm about to drown, and there's nobody to rescue me. But I did get out in a very ingenious way that I describe very explicitly in my book.

In *Hayduke Lives!*, Ed described a similar scene. Then he wrote me a letter, "I remember something about how you got out of the pothole with your boobs." I said, "Oh, no, Ed—it had nothing whatever to do with my boobs. That was how you interpreted it. You had Bonnie get out with suction." Then I said, "Boobs don't suck—or didn't you know that?"

ML: Describe your friendship with Ed.

Lee: People always ask, "Wasn't Ed a great friend of yours?" And I'd say, "Well, he was a friend. I don't know that he was a great friend." I was never his lover—I was much too old for him—and didn't have that kind of relationship. We were kindred spirits.

Ed always helped me whenever I asked anything of him. If it weren't for him, I don't think I'd ever have gotten my book about Glen Canyon published because I first wrote it as a novel, with a fictionalized persona that was me. He came to visit once, and I asked him to read it. Afterward he said, "Hey, you don't need to invent anything. Your experiences on that river and your journals tell the whole story. Forget the persona. Write from the first person. Tell your story honestly."

I said, "I can't write my experiences in the first person, because I start to cry every time I put myself back there. That's what I do when I write."

Ed said, "*Ten Thousand Goddam Cattle* is in the first person." I said, "It is?" I picked it up and sure enough it was. But the book isn't about an emotional experience. It's about cowboys and their history as they told it in their songs and my research to find the names of the cowboys who wrote them. It didn't tear me up like the loss of Glen Canyon.

It wasn't like somebody had come in and cut off the legs of my lover and all that showed up was his head. And when I think about that loss, I start to cry, like I'm doing now, it happens every time. I go back there and I have to remember that it's drowned.

I really don't think that I would have gotten around to writing *All My Rivers Are Gone* [renamed *Glen Canyon Betrayed*] about my trips through Glen Canyon if he hadn't come through and read the novel and said, "Get on with it, Lee." Thanks, Ed.

ML: What was it about Glen Canyon that captured your heart?

Lee: I loved the calm, quiet places on the river and in the canyons. It was serene. It was a canyon with hundreds of cathedrals in it made of native stone. And it had a reverence to it that I didn't even recognize the first time I went down. I just felt a strange difference about it, and it didn't occur to me until the third or fourth trip that this is a private place.

Glen Canyon was my sanctuary. It was my everything. And as time went on, it became my lover. It was there that I could be my most natural self. I used to think, I wonder if you can love a place more than you do a human being. And I've come to the conclusion that you really can.

The Grand Canyon is powerful, majestic, overpowering. But it was very different when you put your boat in the water at Glen Canyon. You're not thinking ahead about all the terrible rapids that you're going to go through, and how your heartbeat goes up and your adrenalin rushes in. When you're in the Glen, what you're thinking about is the tranquility of the place, the quiet water, and the eternal green on the banks with those towering 300- to 1,500-foot sandstone walls.

Then there were the side canyons that took us into their hearts, sometimes long, sometimes short, many with perennial streams, so rare in our desert environments. One of the most impressive was the one we named Little Arch Canyon. Just as we went in, about three hundred feet up on the right, a part of the wall had broken away from the main one, and just weathered away underneath was this beautiful little arch. It was probably about half the size of an ordinary living room.

Little Arch Canyon had a very insignificant entrance. First you had to get by a choke of willow branches and a few tammies [tamarisks]. But once you got in, the canyon narrowed down to what people call slot canyons today, a word I don't like. A slot—that's something you find in Las Vegas. I call them fluted canyons because the fluting and curving of the walls sometimes looks like weaving. The canyon's narrow floor was full of maidenhair fern. As we walked up, we tried not to hurt the fern, and yet we had to put our feet down. When you put your hands on the walls, you'd still be touching fern because it grew up about five to six feet from the bottom.

And then there were the tapestry walls that came down on both sides, patterns that looked just like a Spanish shawl. If that isn't a scene that just blows your mind, then nothing can.

When the canyon widened out, there were redbud trees, and more willows, and other trees, and little lizards all over the walls. Sometimes a great big pool of brilliant sun would come down, just like a spotlight. The reflection of that one light on the canyon walls was incredibly beautiful. The canyon ended in a waterfall and a lovely little pool.

Two friends—photographer Tad Nichols and river guide Frank Wright—and I went in there three or four times over the years. One day I finally said, "You know, I really want to get up that one wall." You could almost see around the next bend. It was just teasing us to get beyond where we couldn't quite go.

TAD NICHOLS, *IMAGES OF A LOST WORLD, GLEN CANYON* (1999)

Tad Nichols fell in love with the magic of Glen Canyon during the 1950s. His book, *Images of a Lost World, Glen Canyon: Photographs and Recollections* takes readers on a powerful journey down the 162-mile stretch of the Colorado River through the canyon, the wilderness that no longer exists, and the human history now buried underneath the reservoir's waters. The book includes short essays by Frank Wright and Katie Lee.

Nichols had a background in geology and anthropology and was a student of Ansel Adams and Brett Weston. His photographs were often published in *Arizona Highways*. Nichols made nature films for Walt Disney and documented scientific expeditions, one to Mexico's Paricutin Volcano, which erupted out of a cornfield in 1943 and grew to more than 1,300 feet within the year. Nichols died in 2000 at the age of eighty-nine.

We decided that we would try and chip enough little handholds, just minor ones, to get us up beyond this waterfall and into that hidden place. Up to this time, we had never, ever taken a pick or made any steps. We never damaged the canyon.

We made one step in the pool that night at water level, knowing it would be covered up when the monsoon rains came and filled the pool with more water. We didn't have to make a second step because we found a small hole covered with moss, and all we had to do was put a stick in it. The next morning, we went in and chipped another step farther up by standing on the stick. That was enough for me to get up, followed by Tad and Frank.

We wove through a labyrinth of stone, as smooth as the walls of a house, beautifully sculptured, and the walls were like silver and looked like they just had raindrops all over them and little stone pockmarks. When we came to the end we found we had stepped into a perfect stone teepee, with a skylight that was no bigger than the length of two of our arms put together and this beautiful spiral hole at the top where the water siphoned down and then dripped along the sides. We just stood in this bowl of stone and just breathed.

As that light shone down into this teepee, I had the feeling that we might have been the first humans to have ever been in that spot. That's quite a feeling. It does something to you. I can't explain it. It just makes you feel like you're part of the earth.

ML: After the dam, others who went down that river never wanted to go back. They didn't want to see what was destroyed because they couldn't take it. But you did go back. Why?

Lee: I went back to the Glen three times as the reservoir filled. I don't know why I wanted to torture myself and look at it, but I wanted to see some places.

Before then, part of the Glen's wonderful mystery was if I couldn't get back there as often as I wanted, I could always imagine what was there. Now that feeling is destroyed. I have blocked many memories and cry.

The third time, I went into Hall's Crossing, where the water had come halfway up that thousand-foot wall. It was probably about five hundred feet deep there. I didn't know what I was going to see. I came in at night and I stayed in Frank Wright's trailer.

The next morning I was almost afraid to go out because I heard all this racket. I heard motors revving and bulldozers scraping. There was even an airplane that came in and landed that morning at an airstrip, which recently had been made.

When I went and looked over the edge of the canyon, I just went down on my knees. I couldn't believe this trench, wall-to-wall water, nothing visible, all this slimy, foamy stuff licking into these private nooks that were the side canyons that we'd enjoyed. It was just devastating.

I had a little runabout, which I called SCREWD RIVER—screwdriver

Katie Lee Nymph. Photographer Martin Koehler. Northern Arizona University, Cline Library, Katie Lee Collection.

with a space between the D and the R. That same day, I went downstream toward Little Lost Eden Canyon, which was truly lost. I recognized some of the canyons only because of the mileage markers. All the parts that we had walked up were drowned. Many of the places that I could get to were totally uninteresting.

All I could think about was the beaver drowned in those side canyons because they were backed up with driftwood and couldn't get up the walls. The beaver had built hundreds of little dams trying to stem the tide, and you'd see them floating on these patches of wood and they looked just totally bewildered—they didn't know where they were. There were no birds. All their trees, all their greenery, all the willows, all the ash, all the squawberry bushes—everything was gone, wall-to-wall water. No life at all.

I did manage to go into Little Arch Canyon. The reason I recognized it was because the little arch was now twenty feet over my head, not three hundred, and I recognized the sluiceway it formed or I wouldn't have had a clue. I was halfway up, when the walls began to close in, and I cut the motor. The silence rang. No wake, no wind, no whisper of a breeze. Above the water, a brine line rose, higher than my reach, and was covered with blooms of dried algae. I went as far as I could and then sat on the bow and pushed against the walls until I couldn't get any further.

Sunlight shot almost directly down, lighting the green algae-covered slick rock underneath. I could see into the depths at least a dozen feet because here was light in the canyon. As I came around the bend, I looked down into the water. I thought that I was probably near the pool where we'd made the steps. Yes, there it was, the light perfect, shining through the smoke hole and against the slanting walls of the stone teepee. I dove down into the water about six feet. Sure enough, there was the hole into the teepee where we had stood in the twilight bottom of that bowl of stone, the timeless womb of Mother Earth, the first holy place I had ever been.

And now I'm crying again. Why do we destroy places like this? What's the matter with us? Makes me mad all over again.

That was the last time I went back. I said to myself: I cannot deal with this. This is like my lover is in a wheelchair, and he's immobile. He can't move anymore. I'm never going to go back and watch him die. I thought that human beings had sensitivity and conscience, something that would keep us from doing harm to such beauty as that. I guess I was wrong.

I'm angry. I'm dead angry. And you know something about anger? Anger is a very strong emotion, and I have learned that it works just as well—if not better sometimes—than love. But it has to be directed. And if you direct your anger, you can use it as an energy force. And that's what I've tried to do through my years of activism to restore the canyon and let the Colorado River run free.

I'm angry at these fat, gutted, fat, tired pigs on their four-wheel-drive machines going all over the sandstone, the beautiful sandstone that took hundreds of thousands of years to make, and cover it with their black skid marks.

When I hear that these people might again be able to get into parts of Glen Canyon when the reservoir is dropped—I'm almost glad sometimes that it is under water and they can't fucking well get to it. So there. Now I'm crying again.

ML: What should be done now?

Lee: I'm quite realistic about the certainty that although Powell Reservoir will never be full again, it will be a lengthy time before it becomes a wall-to-wall puddle; and realistic also about the necessity of continuing to talk about protecting what is there. The Glen's ecosystem was and still is intricate, fecund, seminal, and, above all, fragile.

As drought and warming climates reveal more of the Glen's side canyons, there needs to be a change in custody as well as how it is named. We need new terminology to tell people that this is a protected place where only a few can go, not a recreational area full of concessions, railings, ropes, bridges, paths, signs, trail markers, parking lots, gas stations, and pay stations. National parks and recreation areas are playgrounds for everyone, at any time.

It's time we came up with a new designation, maybe something like a biopreserve, to indicate that Glen Canyon is a place where ecosystems have been destroyed and must be given time to restore themselves as water levels decrease. They won't have a chance if hordes of people descend on it. Invite a herd of buffalo into your rose garden and you'll know why. Australia's got thousands of protected places where everybody and his machine can't go.

In our pain and in our panic to save the rose we may have to grab the stem. But any time somebody comes up with something new, it's: "Oh, we can't do that." "Oh, that'll just wreck something else." Get off it and move on, for Christ's sake. People are such stupid shits.

ML: What can you say about the government's labeling of environmentalists?

Lee: Today, people that protest for wilderness and march against a coal-fired plant or an oil or gas pipeline are labeled as eco-terrorists. That word makes me laugh.

It came from somebody, probably a Republican, never mind, I'm sure it was a Republican. We know who the terrorists are. They're the government and the corporations ripping the land apart.

We're supposed to be a free country and be able to say how we feel, in front of a crowd, in a small room, around a campfire, wherever. I'm no terrorist. I can get up and speak my piece or sing or show slides, but I don't get out and rabble-rouse much more than picking up a few survey stakes once in a while. I think my way is much more effective.

I have some bumper stickers on my car that say it pretty much like it is. One says, "I love my country, but I fear my government." Another says, "End of Lake Fowell," because I took the "Friends of Lake Powell" Chamber of Commerce sticker and cut off the F-r-i, leaving "end" and putting the F over the P. They don't make that bumper sticker anymore. Another says, "Restore Glen Canyon: Free the Colorado."

I'm amazed at what this [Trump] administration has done to put fear into people who show disagreement with them. I'll never forget the day when a woman came up to me at the parking lot at Safeway and said, "Oh, I like your bumper stickers, but aren't you afraid to show them?" I said, "Lady, what's happened to you? You do not have to be afraid to be an American and protest if there's something you don't like about the government. You have the freedom to speak." She said again, "You know, I'm afraid."

Dear God. That's awful. I'm not afraid. I'll put my feelings out there anytime, anywhere. That's my protest. So sue me!

Oh, yes. I nearly forgot about my license plate. It says, "Dam Dam." The Department of Motor Vehicles asked me what is behind the meaning of my personalized license plate. I told them, "That's the name of my sheep ranch."

ML: I remember you saying that protesting the dam was like trying to put out a fire with a teacup, so why do you keep protesting?

Lee: I'm doing whatever I can. I can't hike the canyons anymore, but I can tell people why the Glen was a holy place.

When my friends learned about the filling of Glen Canyon, many of us were angry and that got us into being activists. But that was the 1950s, and like many, we were individuals who didn't join organizations. I didn't even join the Sierra Club.

We tried to protest—we wrote letters; we took people down the river—but there were never enough of us put together to do anything politically about getting rid or protesting the fact that this dam was going to envelop a place that should never be. As my friend Martin Litton said, "If you don't try and lose, then it's a heartburn. If you've tried and you lose, you know you did the best you can."

THE "CONSERVATION CONSCIENCE" OF MARTIN LITTON

Clyde Martin Litton was one of the earliest conservationists to protest the building of a dam on the Colorado River in Echo Park, another at the north end of Glen Canyon, and a third one near the Marble Canyon Bridge in Arizona.

Litton fell in love with the Colorado River when he first rafted it in 1955. In 1964, he led a river trip down the Colorado with, among others, prominent environmentalist David Brower, photographer Philip Hyde, and author Francois Leydet. The trip led to the publication of Leydet's book, *Time and the River Flowing* (1964), which included photographs by Hyde and Ansel Adams. The book helped catalyze opposition to the dams being proposed on the Colorado River.

Litton also fought to save California's redwoods and fought against the logging of giant sequoias in Sequoia National Forest and Giant Sequoia National Monument. As travel editor for *Sunset Magazine* from 1954 to 1968, he published a cover story titled "The Redwood Country," which aroused the public fervor needed for establishing Redwood National Park in 1968.

Litton authored *The Life and Death of Lake Mead* (1968). He has been featured in such documentary films as *Monumental: David Brower's Fight for Wild America* (2004) and the award-winning *River Runners of the Grand Canyon* (2012).

David Brower is credited with calling Litton his "conservation conscience."

Litton died in 2014. He was ninety-seven years old.

Dave Brower, who was executive director of the Sierra Club, fought against the Echo Park Dam in Utah's Dinosaur National Monument and helped save it but did not fight for saving Glen Canyon. It was a mistake he has often said he has regretted.

For me, if you love something like that and your life has been changed by it, then you're going to stand up and fight for it. You can't just sit there and let anger eat at you. But if you put your anger into action, that can be your life. And I guess that's sort of what mine was like. And that's what Dave Foreman's is like; and what Jack Loeffler's is like. I believe that that's what Ed Abbey felt about the desert. We don't want every place on the planet to be damaged. None of us can quit protesting—it's part of who we are. I fight because it is instilled in me. It's in my soul.

———

In 2017, Katie Lee died peacefully in her home at the age of ninety-eight.

5 | KEN SLEIGHT

Biography

When Ken Sleight returned from serving in Korea, he went to college at the University of Utah, graduating in 1955. For three years, he worked for Firestone Tire and Rubber. He quit to become an outfitter taking people down the Colorado, Green, and Escalante Rivers in Arizona and Utah.

He first ran the Colorado River through Glen Canyon in 1955. When the Bureau of Reclamation announced plans to dam the canyon and flood 186 miles of river, he became an environmental activist. In early 1967, Ken was elected president of the Western River Guides Association and brought environmental concerns to the forefront. Even when Reservoir Powell drowned the canyon, he never stopped trying to restore the free flow of the Colorado River.

From 2014 to 2016, the *Canyon Country Zephyr* published a reprint of earlier articles Ken had written for the *Zephyr* called "Ken Sleight Remembers." Sleight touched on places he loved, like Arches or Escalante; characters he knew, like Harry Aleson, a river guide in Glen Canyon; and on some of the battles he fought on behalf of indigenous peoples who live on the Colorado Plateau.

As one of Edward Abbey's close friends, Sleight became the inspiration for the character Seldom Seen Smith in *The Monkey Wrench Gang*.

When Sleight and his wife, Jane, purchased Pack Creek Ranch near Moab, Utah, in 1986, he celebrated his friendship with Abbey by naming several of the roads there Abbey Road, Desert Solitaire, and Seldom Seen.

In 2012, Sleight was inducted into the River Runners Hall of Fame, located at the John Wesley Powell River History Museum in Green River, Utah. In 2018, Sleight, Ryann Savino, and Martha Ham created the museum exhibit *Glen Canyon: A River Guide Remembers*. The exhibit takes visitors on a trip through Glen Canyon with a remarkable collection of historic landscape photographs, Native American artifacts, boats and river gear, passenger portraits and journals, and handwritten-packing lists.

Sleight is currently working on his memoir.

My film crew and I interviewed Ken at Pack Creek Ranch, Utah: the first time at his home, the second time outside the cabin that Ed Abbey used when he was writing, and the third time in Ken's workspace, the Quonset hut, where he has many boxes of his extensive archives.

———

ML Lincoln: How did you and Ed Abbey meet?

Ken Sleight: Right after I read *Desert Solitaire*, I became very interested in it. I sent Abbey a little note telling him how great it was. He wrote back, "Ken, we've got to get together for a beer." Here we were in the same town, knew about each other, but never met.

After Arches, Abbey became a ranger at Lee's Ferry. One day, I took a few boats and gear down to the ferry to get ready for a trip down Grand Canyon. While I was unloading, Peggy, my helper, tapped me on the shoulders. "There's a ranger coming; tall, lanky guy." I looked up and there was Abbey with his inspection clipboard. I had expected to see him, and he had expected to see me. It was a real moment together on finally meeting.

Then what he did was not like most other rangers, howdy and good-bye. He stayed there and started pumping up a doggone boat, and then another one. He worked for two hours 'til we got all the boats ready to go for my party that was to come the next morning. After that, we pulled some sandwiches together, and we ate there on the boats, along with some beer. We started to have a little more beer, a little more beer,

Ken Sleight on the oars. Photographer Bill Adams.
Courtesy of the Collection of Ken Sleight.

and spent most of that night cussing out the damn dam. That night was
the beginning of The Monkey Wrench Gang, because we talked far into
the night about the evils that had happened in Glen Canyon. We both
knew much about the canyon.

ML: Did you and Ed ever monkeywrench together? I did hear a story
about your antics with Ed on the road to Bull Frog Marina.

Sleight: One day, Ed Abbey came to see me and says, "Let's go over the
Henrys for the day and camp out." So he rolled over in the morning. He
had a big box of beer cans in the back of his truck. I said, "You going to
the dump?" "Yeah, that's where I'm headed." I went in and grabbed a
whole box of beer cans, and put 'em in the truck: "If you're going, then
take all my stuff."

Eventually, we went down the spanking new highway built all the
way to Bullfrog Marina, black and beautiful as a road can be. We
drove to the sign that said Glen Canyon National Recreation Area and
stopped. Truck after truck was hauling these great big boats and lum-
bering down to Bullfrog Marina on Lake Powell.

I had read John Wesley Powell, who named the Glen during his 1869
survey. I had gone down on many trips, and Glen Canyon became home
to me. To me, it was mine. I thought of all those canyons destined to be
destroyed. Abbey felt the same way. When you're in an area like that it
becomes yours.

Abbey turned around, thought a minute, thought some more, and
said, "Well, we'd just as well do it, just as well do it." We got out of the
truck, grabbed the boxes of beer cans, and watched them lift right up
and float out of those boxes and splatter down on the highway. What a
beautiful thing!

Abbey's been criticized about it. I've been criticized about it. "Why
would you do that? If you're an environmentalist, why would you
throw beer cans on the road?" After a day of thinking about how they
wrecked and destroyed the Glen Canyon, and seeing all those big boats
going down, polluting and trashing the whole reservoir, we got angry.
At that moment we just wanted to monkeywrench.

It was totally wrong but apt.

ML: Can you talk about when you and Ed Abbey lived together at Green River and then at Pack Creek Ranch?

Sleight: After we met at Lee's Ferry and became friends, we bought a little melon and alfalfa farm and a one-room shack at Willow Bend in Green River, Utah. I was taking care of the place and doing the farming and had plans to do all this stuff. But neither one of us really had time. I was a river and backcountry horse-pack guide. Ed was writing and lecturing.

We had an affinity with each other. In so many ways we were quite alike. There were only a few things on which we disagreed pertaining to the farm. We were taking care of the fence line, and I was cutting down rabbit brush, when Abbey asked, "What are you cutting that down for?" I said, "It's rabbit brush, just a weed. If it stays, it'll catch fire and burn our fence line down." He became very antagonistic to my comment and took offense at cutting down a living green plant that was native to the area.

That's one of the few differences we ever had. We had a great hour or two discussion about it over sandwiches and a beer. We listened to each other and, in the end, I just left the rabbit brush be. When I look back, I laugh like hell about his concern about a common weed. But it also got me thinking that when people are concerned about one thing that means a lot to them, you listen.

We were in Willow Bend when Ed brought me the manuscript *The Monkey Wrench Gang*: "Read it and tell me what you think." I took it down the Dolores River and read the whole damn thing in one day. And the next day, I read it again. It caused me to laugh like hell. I knew it was good. It made an impact much greater than I first thought.

ML: Were you Seldom Seen Smith in *The Monkey Wrench Gang*?

Sleight: A lot of people ask me that. You know who Seldom Seen Smith is? Ed Abbey himself. All his characters—the dialogue, their actions, and so forth—radiate back to his philosophy and what he experienced.

I can see that Seldom Seen is a caricature of me. I recognized the similarities between Abbey's thoughts and my own because we thought a lot alike. Abbey picked his friends, sometimes a motley group. We choose our friends because they think like us. There's no mystery about that.

Around the campfire, Abbey was as amusing in his quiet way as he was in his books. He was also a great listener. A lot of the things that went around the campfire showed up in his books and articles verbatim or very close to what he heard people say. After everything was quiet, Abbey would go off and start writing notes. It was something to observe.

When I read some of his expressions or his dialogues for Seldom Seen, I have thought, yeah, I could have said it that way. But in my opinion, Seldom Seen Smith is Abbey, with a token of maybe Sleight. That's the way I look at it. And if Abbey were here, he'd probably say the same thing.

ML: Where did the name Seldom Smith come from?

Sleight: Even though Abbey and I were great friends, sometimes he wouldn't see me for a month. "I haven't seen you for a long time," he'd say. When I would come back from my river trips after putting myself out for clients and new friends, all I'd want is just to get off on my own until the next trip. That's how in Abbey's mind I was Seldom Seen. That's where the name comes from, I'm sure. Is that right, Ed? He was a great one to put tag names on some people that were humorously apt.

ML: When did you move from Willow Bend?

Sleight: Eventually, we sold the farm at Willow Bend because we couldn't make the payments. We weren't that rich, and so we let it go to a mutual friend.

In 1986, my wife Jane and I bought the land and historic cabins at Pack Creek Ranch, just south of Moab. Abbey came up here with us. He and his kids lived in the red house, which we called Roadhouse, with a tiny cabin right out the back door, which became his writing retreat. He really enjoyed working there.

When Abbey would go into his cabin, he didn't want any

interruption. If I heard him typing when I came up during the day, I wouldn't intrude. Nor would I let others intrude. He wanted privacy so much.

Everybody wanted a part of Abbey. Every time he went out speaking, people wanted to meet him.

They knew he lived up there, but they didn't have his phone number. "I don't want to meet people," Abbey told me, "I've just had enough." Reporters would call me and say, "I'd like to interview Ed Abbey." He could have had one person after another taking up his whole time. When would he write? So I helped him out. Most of the time people had to come through me to get to Abbey. I felt like a protector of his privacy. Funny thing is I start feeling like Abbey when there are a lot of people wanting my attention, and I can't quite get my thoughts together.

Both before and after Abbey died, Pack Creek became a place for gatherings of environmental activists, which became a series of events, musicals, book reviews, and lectures with environmental themes. One that was filmed was called *Conversation at Pack Creek*.

ML: Let's talk about White Mesa Mill, south of Blanding, Utah, which I passed on the way up here. As you know it's the only licensed uranium mill in the United States. I stopped to read the entrance sign. I couldn't believe that it only talked about the lack of injuries on the job site. But what I've heard you talk about are the incidences of cancer caused by uranium mining and processing operations.

Sleight: With the nuclear era came a lot of uranium mining in Utah. And if you're going to mine, you've got to have a place to process that ore to make it into yellowcake and a place to keep the waste. They built many mills near Ute and Navajo land during the cold war.

The White Mesa Mill still dismays me. I've been in opposition to it ever since the land was given to them by the Bureau of Land Management [BLM]. It was even questionable that they had the authority to do so. The mill was built right over some old Ute Indian ruins and burials, and many objected to placing it right on sacred sites. It's just one aspect of this whole thing.

At first, the plant was just going to take care of the uranium ore that was mined around the Colorado Plateau. Then they wanted to bring in what they called monitor retrieval storage, the high-level radioactive stuff, and store it for a little while before it went on to its final destination to be buried. Utah governor Scott Matheson, who served from 1977 to 1985, said he wasn't going to allow that, and he fought like hell to keep it out. And he did. They still haven't found the place to dispose of it.

They did allow low-level radioactive deposits to be brought in from Eastern and Midwest states and from foreign countries, like Japan and Canada. The tailings grew and grew. I always questioned whether this plant could safely store radioactive material that lasts for tens of thousands of years among the canyons in our little area. We fought against having it brought in, in the first place.

I remember coming back from the torch relay during the 2002 Olympics through the Navajo reservation. Thousands turned up in Monument Valley, and I watched the torch pass from person to person. The Navajos were very excited by the ceremonies.

But on the way back from that great occasion, the wind came up, and a big black cloud of darkness came down the valley and crossed Highway 191, south of White Mesa Mill. It eventually drifted all the way through much of the reservation. I drove through that black dust cloud. I thought that it must be harmful. I followed this cloud all the way up to where it was coming off the tailings at the mill. I took pictures and sent copies to the San Juan County commissioners. The company just haphazardly heaped the waste piles, without covers, right near the highway. The wind was still taking dust off the piles when I walked into the plant. I called attention to this to the authorities; others did likewise. They did nothing.

When I went to the next San Juan County commissioners' meeting to protest, they asked, "Why did you drive up there if you knew it was harmful." I answered, "It was the right thing to do."

Those tailings made people sick. Ask the people who work at plants like the mill who get cancer and died sooner than they might have. It was a huge health problem. We called for full-scale epidemiological studies for years. None were done, other than a few minor ones at the Monticello

Mill, which is now closed. Later they found increases in cancer and other problems, but because many of the Native Americans didn't have adequate records, they were deprived of government compensation.

RADIATION EXPOSURE COMPENSATION ACT

In 1990, the US Congress passed the Radiation Exposure Compensation Act (RECA). It compensates people who contracted cancers and other life-threatening diseases as a result of being exposed to nuclear testing at Utah test sites in the 1950s (downwinders), participated in nuclear weapons tests, worked as employees in uranium mining and milling, or transported uranium ore.

Even with amendments to RECA, many people have found it difficult to provide the paperwork required to provide employment, residency within the designated areas, and marriage certificates. Nevertheless, according to a report published by the US Department of Justice submitted to Congress in February 2016, more than $2 billion has been awarded since the program's inception to approximately 31,000 claimants—$264 million to Native Americans of seventeen different tribes. That said, the report also states that the majority of the awards went to downwinders. "As of 16 March 2016, successful claims had been awarded to 19,555 downwinders, 3,963 onsite participants, 6,214 uranium miners, 1,673 uranium millers and 328 ore transporters." (https://www.justice.gov/jmd/file/821056/download)

So nothing gets done, and the White Mesa Mill continues on and has the sign you saw about their safety record. I think it's an unsafe plant, always have. And that's what irritates me, is that all this evidence is out there and they continue on. We're ignored. Our Radiation Control Board didn't put the brakes on either.

It's very dismaying. You fight and fight and fight, and it doesn't do much good.

THREATS TO WATER CONTAMINATION BELEAGUER WHITE MESA MILL

For the last five years, members of the Ute Tribe, with support from the Grand Canyon Trust, have claimed that there are leaks in the liners underneath the mill's tailings ponds and that contaminated water has been found in the groundwater beneath the mills. According to Scott Clow, environmental program director for the tribe, the contaminated water appears to be moving toward the nearby town of White Mesa. According to him, the acidity of the water has increased, and so have concentrations of potentially harmful substances, such as heavy metals. If true, then contamination poses a potential long-term threat to the Navajo aquifer, the main source of drinking water for southeastern Utah and northern Arizona.

State regulators deny the threats and say the pollution is due to other sources.

Meanwhile, uranium mining is on the uptake in the Southwest and operating permits for new Southwest uranium mines continue to be approved by the BLM.

In 2018, permits submitted by Energy Fuels Resources, White Mesa Mills' owner, were approved for the production of Vanadium from waste ponds located on the property of the mill, with known toxic potential to employees.

The mill is unlikely to be closed because it is the last mill in the United States to process uranium.

Since then, I worked closely with the Navajo and the Ute, fighting for better living and working conditions. They are such a neglected people. What battles we've had on their behalf! I have a lot of comforts around me, but I feel that they should have the same as the rest of us. Many live in deep poverty and there's high unemployment. Here in Utah I see people trying to keep those good things from them, whether it's improving healthcare or their standard of living. I don't see the government coming to their rescue, even when they could help.

Sometime during that period, I remember launching a drive to register Native Americans to run against the white Republican power structure in San Juan County. The campaign was dubbed "Niha-Whol-Zhiizh," which means, "It's our turn." I so agreed with them.

VICTORIES IN SAN JUAN COUNTY, UTAH, CONTINUE TO BE CHALLENGED

In 2018, voters in San Juan County, Utah, elected Willy Grayeyes to serve as county commissioner by a vote of 973 to 814 over Republican Kelly G. Law. For the first time in the county's history, Navajos dominated the three-person board. (Navajo Kenneth Maryboy was elected in 2006.)

Unfortunately, the election continues to be legally challenged by Law who claims Greyeyes is not a resident of the county. In January 2019, Seventh District Judge Don Torgerson ruled against Law's challenge and declared Greyeyes was a resident. Law's attorneys promptly appealed the ruling and filed it in the Utah State Supreme Court.

Also, the redistricting of the voting boundaries of San Juan County that occurred in 2017 continues to be legally challenged, including the population estimates that led to it. The redistricting was an acknowledgement that Navajos have been the dominant population for many decades in San Juan County, and that the boundaries of previous voting districts gerrymandered against them.

Finally, the majority of Navajos in San Juan County (as well as Hopi and Ute Tribes) supported protection of the Bears Ears National Monument, which was established in 2016 by President Obama. In 2018 President Trump issued an executive order shrinking monument boundaries to make way for uranium, coal, and oil and gas extraction. Several lawsuits challenging the order have been filed.

According to San Juan County administrator Kelly Pehrson, as of March 2019, these controversies have already cost San Juan County several million dollars.

ML: You were an activist long before you met Ed Abbey? What first turned you into one?

Sleight: The dropping of the bomb at Hiroshima and another one on Nagasaki really changed my mind about government in general and turned me into an avid antinuclear activist. It was such an atrocity to kill so many civilians, and so needlessly. The war was nearly over. All they had to do was wait the Japanese out.

Even before that, the government told lies and misled the public about the nuclear testing they did in the Nevada desert in the 1950s. Big clouds of radioactive dust settled over people downwind, killing many, getting many sick, and contaminating the milk of livestock and wild animals. Many children were born deformed.

A lot of my kin succumbed to cancer. I think that's why I got cancer a number of years ago. I've overcome it so far, knock on wood. But a lot of people weren't so lucky.

ML: Didn't you stand in front of bulldozers a few times?

Sleight: In 1990, the BLM decided to chain Amassa Back, just south of my land at Pack Creek Ranch at the foot of the LaSal Mountains. You know what chaining is? Hooking a big anchor chain between two enormous bulldozers and plowing up whatever is in between—sage, rabbit bush, pinions, and junipers.

A bunch of us went to the BLM and said they needed to do a more adequate environmental analysis. To us, chaining was an invitation to overgrazing and erosion. The authorities refused. When we informed them about the Native American sites up there, they told us they would flag them so the bulldozers could go around. I got the schedule of when and where they were going to be.

Soon after, when the bulldozers started up, I got on my horse Knothead and went down there. They were mowing everything in sight, even the ruins. The BLM hadn't provided the bulldozer operators with monitors to tell them where and where not to go. That pissed me off. I rode in front of the big monsters coming toward me and stayed there. When they stopped, I said, "Well, you can't go on. There's no monitors on the bulldozers to tell you where the archeological sites are." They called BLM and county law enforcement. Although my horse reared a couple of times, we stayed our ground. He was a damn good horse.

When the authorities got there, they grabbed my horse and asked me to dismount. They dragged me off to the side and told me that I had no right to stop the bulldozers. Because I was running for the Utah's House of Representatives, they warned me it wouldn't look good if they charged me. I thought to myself, well, so be it. I had expected that they'd charge me with something, but they didn't.

Half an hour later, they proceeded with the chaining.

Out of that incident came a meeting with two or three of my friends and Utah's BLM director. After we told him our story, the BLM responded by calling for a temporary moratorium on chaining. "We also are going to do environmental studies on site-specific areas."

It was one of the battles we actually won. We didn't win the whole battle, yet we had an influence on changing policy. And out of that came more scrutiny of the practice of chaining our lands. So I felt good about that.

It was because of direct action. I learned that if your conscience tells you there is an unjust law or regulation, you should do whatever you can do to stop it. Your conscience is even above the law. However, I always put the limit on doing no physical damage to humans or property. You can do everything you want as long as it's nonviolent.

Civil disobedience works. It goes back to Thoreau and Gandhi and many others. It works. It tells the public you're serious. It's an example of nonviolent monkeywrenching. Passive resistance or direct action is a real good way to bring attention to "evil." I'm all for it.

ML: You led hundreds of trips into the wilderness and protested against the building of Glen Canyon Dam. Has any place captured your heart like Glen Canyon?

Sleight: Like a good woman? Yeah. Sure. A lot of places: Havasu Canyon, Machu Picchu in Peru, the Yukon River in Alaska. There are a lot

Ken Sleight at protest as he is pulled by Forest Service personnel, circa late 1980s. Photographer unknown. Courtesy of the Collection of Ken Sleight.

of beautiful places everywhere you go on this earth. Every community's got their beautiful places, right? The thing about Glen Canyon—you always wanted to come back to it. I spent a lot of my life up and down the Colorado River through that canyon.

The destruction of Glen Canyon is the greatest inhumane act against the environment that I knew in my lifetime. It meant a lot to me because I was there and I watched them destroy thousands and thousands and thousands of sacred sites.

Others and myself fought like hell against it. But I was in my twenties and didn't know about direct action. I could have done much more to stop that dam, but I didn't know how.

David Brower, who was the executive director of the Sierra Club in the 1960s, bless him, put in a big advertisement in the *New York Times*, "Should We Also Flood the Sistine Chapel So Tourists Can Get Nearer the Ceiling?," which sparked a nationwide protest against the planned dam project at the confluence of the Green and Yampa Rivers, Utah, in

Dinosaur National Monument. It did work. Brower made a compromise to let the dam at Glen Canyon be created if the Bureau of Reclamation would abandon a dam that was proposed at Echo Park, which would have flooded Dinosaur. A lot of environmentalists supported the Glen Canyon Dam construction because they thought it wasn't a big deal. They didn't know the consequences of the dam to the Glen. That made me very angry. Once they won no dam construction in Dinosaur, environmentalists thought they had won the whole game. They turned their backs on Glen Canyon.

In 1970, water from Lake Foul began to flow up toward Rainbow Bridge National Monument. Then I met with Brower, Ted Turner, and others, and decided we'd sue the bastards. That was one of the first times that I took an active role in saying something should be preserved. We filed our lawsuit with the US District Court. Chief Judge Willis Ritter ruled with us and halted the progress of the reservoir into Rainbow Bridge National Monument boundaries. I was the most happy person in the whole world after we won.

Then the decision went all the way to the US Circuit Court of Appeals in Denver. The Bureau of Reclamation appealed the District Court decision. The Circuit Court, presided over by Judge Lewis Powell, ruled against us. Then we tried to take it to the Supreme Court and they refused to hear the case. We lost. It taught me a lot. It was especially galling to me.

A few years later, when Judge Powell became Supreme Court Chief Justice, he said it was one of the worst decisions he had been involved in as an appeals judge. It has been a sticking point in my mind until this day.

In the planning stages prior to the building of the dam, the law said that Rainbow Bridge would not be impaired by this reservoir. What was most unforgivable and heartbreaking was that the federal government broke its own law, which said that the water levels of any reservoirs could not encroach into any national park or monument.

I used to be able to lie down on the slick rock and look up at the arch and listen to the Canyon Wrens. The little spring and redbud tree that was growing next to it was flooded. It was very hurtful. When the water came up, I had no further enjoyment of those experiences.

I knew for years that they were going to dam it, but I wasn't prepared for that defining moment. It's like going to the guillotine: You know it's coming, but until that moment you're not really prepared. I couldn't visualize it internally. It broke my heart.

When the Bureau of Reclamation closed the cofferdams and started letting the water in, I was surprised how fast the water came up and filled all those little side canyons where I used to take people.

When we came back to Glen Canyon that first year, before the waters completely filled it, I poked my boat up into some of the side canyons.

In Music Temple, the water climbed over pictographs and petroglyphs and covered the Powell inscriptions dating back to 1869—yes, I could take my hand down beneath the surface of that water and feel them, but it wasn't the same.

Across from there is Hidden Passage where I took my boat as far as it could go. The big mud bank was gone. We used to trample through and it was fun for me, but maybe not for everybody. Walking up the narrow, sinewy canyon passageway used to be the greatest hike. The wildlife was drowned out. There were no more freshwater bluegills. Now all you can see were little lizards on a stick of wood, just floating on the water surface.

I was there to see the waters come up into the big amphitheater, drowning it. Each trip, the water got higher and higher until it overwhelmed a little waterfall there and destroyed it.

Cathedral in the Desert was a cathedral, no doubt about it. I used to have to part the willows in order to get into it. I'd never felt so good in such a sublime area in my whole life.

When I ran trips, we did a layover at Lake Canyon to see many Anasazi [ancestral Puebloan] sites. It was dense with human history, but the water, at that point, had drowned them out.

The flooding of Glen Canyon was a wholesale destruction.

If you ask why I am an environmentalist, it's because I saw so much devastation right in front of my eyes.

So be it. Glen Canyon is a dear, dear subject.

ML: What is wilderness to you?

Sleight: Freedom. To get off the road, get off the trails where there are no people, where you might have some adventure, where you might be at risk because you are at the mercy of the wild. There certainly are more regulations now, but back then, there was nobody to tell you what to do when you found yourself having to face survival and muster through. You had the freedom to do what you wanted, right or wrong, to make mistakes, and figure out how they might affect your life. It gets you to understand who you are on your own. It's very personal.

ML: So many defeats. What keeps you fighting?

Sleight: Yeah, there's been a hell of a lot of defeats. You get to a point where you want to stamp your feet, yell, and make your voice heard. At least you have a feeling of doing something.

I plan to make the most of whatever time I have left on this earth and continue protesting against what is unjust. It's still worthwhile.

Today there is renewed energy from younger activists, like Tim De-Christopher. He listened to his conscience and rebelled. He used civil disobedience to protest the injustice of oil leases without environmental impact studies. And he was ready to take the consequences.

He was so right to do what he did to protect the environment. I support him all the way because of that. It's a very emotional thing for me. I know how he feels. And he's said what he feels. We need more of that type of person.

ML: After all the years of protest, what might you like to tell young people, what advice would you like to give them?

Sleight: There's a time to rebel against unjust laws. But it comes down to this: how far do you want to go to protect what you've got?

Ed and I talked about that, the monkey wrench. You get up and say, okay, bring your monkey wrenches out, and go at 'em. What do most people think about when you say that? They think, you're going to throw the monkey wrench into the machines.

That's not all of it. Your monkey wrench is your talent. I've thought a lot about it. It might be speaking. It might be teaching. It might be writing, like Abbey. You might be a lawyer and file lawsuits.

Do you see what I mean? I guess it comes down not only to talent but expression. I tell people to express themselves, to find their ultimate creativity, to throw their talent and their everything to make this a better place to live. That's what's worthwhile: to use power and creativity to rectify the wrongs of the world. Abbey's monkey wrench is a symbol of "let's do better." That's what I subscribe to.

6 | DOUG PEACOCK

Biography

Author and naturalist Doug Peacock has published widely on wilderness issues ranging from grizzly bears to buffalo, from the Sonoran Desert to the fjords of British Columbia, from the tigers of Siberia to the blue sheep of Nepal.

A disabled American veteran, Peacock served two years as a Green Beret medic in the central highlands of Vietnam, chronicling his experiences in two memoirs. *Grizzly Years: In Search of the American Wilderness* (1990) follows Peacock's recovery from the wounds of war by immersion in North America's wildest lands, the realm of the grizzly bear. He credits grizzlies with saving his life and has since become a passionate advocate for the bears, camping extensively in Yellowstone and Glacier National Parks to document their struggles through film, photography, writing, and lecturing. His second memoir, *Walking It Off: A Veteran's Chronicle of War and Wilderness* (2005), delves more deeply into the trauma of war and the healing power of wilderness. He has worked with Vietnam, Iraq, and Afghanistan War veterans to help them find the solace that fighting for wilderness can provide.

Peacock was named a 2007 Guggenheim Fellow and was awarded the 2011 Lannan Cultural Freedom Fellowship for his work on archaeology, climate change, and the peopling of North America. He published his work in 2013 as *In the Shadow of the Sabertooth: Global Warming, the Origins of the First Americans, and the Terrible Beasts of the Pleistocene.*

Sabertooth won the 2014 High Plains Book Award in the Science Category. His other books include *¡Baja!* (1991) and *The Essential Grizzly: The Mingled Fates of Men and Bears* (2006), which he coauthored with Andrea Peacock.

Peacock was the subject of *Peacock's War* by Earthrise Entertainment, a 1989 feature film about his experiences in Vietnam and his work with grizzlies, which premiered on PBS's *Nature* program and won grand prizes at the Telluride Mountainfilm and Snowbird Film Festivals. More recently, he was featured in *Grizzly Country*, a short documentary by Ben Moon that won the 2019 New York WILD Film Festival Conservation Hero award. He has appeared on many television shows including *The Today Show*, *Good Morning America*, and *Democracy Now!*

Peacock is the founder of Save the Yellowstone Grizzly, a nonprofit dedicated to the protection of grizzlies in the lower forty-eight states. He cofounded Round River Conservation Studies (together with Dennis Sizemore), which has contributed to the preservation of more than thirty-five million acres of wilderness. He served as the organization's board chair for twenty-five years.

Two interviews were conducted with Doug: one at Chico Hot Springs in the heart of Paradise Valley, Montana; the other at his home outside of Livingston, Montana. As I left the interview, Doug tapped the doormat with his cane. It reads, "Come back with a warrant." Doug said, "This is for the Feds."

Doug Peacock lives with his wife, their two collie dogs, and an orange tabby cat in Emigrant, Montana. (www.dougpeacock.net; www.roundriver. org; https://elkriverbooks.com)

———

ML Lincoln: How did the Vietnam War change the course of your life?

Doug Peacock: The day I flew out of Vietnam was March 16, 1968. Our helicopter got shot at, which is not a big deal. However, I was over My Lai at the time, and I didn't know about the massacre that happened until a year later. I flew right over it! That event staggered me and changed my life.

THE MY LAI MASSACRE

The mass murder of between 347 and 504 unarmed South Vietnamese men, women, and children by US Army soldiers occurred on March 16, 1968. The soldiers were flown in by helicopter to the village of My Lai and surrounding hamlets. Women were gang raped, livestock and homes burned, water sources fouled.

Although the massacre was covered up by the US Army, hints reached newsman Seymour M. Hersh, who began sniffing for information. In late 1969, Hersh wrote up his research for a newspaper called *Dispatch News Service*. His exclusive exposé led to front-page stories in the *Washington Post* and the *New York Times*. In 1972, Hersh published a two-part essay about one of the Vietnam War's most heinous crimes in the *New Yorker*, which won him a Pulitzer Prize (https://www.newyorker.com/magazine/1972/01/22/i-coverup).

The only person to be accused of a crime was a platoon leader named Lieutenant William Calley Jr., who was found guilty of killing twenty-two people. Although he was given a life sentence, President Nixon reduced it to three-and-a-half years of house arrest at Calley's home in Fort Benning, Georgia.

Hugh Thompson, one of the helicopter crewmen who helped fly the soldiers into the villages, testified against Calley at his trial, and Thompson was publicly vilified for many years. This was because the story about three helicopter crewman who landed to try to stop the massacre was also squelched until 1998, when the US Army awarded them the Soldier's Medal for their heroism.

After Vietnam, I was like a lot of other Vets. I was really out of sorts.

Doug Peacock, Green Beret, 1968. Photographer M. E. Peacock.

Couldn't be around people. All my life, the one place I've always been comfortable is in the wilderness. When I got back, I went to live in the woods, sort of like a wounded animal crawling back into the brush. As the snow melted I went further and further north, until July when I ended up in the Wind River Range in Wyoming.

By early October, the weather turned bad, and I felt the first signs of another malaria attack. I had a lot of malaria when I was a Green Beret, so I knew what to expect.

I decided to go back into an area that I knew in Yellowstone that had hot springs on a creek, pitch a tent, and just kind of soak—like the old spa notion—and regain my health. One day, I was in this little pool about the size of a big bathtub in a thermal creek where the hot water tumbles over you. It was a brisk day—you could hear lodgepole pines being uprooted—must have been a 40-mile-an-hour gust.

As I was soaking, I caught some motion off to my side across the meadow. About 250 feet away, a mother grizzly with two yearling cubs was grazing. I didn't know anything about grizzly bears except to stay away from mothers and cubs. I decided to climb a tree. I waited until the bears were looking in the other direction and stood up. I blacked out because of the whirlpool-like effect of the hot water. As I started to fall, I grabbed at the tree, and it cut a big gash in my forehead.

But I was terrified, so I got up the tree anyway. When I got to the top, I discovered it wasn't much bigger than a Christmas tree. So now the blood is pouring down my face, and I'm seven or eight feet up, perched at the top like some kind of silly meadowlark.

That mother grizzly and her yearlings came around, eating this kind of blue-gray grass, sometimes grazing within fifteen feet of me. They were right there, and I was up this little stupid tree. She never even looked at me. Meanwhile, I'm freezing my ass off.

Those bears got my attention. I decided then that since the bears had sort of saved my life that it was payback time. My friend Ed Gage gave me a Bolex movie camera and said, "Go film those bears." I managed to raise about $6,000 and moved into the backcountry in Yellowstone to study grizzlies. In a way I never left.

From then on, the presence of the grizzlies colored the way I saw everything. They dominate the total ambience of a place. You can't ignore them. They're the most important thing out there—it's not about you and your problems. And I found that incredibly useful, therapeutic in every way.

I hung out with grizzlies for four to five years, living with them, off and on for decades, camping in Yellowstone National Park. I watched them for thousands of hours, call it old-fashioned bear biology, the way naturalists like the Murie brothers did in Alaska. Adolf Murie wrote *The Grizzlies of Mount McKinley*, which was probably the most readable of all the grizzly books.

I began noticing fewer and fewer bears. From 1968 to 1973, about 270 grizzly bears were killed in the Yellowstone ecosystem, which was virtually the entire population. We don't know, but the numbers went as low as maybe 80 or 100 grizzlies. They were shot at "mortality sumps," typically at garbage dumps in Montana border towns like Cooke City, West Yellowstone, and Jardine.

ML: Last night we were talking about people killing animals without any kind of compassion. Is that because they fear them?

Peacock: Our culture so fears the unknown that it becomes a driving force when you talk about people fearing wolves, fearing bears, fearing wilderness, fearing everything they do not know. I think the source of that fear is that as we get further and further from our origins, we fear the unknown even more. We didn't evolve in cities; we were basically creatures of the savanna, whose remnants we call wilderness. We are losing touch with that.

One of the lessons of going out and living with the grizzly bear, for instance, is not his ability to kill. It's not his awesome muscular strength that you learn. Sure, a grizzly bear can kill and eat you anytime it wants to, but it doesn't. That is amazing restraint. I think out of it we learn tolerance, and that's a kind of enforced humility. And humility really is the emotional basis behind reason, behind having an open mind.

When I say that we want to save grizzly bears, I'm also saying people are going to have to learn how to live with them. They once lived very well with us. On this continent, humans and grizzlies coexisted for as long as people have been here. It's only been the last two hundred years that that equation has stopped. But human tolerance is going to have to open up a lot more than just letting a bear wander through your yard, because now we have a common fate.

Yellowstone is an island ecosystem. The grizzlies that live there, and other animals, have a very difficult time trying to get up north to Glacier National Park. The problem with the weather heating up is that animals that can't fly or swim are going to have to go up the mountain. And the animals who then live at the tops of mountains, if they can't go north, they're going to go extinct. If you wanted to really save the grizzly in Yellowstone, you'd have to enlarge your vision and give them a way to go north, some kind of connectivity.

ML: You came out of the Vietnam War with Death Eyes; that death against animals and genocide of people are the same. What do you mean?

Peacock: I saw that the forces of death in the world are the same—the genocides, the destruction of bison, the dehumanization of other races and cultures—it's all connected. We just herd 'em up into ditches and corrals and slaughter 'em like pigs. These dark forces draw from the same well.

I came out of that war with Death Eyes. It's a real thing in my life. And the only person I've really ever talked to about it is author and activist Terry Tempest Williams.

To see with Death Eyes means basically you've gone beyond—that you've had some kind of experience, horrific, traumatic, or comparable to those things, that forever changes your life. That's what happened to me in Vietnam.

In shamanistic societies and some tribal cultures, once those who had experienced Death Eyes came back to the tribe, they were given ritual scarification or tattoos to denote to other people around them that they have seen beyond and had Death Eyes. And it was also a warning to maybe be careful and stay away from them a little bit.

In the preliterate Sumerian society, one of the goddesses descends down into the earth and is forced to face the underworld. When she reemerges, she becomes a hideous person—she's really very angry and lashes out. Her story had many parallels with returning Vietnam veterans with post-traumatic stress symptoms [PTSD]—overly cautious, jumping at sounds, angry with a deep anger, which hasn't found its place or use quite yet.

On the other hand, to see with absolute objectivity, to see completely from the outside, to see before judgment—is very useful. But you pay a tremendous price for it at the same time. It's a liability all your life, one you can't shed. It's not like taking a badge off. You try to be as compassionate and creative as you can be, and, at the same time, you know that within you live seeds of deep anger and even destruction. The capability is always there.

Once Vietnam was behind me, I've found that is probably the most useful insight into my own psyche. That's not the most useful talent to live with in a society. It's probably why I spend so much time out in the wilderness. Even when I was married and had children, I'd be gone six months out of the year, just to give everybody a break.

ML: Where did you meet Ed Abbey and how did he influence your life?

Peacock: In the winter of 1969, I met Ed in Tucson. I had been invited to William Eastlake's house—the grand old man of southwestern letters. I drove my motorcycle on the desert roads until I found the house.

> The winter air had chilled me and my hands shook as I pulled out a baggie of Bugler tobacco and rolled a joint-like cigarette. The cold palsied my fingers and I had trouble striking a match. The man sitting next to me gave me a light. He was tall, rangy, with a short dark beard. We talked about mountain lions, a subject he was up on, because he had just written a piece for *Life Magazine*. He worked as a seasonal ranger at Organ Pipe Cactus National Monument in southwestern Arizona and his name was Ed Abbey. He invited me to visit.
>
> A week later, I threw my sleeping bag in my jeep and drove to Organ Pipe bearing gifts: a six-pack of beer and a bottle of whiskey. That is how you visited people in those days. (*Walking It Off*, p. 28)

At that time I met Ed Abbey, he noticed that I was sort of a wild character. Among people he knew, I was probably the angriest, craziest, most militant, not in a political sense, but just in a personal sense. My craziness was also a cross to bear for him, because every time an explosion would go off, I'd jump into a ditch and do shit like that. Abbey bore it well. And that's why he became my friend.

I was very strong in my viewpoints, and I was very physical. It was Abbey that first noticed all that great anger and militancy, all those talents and skills, going to waste.

Ed Abbey gave me this notion—that maybe the only thing worth saving at all was wilderness. In Abbey's view, what is being destroyed is our home. The wilderness is as much of a home as we'll ever have, all we ever needed.

Abbey believed in freedom and dignity—especially when it comes to issues of wilderness. These weren't just goddamn words, they were a way of life. I agreed with them forty years ago, and I'm still fighting those battles today.

ML: Many of these themes became part of his novel *The Monkey Wrench Gang*. Most say the character Hayduke was you. Can you talk about that?

Peacock: The only thing worse than reading your own press is becoming someone else's fiction. I don't think Ed Abbey chose me as a model for Hayduke. I was just there. I was who Ed knew. I was also the one that gave him all the counterinsurgent literature that I'd gleaned from my demolition days, when Green Berets improvised explosives of one kind or another.

Basically, Ed Abbey didn't create characters; he didn't create material. He stole things, which is the prerogative of a really good novelist. When you're sitting around with him, drinking the horrific rum gimlets, and you told a joke or you had a great line, Ed would get his pad out and write it down.

The character Hayduke is a fictional character. Ed Abbey made him up. Hayduke became kind of famous—"Hayduke Lives!" was scribbled on bathroom walls across the West. There were literally a hundred people writing letters to editors saying, "I am the Hayduke." And that is so pathetic and sad, not to have a vital life of your own.

By the time *The Monkey Wrench Gang* was published, I had started full-time trying to save grizzly bears, so I had my own life. I was a cinematographer, and I worked as a backcountry ranger and as a fire lookout. I was earning four whole thousand bucks a year, trying to support a family.

A lot of Ed's own personality went into those monkey wrench gang characters. Physically and in broad brushstrokes, he took people he knew around him—his ex-girlfriend Ingrid Eisenstadter and two dear friends of a very different ilk—Ken Sleight and John De Puy—and imbued them with some notions of his own.

He pegged Doug Peacock as a wounded warrior, who still loved the earth and had somehow survived a terrible ordeal, in this case the Vietnam War, but somehow had retained the elements in his own humanity. This was a full six or seven years before anybody even recognized such a thing as post-traumatic stress disorder. For that alone Ed deserves so much credit.

As a character, Hayduke was a dolt. A dolt doesn't have the luxury of thinking. Abbey sort of stopped short of imbuing him with powers of analysis or a rational explanation for his base behavior. That was Ed's own input into this character. I think it's brilliant, and I loved him for it, still do.

But, you know, there might have been a philosophical base. Ed didn't bother with it in the book. It would have slowed down the action. It's a good novel—well to leave it alone.

And yeah, Lippincott, the publisher, had some concern that the character Hayduke was too close to the real Peacock. So their legal staff had Ed Abbey write me the most embarrassing, spit-dribbling, kind of awful stuff, such as "Oh, only the good parts of Hayduke are Peacock."

When I got down to Moab, where Ed lived, we took a little hike up Mill Creek, which is right out of Moab. I had the letter with me. When we got to the petroglyphs, we burned it and let the wind carry it away. Neither one of us ever spoke to the other again about Hayduke or his origins. Never came up.

ML: Monkeywrenching survives. Is it still relevant?

Peacock: Today, monkeywrenching as this literal going-under-bulldozers thing—it's too late for that. It's not just destroying the tools of technology. It's more a metaphor for standing up for what's right at the time.

Our survival is so collective today. We've got to take the tools that would basically sabotage the destruction that's going on toward

Earth and deal with it in a really creative way. It will involve all our talents, all our skills, and all our militancy, to fight these battles. And that means taking an individual stance every day for what you see as wrong and perceive as right and act upon them. This is going to entail some element of risk on your own part. It's very much like monkey-wrenching because what is right is not always legal and vice versa. Today, monkeywrenching is mostly relevant as a symbol for the re-fusal to compromise.

ML: Where does the environmental movement fit into this battle?

Peacock: The mainstream environmental movement took an ass-kicking, especially during the last eight years of the Bush administration. And it wasn't just limited to the Bush administration. It was assumed some-where along the line that in order to make changes to save parcels of wilderness and a wild animal here and there, they had to make deals and compromises. They had to make alliances.

I'm cautioning that it's probably bad to make an alliance or a com-promise with resource extraction industry, logging, or mining corpo-rations. I am saying that this is where some money for environmental groups comes from whether they like it or not. They became organized much like the corporations they were opposing. It made them lose their way. They lost their anger.

I thought there would be all kinds of Ed Abbeys coming out after he died, filling his great big lecherous shoes. But for whatever reason, there aren't, and they didn't.

ML: What do you think of the Wilderness Act and our national parks?

Peacock: The best American ideas we've ever come up with are the Wilderness Act, the Antiquities Act, and the Endangered Species Act. You could always want more, but what we've got is pretty good. These are political tools for seeing, for having a vision. Sometimes the vision is incomplete. But remember, national parks are political organizations. The secretary of the interior has all the political choice of whichever spit dribbler is in office at the time. People drive to a national park and all of a sudden they think they're in a different place, like a public zoo or a museum of some kind, when in fact they are in living ecosystems. That mentality permeates management, too.

ML: After reading your book, *In the Shadow of the Sabertooth*, I became curious about your transition from studying grizzly bears to the migrations of humans into North America. How did this come about?

Peacock: What's at stake here is not just the fate of the lynx and the grizzly bear. It's also the two-legged hominoid. Today, bears and humans have pretty much exactly the same chance of survival.

One of the things that fueled my interest in the peopling of North America was that the grizzly bear came over about seventy thousand years ago, the same geologic time as did the first Americans, perhaps fifty thousand years later. It had to be the most incredible time on earth for humans, because they came into a continent with all kinds of beautiful and now-extinct species, filled with carnivores you don't see anymore, like short-faced bears that are three times as tall as a grizzly and could run like antelopes.

But my interest in archaeology started when I was about nine. I was at a Boy Scout camp in Northern Michigan. I walked around and picked up this odd flat object, a stone. When I showed it to my father, he told me it was an arrowhead.

Because I didn't like school that much, I spent all my time from the time I was about ten until I graduated from high school either hunting pheasants or looking for arrowheads. My mother would drive me out and drop me off in the country around Saginaw, Michigan, and pick me up at dark.

It's where the Great Lakes at various times left beaches, the remnants of which became sand ridges. When I was fourteen or fifteen, I discovered that the topographic map with the contours every five feet showed every bump, every ridge, and these ran through wild places, where I'd walk around looking for blowouts. On these ridges were arrowheads that were different from the ones down by the river. I also found no

Doug Peacock, polar bear expedition, Somerset Island, High Canadian Arctic.
Photographer Rick Ridgeway.

pottery. What this meant even I could figure out as a fourteen-year-old; these sites were pre-pottery, pre-agricultural sites.

One day I was walking a ridge and found a red ochre anthill. By this time, I knew a little bit about how you were supposed to dig scientifically. When I got down to about fourteen inches, I started to brush off copper beads and tiny pieces of bone. That's when I called the University of Michigan. Some archeologists came down and found a burial of an infant or stillborn child wrapped with about a thousand copper beads.

Many years after Ed Abbey died, I gave a private reading at Clarke Abbey's house from my book *Walking It Off*. Many old friends were there. When I finished, one of them came up with a cardboard box. It was a bunch of Indian artifacts that I collected thirty years ago and had lent his wife, who was a schoolteacher. I didn't open the box until I got back home. When I saw the arrowheads and axes and other beautiful artifacts, it struck me immediately: I had to take them back.

During the summer of 2008, I flew back to Michigan with this box, rented a car, and got a set of camo fatigues and a trowel. Some of the places where I found these arrowheads were still in wonderful wilderness areas and in a bird sanctuary called the Shiawassee Flats—so it was easy to put them back. But in other places, townhouses had been built. I'd have to low crawl through the shrubs, dig a hole in somebody's flower bed, stick arrowheads back in and get the hell out of there before I got shot. I had to move around one step ahead of the cops while I drove the roads and snuck into neighborhoods.

So after I reburied all the arrowheads, I decided that I'd go live off the land, much like the Ancients might have, and write about these things. From my early interest in archeology, I always wondered how people lived a thousand years, ten thousand years ago.

When the human beings first got here, it was the largest unexplored wilderness in the history of our species. We had two continents and no people. Here was the greatest human adventure of all time.

What also interested me is that this was a time of great climatic change. The weather was warming and allowing the glaciers to recede and people to come down the coast and maybe down the corridor into

Montana from Alaska. And about twelve thousand years ago, there were incredible extinctions happening because of catastrophic natural events—such as global warming, sea rise, and also overhunting. And yet those people, even with so much change going on in their lives, successfully mastered territories and technologies and thrived and lived.

ARCHAEOLOGY AS A TEACHER ABOUT CLIMATE CHANGE

What lessons can be learned about climate change from the ancestors that first inhabited North America? Doug Peacock's book In The Shadow of the Sabertooth: A Renegade Naturalist Considers Global Warming, the First Americans and the Terrible Beasts of the Pleistocene (2013) thoroughly explores the answers. The ancestors that Peacock studies are the Clovis people that came to this continent from Siberia thirteen thousand to fifteen thousand years ago. They learned to survive against such large predators as saber-toothed cats and gigantic short-faced bears in the brutal and changing climate that was imposed by the Ice Age. Deeply personal and haunting, Peacock takes the reader on treks to the tigers in Siberia, the canyons and arroyos of Mexico and the America Southwest, and the wild coasts of Alaska and the Pacific Northwest. Peacock warns that the impacts humans will face today from global warming will be more drastic than those experienced by our early ancestors, perhaps leading to the death of large mammals, the depletion of the ozone, and the extinction of many species, including our own.

Today we are again facing great climatic changes. Will we be up to the muster? I don't know. We're talking about the death of countless millions of people from starvation, sea rise, typhoons, epidemics, water shortages, or war. More species are going extinct and extinction rates are higher now than during the great extinction in the

Cretaceous, when an asteroid wiped out the dinosaurs. It's coming so fast.

Where are we going to find the intelligence, the courage, and the humanity to face those changes? Basically, we're going to have to love someone's uncle who lives in Africa or Asia as much as we do our own child. And until we're capable of that kind of human compassion, we're going down the drain.

This is something that's going to stretch our brains, and I'm not sure we will get out alive. If we do, it's only because we will have preserved enough wilderness that will allow us and other animals to survive and evolve in their native habitats, which are also our home.

This is a time of great pessimism, one that affects our daily lives and those of our grandchildren. But at the same time, we have to retain our optimism and fight. And the real force, the real army that will fight for the earth is our children, our younger people. I have great hope for the new generation. When I travel around and lecture, they are the ones that give me the most hope.

ML: What are the lessons to be learned?

Peacock: I came out of the Vietnam War as a warrior looking for a war worth fighting. It certainly wasn't Vietnam. I was looking for my own battle, one that I could fight honorably and justly.

I believe that in wildness is the preservation of ourselves. So it's no mistake that the battle for the American wilderness is exactly where I started out. It was holistic. I'd seen the wholesale destruction in Vietnam by the machines of war. When I came back, I saw the same things going on in the American West. They're still going on.

My assumption has always been that that which evolves does not persist without the conditions of wildness that created it, the conditions of habitat that sustained it. What we evolved from was the natural habitat everywhere on earth whose remnants today we call the wilderness. And it's the wilderness that's the most important. So that's what I decided I would take on. That was going to be my life—taking on the forces of that destruction. There was no transition between antiwar and being pro-wilderness. It was the easiest parallel thinking I'd ever done in my life.

To survive is natural. Now is our time to concentrate our strengths and organically connect with that which gave rise to our species, which is the earth itself. It's going to be a hell of a fight.

7 | JACK LOEFFLER

Biography

Jack Loeffler travels throughout the American West and Mexico recording folk and indigenous music and making stereo recordings of natural habitats. He conducts hundreds of interviews with authors, hippies, philosophers, scientists, ranchers, cowboys, and indigenous peoples. He has produced more than four hundred documentary radio programs for Community Public Radio.

Jack is a dedicated activist and aural historian on behalf of indigenous and native cultures. He helps preserve the bioregional ties to their sacred homelands, fights for their economic rights, and promotes their wilderness values. His latest radio series is called *Restoring Indigenous Mindfulness Within the Commons of Human Consciousness.*

An accomplished musician, Jack spent two years as a US Army bandsman and several more as a jazz performer. After he moved to Santa Fe in 1962, he became curator at the Museum of International Folk Art, curator at the Laboratory of Anthropology, and music director for the Center for Arts of Indian America. In late 1969, he cofounded the Central Clearing House in order to document and thwart areas of environmental jeopardy in the Southwest.

In 2017–2018, Jack cocurated an exhibition at the New Mexico History Museum titled *Voices of Counterculture in the Southwest* that resulted in both a book and radio series of the same title.

He has authored eight books, including *Adventures with Ed: A Portrait of Abbey* (2002); *Healing the West: Voices of Culture and Habitat* (2008); and *La Musica de los Viejitos: The Hispano Folk Music of the Río Grande del Norte* (1999). In 2019, the University of New Mexico Press will publish his memoir, *Headed into the Wind: A Memoir*.

Jack was awarded a 2008 New Mexico Governor's Award for Excellence in the Arts and the Edgar Lee Hewett Award for Outstanding Service to the Public by the New Mexico Historical Society. In 2009, he was honored as a Santa Fe Living Treasure by a volunteer organization of the same name that honors elders who have served the community with "kind hearts and good deeds."

Jack narrated ML Lincoln's documentary film *Wrenched*.

I interviewed Jack three times: once in Moab, Utah, and twice in his home outside of Santa Fe, New Mexico. There he showed me an original manuscript of *The Monkey Wrench Gang*, which Edward Abbey had given him, with a beautiful leather binding that his wife, Katherine, crafted.

———

ML Lincoln: How did the Navajo way of life influence you?

Jack Loeffler: Living in a hogan at Navajo Mountain in Southeastern Utah from June to December 1964 was one of the profound periods of my life.

Everything expanded and opened up, not just my mind, but my heart and my soul. I began to hear the relationship of humankind to habitat. I think maybe that's where I started really listening.

I was honored to have been adopted into the family of Maggie and Eugene Holgate who asked me to move into a hogan that had been built by one of their sons. He had passed away when he was living in Flagstaff, Arizona. It was not a *chindi* [ghost] hogan because no one had died in there. There may have been a ghost of a centipede that I killed, but other than that there were no ghosts.

One of the things that's really interesting about the Navajo people is that they live in small clusters. They don't live in large communities, as do the Puebloan people. In the cluster where I was, four or five hogans were inhabited by different family members. The only person who spoke any English was Jamie Holgate, who was twelve years old. [Holgate later became the Navajo Mountain Chapter vice president.]

I had to concentrate on how to comport myself in a way that would not be offensive. Part of the time, I herded sheep. Little by little, the Navajos brought me into their fold as much as they possibly could. I learned that unless one is born into a culture, one can never get more than an inch deep unless one is very lucky.

There I got an inkling of the tremendous factor that the environment has on the evolution of a culture. The Navajo were so shaped by their habitat, so tuned into it, and so loathe to leave it that I realized they had tap roots that went deep and influenced just about everything in their lives.

For example, when my neighbors would go out to herd sheep, in order to protect themselves from the sun, they would take the red earth, moisten it, and put it on their cheeks. Aside from sunburn protection, they were bringing that soil right into their very minds.

Navajo Mountain is one of the holy sacred mountains for the Navajo people. This enormous, 10,300-foot mountain has such a vast and beautiful spirit. When the trees changed colors during the autumn months, I was filled with a burst of life that can rarely be experienced in other places.

Today, I have many dear Navajo friends who have imbued me with their sense of *hozho*, that sense of beauty that seems to fill their souls with the desire and the need to be in total balance and harmony with the universe. When they get out of harmony, they'll go do a healing ceremony. Sometimes that might take as many as nine nights, during which they may sing the beautiful *yeibechai* chant, to help put somebody back together again spiritually.

ML: How did you and Abbey become friends?

Loeffler: In 1968, I knew some of Abbey's points of view from having read *Desert Solitaire*, and I'd met and talked with him a couple of times. He and I had come to the American Southwest from Appalachia, a totally different habitat. He got here before I did. We had each moved from east of the Continental Divide to be in a place where we could see far and be able to wander. We both fell in love with the Colorado Plateau, the centerpiece of the American Southwest, one of the most beautiful environments in the entire world.

Something that happened to each of us independently was seeing a place this beautiful—a place where we knew we had to be—desecrated by industrialism. It was more than either of us could bear. That was one of the things that really brought us together in our friendship. The coal-fired Four Corners Generating Station near Fruitland, New Mexico, became our original focus of what we needed to work on. Stewart Udall, secretary of the interior from 1961 to 1969, once told me that the plume from that plant was the only artifact of human provenance visible from the moon.

Ed became my *compañero*, my camping buddy. I never regarded him as a hero; I rarely saw Ed as the writer he was until after he was dead. He was this buddy that I went camping with five or six times a year for two weeks at a crack, much to the dismay of our wives, who always wondered if we'd come home. We'd take some books along, sit under a tree and read, then look off into the clouds. We spent a lot of time talking with each other in no-holds-barred conversations that let each of us into each other's heads as far as it was possible to get. Ed was somebody I could trust to be at my back, and I hope that he felt the same way.

ML: Abbey said about himself, "I'm a barefoot eco-anarchist." What did he mean?

Loeffler: From my point of view, to try to understand something of Edward Abbey, you have to recognize that deep down in his soul he was truly an anarchist—I think probably a born anarchist—and remained so until he died.

His dad was a follower of Eugene Debs, founder of the Industrial

Jack Loeffler with Edward Abbey, Cabeza Prieta, Arizona, 1986.
Photographer Katherine Loeffler.

Workers of the World and the Social Democracy of America party. He read Walt Whitman's poetry to the Abbey kids night after night. That's probably where Ed first heard, "Resist much, obey little."

In his undergraduate work, Abbey talked about being a barefoot anarchist because he hated cement. He wanted to be able to take off his shoes and curl his toes in the mud, because that's where sunflowers and cottonwoods grow and where we grow. He was a total outdoorsman. From my point of view, Abbey was the person who best melded anarchism and environmentalism. Nobody has even come close to Ed in that respect.

Ed and I talked about revolution a lot: if or when is it justified, should it be peaceful; and if not, when is violence justified? These were themes central to his master's thesis and reappear in his books. What was critical was this, "Cause no harm to any fellow human," because human harm is the kind of terrorism that governments perpetrate and justify as defense of homeland. Within the context of culture, it's looking at the differences between the points of view as held by indigenous peoples, who hold the land as sacred—and newcomers from other continents to this continent— and others who want to turn its habitats into money.

In Abbey's view, the latter are the real eco-terrorists. If you look up *terrorism* in any dictionary, that's precisely what it is—creating harm so that life is terrorized. Our main concern was that any actions in defense of habitat should not mimic government terrorism. And Ed recognized that for what it is—evil. His patriotism was to the land, not to the government.

I should say that Ed regarded anarchism in its highest form as democracy in its highest form. And it really is. It's of the people and by the people, and it's for the people. But Ed evolved that concept to also include for the land that sustains the people and the entire biotic community.

In *Hayduke Lives!* sabotage was justified in the minds of the monkeywrenchers as long as it was used to thwart the tools of the people who tear up habitat. And one of the great speeches by Doc Sarvis is when "the gang" all gathered together, looking out over the Black Mesa Mine:

The eco-warrior does not fight people. He fights an institution, the planetary empire of growth and greed. He fights not human beings but a monstrous megamachine never seen since the days of the late Jurassic in the carnivorous dinosaur. He does not fight humans. He fights a runaway technology, an all-devouring entity that feeds on humans, on all animals, on all living things, and even finally on minerals, metals, rock, soil, on the earth itself, on the bedrock basis of universal being. (p. 114)

However, there was a subtle shift in Abbey's thinking in the fourteen years between the time that he wrote *The Monkey Wrench Gang* and when he finished the final words for *Hayduke Lives!*. In that book, killing happens. There comes a time when a security guard has the drop on both Seldom Seen Smith and George Hayduke and was about to off them. The Lone Ranger takes out the security guard with his pistol, claiming he was aiming for the shotgun but missed, and hit him in the head. The truth is, he shot the man who was about to kill his son, George Washington Hayduke.

One of the things that has always interested me has been Jack Burns, this lone horseman who has ridden through four of Ed's novels. Burns rode through *The Brave Cowboy*, where he revealed himself to be an anarchist. He rode through *The Monkey Wrench Gang*, although very few people were hip to that. In the sequel to that book, it's not revealed until near the end of *Hayduke Lives!* that actually the Lone Ranger is Jack Burns and that Jack Burns, being the father of George Washington Hayduke, is thus the grandfather of the radical environmental movement. Burns also rode through *Good News*, Ed's futuristic Western, which chronologically should have come after *Hayduke Lives!*.

For the first time in Abbey's books, our side took out somebody from their side. By that time in his thinking, the juggernaut of so-called civilization had become so enormous that defense with firearms had become necessary. But in Ed's own words, "By that time, it would already be too late."

Abbey foretold this shift toward justifying violence in his master's thesis, which he titled *The Morality of Political Violence*. Abbey received his master's degree from the University of New Mexico in 1959.

In his thesis, Abbey wrote: "Under the pressure of extreme circumstances . . . all those who are concerned with issues of good and evil—so-called 'men of good will'—may someday find themselves confronted with that critical situation in which all moral alternatives have been eliminated by circumstances, but two: passive submission to unquestioned wrong or the exercise of violence."

I recorded Ed back in 1983. One of the things that he said was that he does all of his defending from behind a typewriter, where other people like Dave Brower and Dave Foreman, to name but two, are out there on the front lines. I'm here to tell you that Ed did a lot of defending of habitat, and the typewriter was nowhere to be tripped over. He was out there doing it. He called it "night work."

Some of us who got into trying to understand how you have to stop the rape of industrialism might have considered doing some strange things to wreck equipment and other forms of sabotage. That may also have been born in the minds of some young veterans because of the sort of training they got when they served in the military. I know that for sure. How are you supposed to react to seeing your homeland being totally laid waste?

But what happened to me and to others over the last fifty years is that we understand that sabotage is not the way to go. It does not lead to a balanced perspective. It further invigorates a police state. Therefore, this is where one gets particularly creative and fertilizes one's own imagination to act accordingly.

ML: How did you find out about what Peabody Coal was planning on Black Mesa in Northern Arizona?

Loeffler: Back in 1969, my pal Bill Brown, a National Park Service historian, revealed to me that Peabody Coal Company had signed a lease with both the Navajo people and the Hopi Tribal Council to create a huge strip mine right in the heart of Black Mesa, a mountain sacred to both cultures, which holds one of the largest coal deposits in the United States and hundreds of archeological and burial sites.

Peabody was going to ship coal by way of railroad from Black Mesa across the Kaibito Plateau to the as-yet-to-be constructed Navajo Generating Station on the banks of Lake Powell in Page, Arizona—or Lake Foul as Ed called it. From there, power would travel through the electric Kachinas, the great power-line towers, all the way down to Lake Havasu, which is situated on the Colorado River, to pump the water out of that lake at an inordinate rate up and over the mountains and into the valleys of Central Arizona.

This became the Central Arizona Project. Ostensibly the water would be used for agriculture. As it turned out, the water was far too expensive for farmers but ideal for developers. Abbey and I discussed at length how the Central Arizona Project was such a grim undertaking, the worst environmental debacle ever visited upon the American Southwest. It invoked the longest water war in American history. In retrospect, it also inspired much of the modern environmental movement. But what was curious to me is that nowhere in *The Monkey Wrench Gang* does the Central Arizona Project appear as a phrase. We talked about it a lot but it never got in there, and I've never understood why.

Peabody would also grind some coal to pieces about three quarters of an inch in diameter and slurry it through a pipeline that would extend 273 miles to the coal-fired Mohave Power Station near Laughlin, Nevada. Additionally, some of the purest water in America would be pumped out of a Pleistocene aquifer at the rate of two thousand gallons a minute [more than three million gallons a day] to slurry the coal. This aquifer had served the Hopi springs that have been running for thousands of years and many deep wells that are used by the Navajo. Peabody Coal Company did not want to use Colorado River water because it would be corrosive to the pipeline. In other words, transporting coal in a noncorrosive way was more important than people drinking pure water.

And what for? Basically to light up Las Vegas and points west. The sacred landscape of the Navajos and the Hopis, a National Sacrifice Area, was being razed and raped in order to generate electrical power to an American culture gone awry.

FOUR CORNERS NATIONAL SACRIFICE AREA

Areas that have become environmental wastelands are often termed *sacrifice zones*. The Eastern Appalachian Mountains were among the first areas to have that term applied. First, its hardwood forests were clear cut; then the tops of more than five hundred mountains were stripped to mine coal seams, poisoning streams and fouling water sources. Disease, despair, and poverty were the disaster's hallmarks for community residents.

In the Southwest, many indigenous communities have felt and are still bearing similar negative impacts of high-cost resource extraction and nuclear testing, many of them located in remote areas. One such area on the Colorado Plateau is known as Four Corners. Here the southwestern corner of Colorado, southeastern Utah, northwestern corner of New Mexico, and northeastern corner of Arizona meet. Sixty miles away is Farmington, New Mexico; eighty-five miles away is Durango, Colorado. Most of the surrounding areas belong to Navajo, Ute, Hopi, Zuni, and other Puebloan cultures. The San Juan River flows through the area.

In 1983, Bullfrog Films released an Academy Award–winning documentary, *The Four Corners: A National Sacrifice Area?* Christopher McLeod, Randy Hayes, and Glenn Switkes produced the film, which explores the impacts of coal and uranium mining and milling and the lung cancers and birth defects that resulted. The film particularly spotlights the devastation wrought by Peabody Coal on Black Mesa from the strip mining of coal and the plunder of its water resources to accomplish it. The area is home to the Hopi and Navajo tribes.

In 1985, the film producers wrote a resource guide as an adjunct to the film. It was published in a social change quarterly called *The Workbook* (Southwest Research and Information Center). The foreword was written by David Brower. The guide highlighted the devastating legacy of nuclear testing and uranium mining and milling to the environment and to its residents. It was a call to action and, topic by topic, helped answer oft-repeated questions: how can we help; what can we do; where can we get further information? The guide also provided a compendium of the names and addresses of approximately seventy-five citizen organizations in the four corners states working for environmental justice and change, and the names of federal and state agencies and legislators. (http://www.bullfrogfilms.com/guides/4cguideSM.pdf.)

ML: How did Abbey feel about this?

Loeffler: He was appalled. He put it this way: "Those rotten filthy swine." Ed imagined a shadow edging across the land. That's how it appeared to me as well—there was a darkening of not just the landscape but of human consciousness itself.

It brings back an incredible array of memories of the way Ed and I were back in those days as young men. The amount of fire that burned in our guts was more than we could bear. It was like Armageddon happening in Paradise right before our very eyes.

Abbey perceived the interrelatedness between corporate economics, industry, politics, the entire scenario, which actually wrapped itself into a whole—the way he defined it, the military-industrial-political complex, corporately driven, was truly one of the great evils manifested in this land. He likened the entire scene unfolding to a kraken, a huge many-tentacled creature that could reach out and destroy.

He wanted to present this whole scenario in *The Monkey Wrench Gang* in such a way that people could enjoy themselves reading the book while being confronted by some of the most important concepts that could be imagined in our time. He realized that if you're going to really inspire a bunch of people to get cracking on defeating this kraken, you had to make it look like fun.

His book did help readers understand that without the Glen Canyon Dam, which guarantees that California, Arizona, and Nevada get their so-called legal apportionment of Colorado River water, that coal strip-mining of Black Mesa for power would not have happened. When you look at a place like Glen Canyon, which existed for at least two or three million years, and think about the presumptuousness of a culture that would plug it, fill it up—in Abbey's opinion and mine—that was an act of terrorism that was indescribably deep and destructive to the natural biotic community and to the indigenous peoples that had lived there for so many thousands of years.

ML: What did you do about Black Mesa?

Loeffler: The reason I work so much with indigenous people and include a few of them among my dearest friends is because inevitably anybody who remains within their respective tradition—Hopi, Tewa, Navajo, Apache, Ute, or whomever—understand that their homeland is sacred and not to be violated. They are our great hope because they contain the seeds of survival potential in the coming decades.

In 1970, I had the great good fortune to be invited by a group of Hopi Elders to work with them. Jim Hopper and I formed the Black Mesa Defense Fund, which resulted in some years of work trying to defend both the Hopi and Navajo cultures against desecration of their sacred landform by the incursion of the Peabody Coal Company.

Part of our effort was telling the story of how the deal for Peabody Coal was illegally ratified and politically betrayed the Navajo and Hopi people.

First, the Hopi Tribal Council was not legally created. In 1936, President Franklin Roosevelt appointed John Collier to be the head of the Bureau of Indian Affairs. Collier appointed anthropologist and author Oliver La Farge to create a Hopi Tribal Council and write a constitution and bylaws to give the United States government a legitimate body with whom to negotiate. Only 15 percent of the Hopis actually voted in favor of this constitution and tribal council.

In no way could that vote be construed as a quorum. Culturally, the Hopis are particularly autonomous. They live in self-governing villages. The notion of a vote is not something that's natural. From their point of view, not showing up to vote is considered as casting a no-vote. The Hopis succeeded in having this council dissolved in 1943.

Jack Loeffler, Gallup ceremonial, Arizona, 1971. Photographer Terrence Moore.

But during the fifties, John Boyden, a former US attorney, got himself hired on by some Hopis as their general counsel by traveling to various villages and organizing a new tribal council. Boyden negotiated the deal between the Hopis and Peabody Coal Company. The contract, signed in 1964 by the new council, leased lands on Black Mesa to Peabody and gave the company access to mineral rights and use of the aquifer, with terms that were particularly advantageous to Peabody and terrible for the Hopis.

What nobody knew was that Boyden was also representing the Peabody Coal Company at the same time. And for this, they paid him $1 million. So it was an enormous conflict of interest. Unfortunately, Boyden's villainy could not be proven until the 1980s, and by then it was too late to stop this terrible debacle.

ML: Was funding for the fight against Peabody Coal problematic?

Loeffler: Not initially. We were provided with a sizeable grant from the philanthropist and activist Harvey Mudd. He inherited a large fortune from his grandfather, Harvey Steel Mudd, cofounder of Arizona's Cypress Mine, and namesake of the Harvey Mudd College.

Then Jerry Mander, an American activist and author, created a fantastic ad for us that we put in both the *New York Times* and the *Los Angeles Times*, which brought in money that supported us for a while. It said something like, "Strip mining the coal out of Black Mesa is like tearing the marble out of St. Peter's Dome." After that, the Black Mesa Defense Fund struggled with funding and began accumulating debt. In 1972, two other friends and I discovered that there were Edward S. Curtis prints available for purchase. [Curtis was a photographer and ethnologist from 1885 to 1926 who focused on the native cultures of the American West at a time when they were on the brink of being entirely wiped out.]

I first stumbled across Curtis back in the 1960s because the Anthropology Museum here in Santa Fe had a complete set of the twenty volumes of photographs that Curtis printed. I became enamored. It was fantastic to discover that we might get hold of a huge collection.

We hired a finder who found the collection in the bottom of what used to be Lauriat's Bookstore in Boston, Massachusetts. A friend and I flew there and went down into the basement, and there in this huge room was crate after crate of Edward S. Curtis prints and the copper plates from which all of the prints were struck. Ultimately, we were able to purchase the entire collection. I had to borrow money to pay my share.

The first crate I opened revealed an incredible copper plate rendering of Chief Joseph, the great leader of the Nez Perce, staring back at me, and it was quite extraordinary.

Ironically, I don't own a single original Curtis print. My favorite was an exquisitely beautiful photograph titled *Mosa*, a portrait of a Mohave Indian girl. I had to sell that photograph in order to purchase a plane ticket for David Monongye to fly to Stockholm, Sweden, to attend the 1972 Conference on the Human Environment. He was a traditional Hopi spiritual leader who became one of my very dear friends and asked me to call him *evava*, which means "elder brother" in Hopi. He was extremely vocal about problems generated by coai mining on Hopi land.

David and three other Hopis refused to get US passports to Stockholm. My wife and I made Hopi passports, and on the backs we wrote, "The bearer of this passport is a citizen of the Hopi Independent Nation. This passport is valid as long as the sun shines, the water flows, and the grass grows." David sprinkled cornmeal and put an eagle feather on each, and we bound them in buckskin. And, by golly, these passports worked to get them there and back again. It was quite amazing.

The nongovernmental organization's [NGO] part of the Stockholm conference included a gathering of Hopi and Navajo Indians and non-Indian prominent activists, such as David Brower, founder of many environmental organizations, and Gary Snyder, the poet laureate of deep ecology, as well as Stewart Brand, Jim and Trisha Hopper, Tom Andrews, Stephanie Mills, David Padwa, Jerry Mander, Melissa Savage, and Huey Johnson. We rented a gallery and set up third world central where indigenous peoples from all over the world gathered nightly.

ML: Did the Black Mesa protest succeed?

Loeffler: No. We gave it our best shot. What we discovered is that politicians, politics, and corporate power are so deeply conjoined, and money is so abundantly fundamental to their efforts, that we couldn't stop it. Finally, we were running on borrowed money and we lost all the lawsuits.

We were totally wiped out because we had not made much of a dent other than to inspire some other would-be environmentalists to get into the act. I feel really good about that. In a way, the Black Mesa Defense Fund helped inspire the modern radical environmental movement.

ML: Didn't you and others have success in stopping the Kaiparowits Power Plant?

Loeffler: Around the mid-1970s, again in Page, Arizona, there was a get-together dinner to really do everything we could all do to stop the intended Kaiparowits Power Plant proposed for southern Utah, which would have been five times larger than the Navajo Generating Station. It could have ultimately generated 10,000 megawatts. That's a huge power plant. And the amount of particulate matter, the amount of nitrous—all of those other gases coming out of there would have been just killer.

Several of us attended, including David Monongye, Ed Abbey, Dave Brower, Malcolm Brown, Alvin Josephy, Brant Calkin, and Dennis Hopper. In the middle of dinner, two FBI agents came in and busted Dennis for having an eagle feather in his hat. He was able to convince them that the feather had been given to him by a Native American and had been properly blessed. Many of us were very po'd at being intruded upon by the FBI.

A bunch of us had been lobbying against the Kaiparowits monstrosity for years. Back in 1972, Dave Brower and I led a back-packing trip down Coyote Gulch, but before we headed down the trail, we visited both the Four Corners Power Plant and then headed north across the Kaiparowits Plateau, looking at what would be destroyed if indeed the Kaiparowits Power Plant went online. Dave's was a powerful environmental voice then, and little by little, a bunch of us had piqued the interest of outfits like the Natural Resources Defense Council, the Native American Rights Fund, and other groups. Abbey's voice had become powerful, and Robert Redford got involved. What had helped early on were the passing of the Endangered Species Act and the Environmental Protection Act and the establishment of the Environmental Protection Agency. Gradually, immediate plans for the plant withered as coal-fired plants were coming to be seen for what they are—implements of the devil, as Ambrose Bierce said in his book *The Devil's Dictionary*. Actually, Redford was burned in effigy in Kanab, Utah, back in 1976 for standing up against the Kaiparowits Power Plant. But even though that plant was shot down back in the 1970s doesn't mean that it won't rise again if corporate powers have their way with the politicians.

That was an environmental battle we did win.

ML: Can you talk about the FBI bust of Dave Foreman?

Loeffler: I think that it was in May 1989, about six weeks after Ed Abbey died, FBI agents with drawn pistols rousted Dave out of bed very early in the morning. Earth First! had been under surveillance for some time, and Michael Fain, an undercover FBI agent, had infiltrated Earth First!. Basically, the FBI was bugging Earth First! phone lines, and at least part of the time, Fain had a tape recorder strapped to his leg beneath his trousers and spent many hours engaging Dave Foreman in conversation, always trying to get him to admit to conspiring to commit sabotage.

Dave always tried to use nonviolent techniques to protect wilderness habitats. He always identified which trees he was going to spike. He stood unarmed in front of bulldozers. He rallied a cadre of young and not-so-young activists to work toward No Compromise in Defense of Mother Earth. Their headquarters were in Tucson, and often Ed Abbey would come to support them in their rallies. Political powers determined that Earth First! was too successful in creating a system of attitudes that were at absolute odds with the prevailing notion of turning habitat into money and growth for the sake of growth.

Dave told me that the FBI spent something like a million bucks to try to entrap him for conspiracy or for committing an act of sabotage. They thought they had him. But they didn't have him. Dave never conspired to commit sabotage. It's true that some Earth Firsters! were caught in the act of attempted sabotage, but they'd been urged on by another FBI infiltrator. Dave pled guilty to one act of conspiracy in order to reduce the prison term of one of the would-be saboteurs—a young woman. He then began yet another career as an influential environmentalist by co-founding the Wildlands Project.

Foreman had asked me to head up the defense fund for paying his lawyers, two of which were Gerry Spence and Sam Guiberson. I asked several folks with 501(c)3s if they would act as fiscal sponsors for the defense fund. Dave Brower at Earth Island Institute was the only one who would, and he did it with great enthusiasm.

Guiberson knew that I did a lot of tape recording and got a court order that enabled me to duplicate sixty-three hours of tape that were used by the FBI to try and convict Foreman. I spent two weeks in FBI headquarters in Phoenix and heard absolutely nothing that made him guilty of anything.

Part of it was listening to conversations between Michael Fain, who was hired by the FBI to be an agent provocateur, and his FBI handler. I listened to Fain say how he was going to entrap Dave, and here I'm paraphrasing, but Fain said he really hated doing that because he thought Dave was actually a good guy. And that made me realize how insidious is the whole process of how the FBI spies on people.

Entrapment is illegal. But that's what the FBI did. It's one of the things that they're using to try to stop the environmental movement, or at least that aspect of the environmental movement that is not so Sierra Club-esque. It's just really incredible what the government will do in the name of whatever they bow to.

At one point an FBI agent came into the room where I was working and said, "You work with tape a lot, don't you? Aren't you sort of an expert?" And I said, "Well, relatively speaking." And he said, "Well, can you help me make better tapes when I bug people's conversations?" I looked at him and adamantly refused. What a bizarre thing to do. Can you imagine that?

Later, at Dave Foreman's trial in Prescott, Arizona, both Dave Brower and I were denied entrance to the court proceedings. This revealed to me yet again how legislation and ethics are at loggerheads when the capitalist system is challenged.

ML: Abbey wrote about wilderness and what it means in relationship to freedom. Why is wilderness needed?

Loeffler: That question has so many ramifications. I'm going to answer it like this: I believe that if the human species has a purpose at all, it's to achieve as high a level of consciousness as is possible. Without wilderness, that highest level of consciousness is impossible. But remember: my generation got to grow up in a time where we could spend a lot of time wandering outside without bumping into other folks. That's where our minds got to soar and where we got our spiritual sustenance.

Now, that's speaking totally to the human need. The planet needs wilderness because the planet is supposed to be a wilderness habitat.

Today many people are so totally involved in their immediate surroundings that they have become estranged from the out-of-doors. In other words, they operate from their BlackBerrys and other fruits of the digital age instead of from piñon trees. The age of virtual reality began almost immediately after Ed died and rearranged our whole system of cultural mores. It had a huge shaping influence on today's younger and even middle-aged generation of people who are so totally hooked into their computer world and the Internet that they have become completely submersed in the world of technophilia, techno fantasy, techno lust. That was probably the worst sort of world Ed Abbey could imagine living in.

ML: When did you forge your views about the desecration of wilderness?

Loeffler: In the summer of 1957, after being drafted into the United States Army, I was put in an army band. Part of our job was to go out to Camp Mercury, the Nevada Proving Grounds, and play music as they shot off atomic bombs at dawn. This happened on three different occasions.

By the end of that summer, my entire mental processes had shifted into some other gear. I realized that I was totally sane in a culture gone awry, one that condones the use of atomic bombs to not only kill fellow humans but to take out entire biotic communities.

When my friend Terry Tempest Williams and I discovered that we were both in the vicinity of one of those bombs going off, it blew our minds. I was playing the trumpet seven miles away from where they shot off the bomb "Smoky," which dumped its residue on the Williams family car as they were driving north past Las Vegas. And as a result, she wrote about the one-breasted women in her family that had cancer and the deaths that occurred. I turned into what I am today, a beatnik cum naturist bohemian with anarchist leanings.

In 1983, a friend of mine, Gary DeWalt, coproduced a documentary film called *Genbaku Shi: Killed by the Atomic Bomb*. It dealt with a crew of air corpsman, as they were known during the Second World War, who were shot down, bailed out of the plane, landed in the sea, and were picked up by Japanese and imprisoned in Hiroshima as prisoners of war.

Tom Cartwright, the pilot of that plane, was taken away from his crew and sent to Tokyo for interrogation. When the atom bomb was dropped on Hiroshima, his remaining crew members died. Tom became a very close friend and was one of the four of us who went out and buried Ed.

TOM CARTWRIGHT'S WAR MEMOIR

Thomas Cartwright's book, *A Date with the Lonesome Lady: A Hiroshima POW Returns* (2002), is a poignant memoir of his experiences during interrogation, his hearing the announcement of the atom bombing of Hiroshima during his imprisonment, his anger at the military's failure to report the deaths of his crew, and his trips to Hiroshima and other locations in Japan after the war to come to some emotional peace. The B-24 plane that Cartwright piloted was named *The Lonesome Lady*.

ML: Can you talk about Abbey's burial?

Loeffler: I had rigged an elevated platform in the bed of my old '78 Chevy pickup under which we could slide Ed's body wrapped in his old blue sleeping bag that I'd packed with dry ice. I put camping gear on top in case I got stopped by a cop. I didn't want to get nailed for hauling Ed's body.

I put the death certificate, which I had filled out and signed, in the glove compartment just in case I did get stopped. I'd hauled away other bodies in my life and found it's always comforting to know that you have something that looks official. But thereafter, it was revealed that I shouldn't have signed the death certificate, because I'm not a doctor who is supposed to officially note when someone has died. But I could tell he was dead.

The four of us couldn't fit in the Chevy, so Doug Peacock took his rig. Tom Cartwright, Steve Prescott [Abbey's brother-in-law], Doug, and I caravanned very deep into one of the deserts of the Southwest.

I don't think Ed and I ever, ever, ever went camping without getting stuck. And, sure enough, even on this last camping trip with Ed dead in the back of the truck, we got stuck in the sand. Tom Cartwright got on one fender and Steve Prescott got on the other fender. Peacock pushed on the grill, and it just fell off. "Geez, what a piece of plastic shit!" Typical Peacock.

It took us a very long time to get to where we finally buried him. We found one of our old favorite campsites and decided that that would be the place.

By that time it was too late to bury him so we camped, the four of us scattered a ways apart because we each felt like being alone. We left Ed's body in the truck, and I slept right behind it. Tom Cartwright remembers that in the middle of the night, a group of coyotes came into the midst of us, right between all of us, including Ed, and started to sing. And we always thought maybe it was a song remembering Ed, sung by the coyotes that he loved.

The next day, what I remember was almost surrealistic. We laid out Ed's body over two shovel handles, each of us carrying one end of the shovel, and carried him up a hill to the place where we buried him and wished him fond farewell into eternity.

I still talk to Ed. I can hear his voice as clear as a bell at any possible time. And I can see him because we walked and walked thousands of miles together, talking and carrying on. And so I hear the timbre of his voice and the feeling of what it was like to have a pal that you could talk with like that. He was my best friend.

8 | SHONTO BEGAY

Biography

Shonto Begay's profound attachment to the land and its sacred relationships to humans were integral to the life of his family and his culture. Even the name Shonto comes from the earth—in *Diné* it refers to the glint of light reflecting off water. He was born in the community of Shonto on the Navajo Reservation, about 120 miles north and east of Flagstaff, Arizona. His mother is a traditional rug weaver in the Bitter Water clan, and his father is a revered and respected medicine man from the Salt Clan.

Begay has been a professional artist since the 1980s, with paintings and drawings that show the lifestyle and emotions of people in his culture, the canyon and mesas he grew up in, and the dangers of environmental encroachment. His art has been shown in more than fifty shows in galleries and museums, including the Wheelwright Museum of the American Indian in Santa Fe, the American Indian Contemporary Arts Museum in San Francisco, and the Phoenix Art Museum. His work is featured in the Arizona State Museum's collection "Connections Across Generations," the Avery Collection of American Indian paintings at the University of Arizona, and several important shows nationwide including the Booth Museum of Western Art, Cartersville, Georgia.

He has written and illustrated several children's books, including *Ma'ii and Cousin Horned Toad: A Traditional Navajo Story* (1992) and *Navajo: Visions and Voices Across the Mesa* (1995). He has illustrated several books written by others, including *The Boy who Dreamed of an*

Acorn by Leigh Casier (1994) and *Navajo Long Walk: Tragic Story of a Proud Peoples Forced March from Homeland* by Joseph Bruchac (2002).

As a spokesperson and activist for environmental rights, Begay supports the Grand Canyon Chapter of the Sierra Club, Black Mesa Trust, and the Save the Peaks.

I interviewed Shonto in his art studio in Flagstaff. He was working on the painting *Watching Us*, which he describes in our interview.

———

ML Lincoln: Shonto, what does your name mean?

Shonto Begay: My name, Shonto, is a Navajo word, which means sunlight on water, the light that plays on the surface. Actually, it means the little light that reflects back on the wall of the canyon, you know, that little play of light. That's the phenomenon that my name means. My last name, Begay, is a very common Navajo surname, meaning the son of. So I'm the son of that phenomenon.

My great-great-great-grandmother's name was [Asdzaa' Shonto] Lady Shonto. This is the name I reclaimed in 1980 because it was where I'm from. Before then, I lived with a US government–issued name. The Navajos in my youth were issued names. We were issued numbers. We were issued religion. That's why a lot of us live with the names of dead presidents and generals and Indian agents. This practice ended in the late sixties.

ML: Shonto, I've read that they took you from your sheep camp and put you in a boarding school. Can you talk a bit about that experience?

Begay: The boarding school experience that I have personally gone through lasted about ten years and began in the early 1960s. This was when the Bureau of Indian Affairs, which was part of the US Department of Interior, "kidnapped" kids off the backs of the sheep trails without consulting their parents, the Elders. A lot of times, the kids that went missing ended up in local boarding schools. You were not allowed to see your parents. You were not allowed to speak your language. You were not allowed to be who you are. I was no exception. At a very young age I was plucked off the sheep trail.

The government's whole educational campaign was assimilation, acculturation, as fast as possible. When we got into the institution, everywhere we saw these signs that we recited every day as a group. We had no idea what they meant. We couldn't read. But we learned to say words that dropped heavy and harsh off our tongues. What we were saying turned out to be, "Tradition is the enemy of progress." That was our experience of how they shed us of our brownness.

We were first given religion by sizes. The shortest kids were Catholic; the medium-size ones were Presbyterian; the tallest were Mormons. The three religions pretty much monopolized. Every Monday, the kids spent the whole day going to US government–sponsored churches. After each summer, when we came back to the boarding school, we were rotated. If you were a Catholic last year, you were Mormon this year. It was just a big ball of confusion.

There were a lot of funny times and a lot of painful ones, but I had nothing else to compare them to. For all I knew, the whole world was full of boarding schools, and all the kids in the world were subjected to these brutal institutions. There were a lot of casualties from that indoctrination. Boarding school was a very vicious time. Of the thirteen young boys that I grew up with in boarding schools, three of us are alive, and now we're probably in our fifties.

I credit a lot of my survival to being able to live outside of my reality, into my own dream, my fantasy paint—drawing and thinking and daydreaming—and that always, always took me off the edge of pain.

But in 1968, with the changes in the civil rights movement, all of a sudden, everything became so lenient. You could speak your language. You didn't have to join a religion. You could go home to see your parents every week. It was so amazingly different that it was unsettling because that's not what we knew. It was really uncomfortable, and we were just waiting for the other shoe to fall.

This is pretty much how it was.

ML: Do you share some of those experiences in your paintings?

Begay: In 2008, I painted *Watching Us*. It's a commentary on growing up in a boarding school and being subjected to B grade Western movies, where Native people, Indians, were bad people. When the cavalry comes over the hill to kill the Indians, the kids jump up and clap. And during playing wartime, none of us wanted to be Indians; everybody wanted to be soldiers and cowboys.

Showing those movies was one way the US government acculturated, assimilated—de-colored us—I guess that's what it was. All the boys sitting and watching the movies are reacting emotionally to what is on the screen, facing with denial, fright, indifference, anger, and tears. Unfortunately a lot of times, it also forced us to crush our innate gentleness, to harden the self to survive.

People ask me: "Who are these faces? Do you know these kids?" And I say: "It's me. It's facets of me, how I viewed or responded to their representation of us, as false as it was. It was a way of telling us how we were lacking as humans." So this painting is a commentary on that—just watching us, watching us. And the light playing through the ears—you know, what you hear burns your ears.

These people are not real that I paint. They're from experience. They're from people that come in and out of my life daily, and mostly just out of that energy of encountering their energies. And just as in every crowd scene there are some people that you're repulsed by; some people that you get closer to; some people you feel really gentle and loving and peaceful toward. The history develops itself, and your emotion follows. It's an amazing process. That's how I make a history of people as I paint, how their stories come out.

And, again, it's just going to the fact that I always lived in the world that I paint in order to survive. My artwork is more than a pursuit of livelihood. It's a way of staying sane, staying alive.

ML: Why did you leave the four sacred mountains area in Northern Arizona as a young man?

Begay: I wanted to move away from the rural life I'd grown up in. I was tired of it. Being raised in a sheep camp was like camping all the time, just moving with the seasons, no electricity, no running water. Everywhere you went you either rode horses or walked. It was dusty and hot and remote. It's way out there.

As a young man, my yearnings were over the horizon. I wanted to go into a city, where my environment was controlled, where I could just slap the wall and the light would come on, where I could turn a knob and the water comes out, where everything was so beautifully composed and geometric.

So I left. I spent many years on my own, outside of the four sacred mountains, looking back in on my own people with the same set of limbs I was born with. What was ironic was that so many people I met were involved in a back-to-the-earth movement and I thought, gee these people are crazy.

In the early seventies, I moved to Berkeley. I drove there in my '54 Ford Comet, saddle, hat, a box of 8-track tapes—all my belongings. I barely managed to negotiate the streets, the traffic lights, to make my way to a home I'd been sent to that was occupied by people in the American Indian Movement. There were urban native activists from just everywhere. I didn't fit in and ended up leaving in the middle of the night and going to the Berkeley campus, trying to find some green area to sleep. I didn't do a fire, but I did use my saddle for a pillow. When I woke up on the grass, a bunch of people were walking by and telling me I couldn't camp there. I got shooed off.

This is looking back to that time from our conversation now. It's taken me quite a few years to really appreciate, love, and reconnect with who I am and where I was from. The very things that drove me from the reservation—the loneliness, the wind, the dust devils in the sheep camps—are the same things that brought me home. But I looked at them differently. Today, those are the things I give thanks for.

The wilderness—the wildness of the land—has always been a source of regeneration, rejuvenation for our people. You'd go into canyons and mesas and seek solace, seek visions, seek some

Shonto Begay. Photographer Hulleah Tsinhnahjinnie.

self-revelation. That's where you're closer to the creation spirits, unfettered by human emotions.

Near my studio up there on the side of the mesa, among the pinon-juniper forests is where my umbilical cord is buried. It's near where I was born. I go back there to recharge and to get fresh ideas.

ML: When I met you at the Braiding Water Conference, we were talking about the recovery of the side canyons of Glen Canyon because of evaporation and drought. And you said in a very, very beautiful way—and it really captured me—how one should treat those canyons. You said, "You must treat them like babies."

Begay: For the Diné [the Navajo], the stewardship of the land, especially the land that's recovering, is like an infant. It is like nurturing a growth of corn or squash, you need the very same tenderness, prayer, protection, and a sense of belonging to Her.

When we place offerings every morning, it is to a young pinon tree; it's to the Grandmother; it's to the earth. The wilderness, the land, is the ultimate mother. She is the final mother. This is what we resort to when we pray and give offerings to the earth. We pray in the name of everything that calls the earth Mother.

That's why we always try to treat these recovering areas, blessed areas, by treading lightly, treading lightly. It always pains me to see all these beautiful landscapes marred, especially if you go north on Highway 89 just beyond Cameron. You see all those beautiful ancient clay hills with tracks of recreational vehicles all over the place.

But when I go back a year later, the tracks are totally gone. It's how nature sheds itself, takes care of herself. The Elders say there is a sense that the earth does take care of herself, just as she takes care of us. So treating her and each other like babies, like infants, being aware, stepping over the crypto-biotic soil, and thinking seven or eight or nine generations hence, is how we try to live.

ML: Thank you. I know that the Navajo Nation is fighting for their rightful allocation of the Colorado River. What is your nation's traditional relationship to water?

Begay: The water of the rivers or streams, the confluence of the Little Colorado, and everything that feeds into the Colorado River, is seen as the blood, the source, the fluid of the Mother and that which engages us in sharing land.

After I returned from Berkeley, I worked as a ranger in Navajo National Monument for a number of years. I was always aware that I was surrounded by a spiral of rivers, a spiral of water, the water that came out of Keet Seel Canyon, that winds around eventually to the Chinle Wash that goes from there into the San Juan River, the San Juan into the Colorado. So there was a spiral that I always saw myself as being a part of. Most all the community names have *water* in them, like Shonto. This is how we always have the longing for that moisture and the sanctity of that moisture, that element, on the tip of our tongues.

ML: You have been talking a little about the Beauty Way, which reflects the Navajo approach to life. Can you tell me more about that?

Begay: The Navajo sense of being in harmony, being in a whole copasetic state of being, has always been about walking in blessed union with yourself, the earth, your fellow kinship, with the animals, the four-legged, the flying beasts, the swimming beasts, the burrowing beasts, and being able to speak your own language. This is how we've always blessed everything around us.

Part of the Beauty Way says: "In front of me in beauty, around me in beauty, behind me in beauty, above me, below me. And then ahead of me, around the bend, in beauty."

So that's our concept of stepping out each day, trying to create each day holy in all senses, stepping into that. And of course, being from an earth-based culture, this is the center of our prayer—maintaining sacredness, maintaining *hozho*, which is the state of being, the state of everything being one union, peaceful.

I also find that I'm very conscious of the Beauty Way when I paint and want my artwork to reflect it. When people ask me why I paint with broken strokes and lines, I say these are the Morse Code to the spirit world. I believe that each one of the broken lines and dotted strokes for me are syllables to the words, to the sentence, to the paragraph and sections of Beauty Way prayers.

With each piece of artwork, I try to create it as another Blessing Way protection ceremony. I work with colors in the most beautiful way that a medicine man and medicine woman see when they perform their duties, very deliberate, very delicate, and very patient. I see my work that way, with each work done, another ceremony done.

And I like to say that my painting, my profession, is all about making peace and maintaining peace among colors, which sometimes consciously creates tension. And the way I put colors next to the other is about being conscious of their own energy interaction.

ML: Wasn't your father a medicine man?

Shonto Begay. Photographer Jeff Newton.

Begay: Yes. My father was a very well-known and respected medicine man. He was probably the youngest one that came out of the Chinle area when he first learned the ceremonies. It took him twenty-one years living with an Elder before he performed his first ceremony. That's the powerful person he was.

He passed on in 2004, but he did leave behind a lot of knowledge for his people. His prayers and his words still ring true in my paintings.

He always told me, told us, that where he's called to perform protection or blessing ceremonies, that afterward, he tells people that if they continued their personal ceremonies in the form of prayers and offerings to the earth, and lived consciously, they would not need medicine people. They would become their own medicine person.

As I grew up, I never saw him as a father figure so much as I saw him as a medicine man. It was like living with a rabbi or the pope.

Everybody always needed him and his services. I was just on the side. Everybody needed his voice to build a line to our people. I was always being told: "We're having this ceremony, we've having a smudging, we're having the Enemy Way. Go get the appropriate plants." And I knew what they were, so I was out gathering. I spent my days walking up to the mesa and the gullies to gather plants that were needed for a particular ceremony.

And at the time, I didn't appreciate it. It was hard, hot, dusty, and sometimes dangerous work. It wasn't until much later that I realized how precious and how valuable everything I grew up with was, including creating sand paintings for healing. I would work on a healing mandala all morning with the Elders, making this delicate, beautiful sand painting, maybe twelve foot in diameter. And of course, the power, the healing power, is drawn from it with the patient. And then before noon, the sand in the painting was swept away.

So in the beginning, a lot of my own paintings were temporary. If something was wrong, I just painted over them. I became not afraid to paint like that. That's why today I tell myself, you've got to paint with nerves.

ML: Paint with nerves?

Begay: Not to be scared, not to be intimidated by your own vision and interpreting it. Because a lot of people do have this silent battle with the blank spaces within.

ML: Like the writer and the empty page?

Begay. Yes.

ML: You talked earlier about the changes that may have affected you and your people negatively, including the mining of coal on Black Mesa by Peabody Coal. Can you tell me about the impact of that on the traditional Navajo people?

Begay: The Elders today say that because we are not placing offerings as often as we used to, praying and talking and being in that communion, we are affected negatively, because we have become detached from Her.

The mining is a blight on the land and on our traditions. That's why many of us are set against it. The disturbance of the earth and its desecration has quite a negative impact. It has caused a lot of environmental health issues.

But then, there's the conflict: many people are surviving on Peabody Coal, by making a livelihood there, including the additional benefit of being allowed to pick over the leftover piles of coal to heat their homes.

There are spaces on the land that the Navajo refer to as the place that is not right, the place that is not the earth itself, but rather what has been done to it. These are the areas that are disturbed in a land once so powerful and so alive, and so giving and taking.

And those desecrations are associated with witchcraft, associated with that whole disrespect of the earth. And that's pretty much what it is for us, a bad, negative energy that exists, that always is among us. The witches are the spirit ones from the old days, punishing us.

Years ago, the desecrated areas used to only be referred to as ones where people were buried or where death occurred. That's why you don't live in hogans where people died. That's why people go away from these areas—because there's a spiritual contamination.

Now there is a physical contamination from the coal dust from Peabody Coal, from the uranium mining, and, of course, from oil extraction. The desecration of the lands has come to be more than just spiritual.

Our people died from the extraction of uranium, the yellow earth, yellow dust. Just beyond Tuba City is where the uranium tailings got placed. I knew people, relatives, that lived there in that little grouping of housing, right across the highway and pretty much everybody I knew eventually died of leukemia. Then it became a Superfund site. It was covered with concrete and the people that were still living nearby were moved away and the houses torn up.

TUBA CITY SUPERFUND SITE

During the 1950s, Rare Earth Metals Corporation built a uranium refining mill five miles east of Tuba City, Arizona, on the Navajo Reservation. The mill processed nearly 800 million tons of uranium ore and produced 5 million pounds of fuel. When the mill closed in the 1960s, tailings from the mill were placed into nearby unlined pits and evaporation ponds, which resulted in air-borne pollutants and soil and groundwater contamination.

Navajo workers were not told of the dangers of working with uranium and other chemicals associated with mining and processing. Many sickened and died of respiratory disease, cancers, and other diseases.

During the 1980s, the area was declared a Superfund site. In 1988, the US Department of Energy (DOE) began to clean up the site by removing soil, demolishing mill buildings and debris, establishing groundwater extraction and monitoring wells, stabilizing windblown materials on forty-five acres by building a disposal cell and capping it with an impermeable barrier, and fencing off the area. The DOE also demolished trailers across the highway, which had been inhabited by Navajos for decades after the mill closed. Hundreds of millions of dollars will still need to be spent cleaning up the Tuba City area and many others located on the Navajo Nation from uranium mining that previously occurred there.

In 2005, the Navajo Nation banned uranium mining on its 27,000-square-mile reservation.

ML: Were you an activist? Did you ever meet other activists, such as Jack Loeffler or Ed Abbey?

Begay: Being a native on this continent, there is never a shortage of causes to bleed for—for the earth and social justice.

When I lived in Flagstaff, I gave my voice to protest putting sewage water on the ski area up in the sacred San Francisco Peaks. My backyard.

TOURISM OVERRIDES DESECRATION OF SACRED NATIVE AMERICAN SITE

Since 2005, various indigenous tribes have protested the use of treated sewage waste for making artificial snow for the ski runs for the Arizona Snowbowl. The popular, all-season destination resort is located on one of the San Francisco Peaks, the volcanic mountains that tower above Flagstaff, Arizona. The resort is located on public lands that are managed by the US Forest Service. Since 2012, some three billion gallons a season is used to make snow for some two hundred plus acres.

For thirteen First Nation tribes, including nearby Apache, Hopi, Hualapai, Navajo, and Yavapai, the mountain is sacred; and the use of sewage water is considered a desecration to the land and an environmental health hazard to people, animals, and plants. Legal challenges to the use of sewage water by tribes and environmental organizations have consistently lost in the courts. The latest was filed by the Hopi Nation, who lost the challenge in November 2018 in the Arizona Supreme Court. Writing for the majority, Justice John Pelander said, "Today we hold, as a matter of law, that environmental damage to public land with religious, cultural, or emotional significance to the plaintiff is not special injury for public nuisance purposes."

To add insult to injury, when skiing opened in that same month, activists were forbidden from protesting at the resort unless they had a ski pass. Native American activist Ray Ray, who led the demonstration in prayer up the mountain, stated, "Am I not allowed to pray and go to the Sacred Mountain that my ancestors and that my people have been praying to long before this was considered America? That a sacred space can be privatized by a company that pays for my religious rights to be taken away, for my freedom of speech to be taken away, is tyranny and malice from the company, the employees, the security and patrons of [Arizona] Snowbowl" (November 16, 2018, www.protectthepeaks.org).

When I first met Jack Loeffler in Santa Fe—it was like meeting a rock star. We became friends. There is a piece about me in his book *Voices of Counterculture of the Southwest* and a reproduction of *The Black Mesa Ceremony*, one of my paintings.

I never met Edward Abbey, but would have loved to. We did the same work in the same areas, though maybe not at the same time. I bought dozens of his books, like *Desert Solitaire*, *The Monkey Wrench Gang*, and *Fire on the Mountain*, and gave them to my children and friends.

I like the activism that my eldest daughter, Enei, and my son-in-law and granddaughters, and all the young people around them are very much involved in. They've protested with Black Mesa Water Coalition. They're giving voice and action to what I've always believed and what I've always lived with—practicing in a private way of treading lightly on the earth and placing offerings and prayers. These young people give these ideas a broader voice, a broader vision, and I enjoy working with them.

They are inheriting the mess we're leaving them, so theirs is a job—as daunting as it is sometimes—now with the mining waste spill into the Animas River and everything else that is happening. They exhibit so much hope in their voices, their strength, their passion. I find myself in a lot of solidarity with them and, of course, support them.

I'm the kind of guy that always looks at his glass half-full. I'm an optimist. I like knowing that something good is coming from what I'm going through individually and what our people are experiencing collectively. The Navajo view has always been that no matter how painful things are, they could have been worse. There's always something that can be seen as an advantage.

I approach the future from the point of view of the medicine man. My father's job was to strengthen the self, the person inside, and teach them to test themselves from within rather than focusing on outside troubles. He gave them the power to heal themselves and awaken the spirit to combat negativity and arouse optimism. He taught me to take the long view, many generations ahead, to have faith that something good will come.

So I have hope for the future.

9 | JOHN DE PUY

Biography

John De Puy hiked many of the Southwest landscapes that he depicts in his striking, modernist paintings and watercolors. According to De Puy, "Everything I am is the land. I spent fifty years interpreting it in painting and fighting lost causes . . . It is this land, its beauty, its myths, and its dreams of wholeness that nourish me."

His parents were devoted to music and arts, and their home was filled with French and German impressionist paintings. In New York, De Puy studied with Hans Hoffman, a German expressionist artist. During my interview, De Puy told me, "Hoffman taught me to look at an image, whatever it is—the landscape, a figure—through the eye. And then you translate it into an inner experience, an inner eye, and then onto the canvas."

His close friend Edward Abbey echoed De Puy's inner experience: "[Although De Puy's drawings and paintings] represent clearly, recognizably, the . . . mountains, buttes, abysmal gorges, . . . it is not the landscape we see, but the one, he claims, is really there. A world of terror as well as beauty that lies beyond the ordinary limits of human experience, that forms the basis of experience, the ground of being."

De Puy's work has been featured in many fine art galleries and museums throughout New Mexico including the Harwood Museum of Art and 203 Fine Art, both in Taos, and the Addison Rowe Gallery in Santa Fe.

I interviewed John at his home designed by his wife, Isabel, and its shape resembles a Navajo hogan. They live off the grid.

He lives in Ojo Caliente, New Mexico, with Isabel and their daughter Noelle. (www.depuygallery.com)

———

ML Lincoln: You have many ties to Navajo country. Can you talk about how it influenced you?

John De Puy: When I began high school, I thought that I would work out in Navajo country as an anthropologist. I went to Columbia University and studied undergraduate anthropology. That dream just disappeared after the Korean War.

During the war, I ended up as medic for the Marine Corps and got blown up when I tangled with a mine. My whole pelvis was shattered, and now I have an artificial hip and part of an artificial femur. That freed me from a life in the workforce! It was a blessing because it gave me a pension for the rest of my life. I retired at age twenty-two.

My buddy Ed Abbey called it "the million dollar wound." He was eternally jealous. He used to say, "Goddamn it, De Puy! We're paying taxes to support your rotten lifestyle! But I know you're gonna' screw them right on to the end, because I predict that you will live indefinitely!"

So when I got back, I was a physical and mental wreck, and I spent almost a year out on Navajo Mountain, in Utah, near the Arizona border. It's one of the sacred mountains for the Navajo. That saved my life. There, Long Salt, an old Navajo *hataali* [shaman], looked at me and said, "Oh, you're not long for this earth. You stay here with me." So I did and became very immersed in the Native American culture.

During that year, Long Salt taught me a form of meditation on the earth. It's very similar to some of the Buddhist concepts—Tibetan Buddhism, Zen Buddhism. Unfortunately, Christianity crushed most of those concepts and set back civilization by, I would say, two thousand years.

When I went on a spirit quest, Long Salt gave me the raven as my protector and guardian. To this day, I talk to ravens when I go on my hikes and about one out of six times, they'll come down and circle around.

I moved to Taos, New Mexico, after spending a year with Long Salt.

ML: When did your family first go to New Mexico?

De Puy: My grandfather was fed up with the Industrial Revolution and thought it was the end of American democracy, which it was. Although he was a kind of socialist anarchist, his whole family were great patriots, and he hated their guts. He came to New Mexico against the wishes of his whole family, and started a ranch in Mora, ran the mill in Mora, and later started another ranch north of Taos. He loved the Southwest and felt quite at home there. He traded with the Navajo. One summer, he worked with John Muir. My grandfather was devoted to wilderness and introduced me to it. He took me out to the Navajo Reservation when I was about six years old, and it's been in my blood ever since.

During the Depression, my grandfather lost the ranch and we had to move to New Jersey, in the Pine Barrens to the south. My father supported the whole family as a merchant mariner. We lived there for ten years. When I was seven years old, I was given a kayak as a birthday present. I'd go out with my dog and camp out anywhere on the rivers in the Barrens.

ML: How did you and Ed Abbey become friends?

De Puy: Ed Abbey and I became friends in 1959, when he was the editor of a bilingual newspaper in Taos, New Mexico, called *El Crepusculo de la Libertad* [The Dawn of Liberty], the name of which appealed to him, of course. He was a devoted anarchist, and the publisher was a devoted Marxist. About two years later, the *Santa Fe New Mexican* newspaper drove both of them out as being pinko Communist, anarchical terrorists.

I was very involved in the Chicano movement [*La Alianza*], which was started in the 1960s by my compadre Reis Tijerina. His daughter was my goddaughter. At that time, Ed was nervous around Chicanos.

Anytime he would go into a bar where they were around, he'd grab his wallet and hide it.

The Chicanos wanted to free the lands they were given under the 1848 Treaty of Guadalupe Hidalgo, which were stolen by the government and the United States Forest Service and given to Anglos. The Chicano farmers in the area were reduced to poverty.

THE TREATY OF GUADALUPE HIDALGO

The Treaty of Guadalupe Hidalgo ended the Mexican-American War (1846–1848) by establishing the Rio Grande River as the boundary between them. Mexico ceded ownership of California, roughly half of New Mexico, most of Arizona, Nevada, and Utah, and portions of Colorado and Wyoming. The amount of land gained by the United States from Mexico was further increased as a result of the Gadsden Purchase of 1853, which ceded parts of present-day southern Arizona and southern New Mexico to the United States.

The treaty explicitly gave Mexicans living in those territories the choice of being US citizens within a year of signing.

They shall be under the obligation to make their election [to become US citizens] within one year from the date of the exchange of ratifications of this treaty; and those who shall remain in the said territories after the expiration of that year, without having declared their intention to retain the character of Mexicans, shall be considered to have elected to become citizens of the United States.

The treaty also gave Mexicans and their heirs the rights to their land grants and other properties they held, and said they would be "inviolably respected" as it would properties held by other US citizens.

What followed was a sad history of the erosion of the clauses of that treaty. Mexican property rights were undermined by legal and legislative manipulation, fraud, graft, and other practices, such that today, very little property remains in the hands of Mexicans. Over the years, they were systematically impoverished and marginalized.

Enter Chicano rights activist Reies López Tijerina, who in the 1960s, by direct action, tried to wrest back the ownership of 600,000 acres of the Tierra Amarilla Land Grant, by claiming the United States was in violation of provisions in the Treaty of Guadalupe Hidalgo. Tijerina exposed the processes by which they were methodically stolen. Although he was correct, his tactics for that era were deemed too violent, hence rendering the cause ineffective. The land still belongs to the US Forest Service.

Ed loved La Alianza. It appealed to his anarchist nature. He became their environmental advisor in spite of wanting them to get rid of all the cows and graze elk, buffalo, and deer. Of course that was heresy among the Hispanics in northern New Mexico. But they loved him, so they listened to him. They thought he was a natural rebel and called him the Emiliano Zapata of the Southwest and eventually adopted *The Monkey Wrench Gang* as their "bible."

For years, Ed would wear baseball caps that said Tierra o Muerte (Land or Death) or Viva la Causa (Long Live the Cause).

In 1967, Tijerina led the only peasant revolt ever to occur in the United States in Tierra Amarilla [Yellow Earth] in northern New Mexico. He and his followers raided the courthouse and freed some of the farmers who were incarcerated. They shot and wounded a state policeman and a jailor. They declared Rio Arriba County, which is Tierra Amarilla, a republic, and called it the Republic of San Joaquin. They issued visas to get through it. Cars were stopped and the drivers asked, "Do you have a visa to the Republic of San Joaquin?" The story of the rebellion was aired over CBS and made the front page of the *New York Times*.

ML: Didn't you and Ed become monkeywrenchers together in Taos?

De Puy: While Ed was editor of *El Crepusculo*, the Melody Sign Company out of Las Vegas, New Mexico, put up forty- to fifty-foot billboards north of Taos, hideous, immense things, advertising cars, motels, and hotels. There were about ten of them coming into this beautiful landscape.

One day Ed and I decided: Enough. We went out with chainsaws and cut them all down. Each of us wanted to save the world. But the funny thing is that about a week later, the owner of the sign company came into the paper to put in an ad for the apprehension of these villains, these crooks, these swine of the earth that had done this. He offered $4,000. Ed, being the editor, took the ad. And suddenly he burst out laughing, and the owner said, "What's so funny?" Ed said, "Oh, I was just thinking of something else—har, har, har." Later he told me: "God! Four thousand bucks, De Puy! I was thinking of turning you in!"

One night we were out working the signs near a big arroyo when we heard voices coming down, and we dove for shelter into the sage. And here comes the town pharmacist who was a member of the town council in Taos, and a poet, who was a friend of D. H. Lawrence, carrying chain saws. They were out hacking down signs. I said, "Boo!" That was the last time Melody Sign Company put signs up north of Taos, because two days after they put them up, they'd all be down again. So they gave up. Ed said these actions were the beginning of what became the book *The Monkey Wrench Gang*.

ML: Two people contributed to the character of Doc Sarvis, the doctor who liked to smoke cigars and tear down billboards in *The Monkey Wrench Gang*. Who would you say they were?

De Puy: Ed said Ralph Newcomb and I were the inspiration for Doc Sarvis. Newcomb went to college with Abbey and they were bosom buddies. I never met Newcomb, but I did know that he and Ed had a terrible falling-out in the early sixties, and they never spoke to each other again. Ed wrote a beautiful chapter about him and Newcomb in

Down the River. It's where Ed speaks about the meaning of life and death.

Then there was myself. Doc was my nickname when I was a medic in the Marines. Although a lot of the words that Sarvis spoke were Ed's ideas, some were mine.

ML: How many billboards do you think Doc Sarvis really cut down?

De Puy: Couple hundred—as well as other things, which we won't discuss. Ed called it night work.

ML: One of the real events fictionalized in *The Monkey Wrench Gang* was about sabotaging a Caterpillar D3. Did you have anything to do with that?

De Puy: Ed and I found this D3-Cat during the construction of that stinking highway down to the Colorado River. The stupid idiots had left the key in the ignition. So we turned the damn thing on and sent it off a five-hundred-foot cliff—made a nice shot when it blew up in flames.

Anyway, I had some land near Monticello in southeast Utah, near Devil's Canyon, where I camped during the summer. One person who had some land right next to mine was Bevin Wright, the son of Frank Wright, the famous river runner. Bevin was the chief of police in Blanding. He'd often stop by after he got through work, in full uniform, pistol on the side.

One night, while Ed and I were standing around the fire cooking, up comes Bevin in full uniform. He pulls up in his car, walks up to the tree we're camping under, and says, "What are you boys eating?" I said, "T-bone steaks. Want to join in?" Ed and I were drinking beer, boilermakers actually. Bevin says sure and sits on a log.

While we're all sitting around and chatting, Bevin looks Ed straight in the eye and looks me straight in the eye and says, "You boys wouldn't know anything about that D3-Cat that went off Comb Ridge a number of years ago, would you?" And Ed—his face turned white! He went around a tree, and I think he threw up.

I saw Bevin wink at me so I knew it was a joke. The reason it was a joke was that the Mormon ranchers who lived around there hated that highway. They didn't want the damn thing built and were happy when the D3 went over the side. But Ed didn't know this! Here's this cop in full uniform, badge, .44 magnum on his hip, looking him in the eye and saying, "You boys wouldn't know anything about that D3-Cat?"

Bevin had the courtesy to explain to Ed afterward that it was no problem.

ML: How would you describe your friendship with Abbey?

De Puy: We were peers. When Ed was editor of *El Crepusculo*, we made a blood oath that he would write about the Southwest and I would paint it. Like me, Ed was a loner. He never joined any organization, even Earth First!. There were very, very few friends he opened up to.

We devoted our life to the Colorado Plateau and the Sonoran Desert. When Ed and I used to go out to the canyons, he'd sit on a rock writing, and I'd sit on another one watching a cliff or a tree until I felt that I was part of them, and then translate it into an inner experience and probably a hallucination.

Ed was a very complicated person, as was I, living in complicated times. I'm not going to practice idolatry in describing Ed, he would not have wanted that. That whole period, with all the romance of it, was just riddled with contradictions—the environmental movement, the social movement. I think we were all totally insane in the sixties. We were trying to save the Colorado Plateau and the Sonoran Desert, the Southwest, and preserve some of the indigenous population, and, in the meantime, fighting with our spouses and each other.

It was the end of the period of the Beats, which was essentially the period Ed and I came out of, although we went in a different direction from Jack Kerouac and Gary Snyder and the rest. It was a time of just incredible turmoil. So in discussing Ed and that whole period, I have to say that it was not all the rosy heroic period that it's sometimes portrayed as. It was a rough time. It killed our marriages. It killed relationships. At times, it almost killed us. It was brutal.

John De Puy with Ed Abbey, while camping on Cedar Mesa, Utah, circa
1980. Photographer unknown. Courtesy of the Collection of
John De Puy.

In the late fifties, our wives left us and took the kids. My wife wanted me to go to Switzerland and work for a bank. Ed's wanted him to go back to Hoboken and work as a caseworker, because she thought he was a failed writer and that he was only capable of stretching her canvases.

We went through hell. We fought like cats and dogs and commiserated with each other about our personal lives.

One time in the seventies, Ed had just lost his third wife Judy to leukemia, and I had just lost my father. Ed was working as a ranger at the fire tower on the North Rim of the Grand Canyon, and we decided to hike down to the bottom through the very seldom-used Thunder River Trail. We spent the night in a rock shelter there, cried on each other's shoulders, and tried to understand life, death, the whole miserable thing. Abbey gave me the absolute, fiery, half-demented courage to go on in spite of any obstacle. You follow your bliss. You go on, whatever the cost.

But when we fought, oh, did we fight! Whew! I mean, this one time I dumped him in Albuquerque with some friends of his whom I found obnoxious. I said, "Ed, you have one more chance to come with me back to Taos." He said, "Have another drink, De Puy." I got in my car and drove back. He had to hitchhike. The next day, he was out for blood. As I saw him coming, I headed out the door and ran for about a mile. I was a faster runner so I escaped his wrath. He was going to kill me.

And so my relationship with Ed was that of a brother.

ML: Weren't you also both trying to cultivate the New York publishing and art world during that period?

De Puy: Yes, but we also loathed it. Our experiences in the Southwest were a long way from the New York art/publishing world.

During much of Ed's writing days, the literary world was dominated by New York publishers, and if you didn't play ball with them, they forgot you. In New York, Ed was considered a regional writer. He hated that. He thought what he was saying was universal. And so did I. It was the same for Western painters like me. We were outsiders.

I didn't play ball with the New York art crowd too well. One incident stands out. I was given this big show in New York and ruined it during the preliminary cocktail party. I was standing by the punch bowl with all these Yuppies and collectors, when this guy comes up and starts working his finger up and down my spine. I looked at the gallery owner, Jacques [Sullivan], and said, "What is this?" And he said, "Well, John, if you're going to make it in the New York art world you have to put up with certain things." I went completely ape shit. I picked up this big round punchbowl, dumped it over this jerk's head, and watched the ice cubes going down his neck. He probably had on a $5,000 custom suit. The gallery called the police.

As I started running out the door, Ed came in. He had just fired his editor at—it wasn't Dutton, it was some other publisher—and he was in a rage because they wanted to cut *The Monkey Wrench Gang* to pieces.

We went down to a bar near Washington Square and got roaring drunk, cursing publishers and art galleries. After the bar closed, we walked up Fifth Avenue, raging and ranting. When we got to a church on lower Fifth Avenue near Washington Square, Ed said, "I wanna pray, De Puy!" When he went up to the church, it was locked. He was enraged: "A church? A man should be able to pray, for God's sake!" And he went out and he found a plank somewhere and started trying to beat the door down. I said, "Ed . . ." I was a little more sober, "Stop it! There are people here. Now stop!" He wouldn't stop.

Finally somebody called the cops. This whole wagon of New York cops showed up, and two big Irish cops just picked Ed up and threw him in the back of the wagon, stuck me in the front, and headed us to the drunk tank for the night. I noticed that the sergeant in charge had an Irish accent and I mentioned to him that my mother was from Dublin and her family name was Erley. He knew the family! We chatted for a while, and I said, "Look, Ed back there, he's"—and by then Ed had passed out—"he's from the hills. He's a hillbilly. He's a hick. He doesn't know what he's doing. I promise you, I'll make sure he never comes back to the island again." Actually, Ed was living in Hoboken at that time. The Irish cop said, "Since you're an Erley . . ." and put us on the tube to Hoboken. "If we ever see either of you guys on this island again, you're going to rot in hell."

ML: Well, that's a story about the great divide. Let's go back out West and talk about your trips with Ed on Navajo Mountain.

De Puy: Ed and I discovered that we both had a great love for Navajo Mountain, and we went on three trips up there. Ed said we circumcised it three times, which was blasphemy.

The third trip was with this totally divergent group of people—a Buddhist abbot, an environmental lawyer, a folk singer, and a CIA spook. Sandy Stewart, abbot of the Bodhi Manda Zen Center in the Jemez Mountains of New Mexico, wasn't Japanese. He was an American Scotsman, who was called by the Zen name Gentei. The environmental lawyer from Santa Fe worked for Navajo Legal Services for a long time. The folksinger, Greenspan, was another disreputable friend of Ed's and mine. Then there was a guy who had been a theater chief in charge of the CIA in Saigon during the Vietnam War. He cracked up under the strain, and when Ed and I met him, he was a wreck, just falling apart. We just said, "Come on." We took him on hikes, we took him on field trips, and we'd kid around about how we'd kill him or he'd kill us. He was a great guy. We kind of brought him back to reality and helped him gradually restore his sanity, so he became our friend.

In the talks around the campfire on that trip, we often talked about the interconnectedness of all species, a concept similar to Zen Buddhism, Native American, and Celts. I gave Ed the sense of the Beauty Way in the Navajo spiritual tradition and the Buddhist sense of beauty and wholeness, the feeling that all of life is interconnected. Although Ed had no use at all for religion of any kind and thought it was the opiate of the masses, he understood that we have an almost mystical relationship with Gaia, the universal earth mother.

We hiked to the north side of Navajo Mountain where there was a canyon going down toward the San Juan River, a very remote area. Hardly anyone had been down this darn thing, big cliffs on either side, straight up. We came to a place where the stream became a waterfall, going over a chute and down about thirty to forty feet to a pool. Ed and I looked at each other and said, "No way. We're going to go back out and up and around on top of the mesa and down." And Sandy, this little Zen Buddhist priest, bald, wearing frigging sandals, for God's sake, looks down, meditates for a minute, strips his clothes off, puts them in a bag, throws them over, breathes a few times, and dives off into this pool. We thought, he's dead. But he made it.

Up until that point, Ed and the rest of us were kidding this little Buddhist monk to death. I mean, we'd be eating steaks and drinking Scotch around the fire. Sandy would be eating some long stringy green seaweed in this horrible stew that he made. And we'd be laughing, right? We thought he was a joke, or at least Ed did until he pulled that stunt. Now he would just say, "Whoa! This guy is for real!"

Ed was fascinated with Zen Buddhism after that trip, and he and Sandy had this long, very philosophic correspondence about the nature of the universe and life and death.

ML: Abbey described the Maze on the West side of Canyonlands National Park as terrifying. When you and Ed went into the Maze, he wrote something like this in *Down by the River*: "Death, the inexplicable disappearance." How did death become conflated with journeys into the Maze?

De Puy: I'm surprised Ed lived to be sixty-two because from way back he had this lifelong fixation on death. He was like the medieval knight in the Swedish film *The Seventh Seal* who played chess with the personification of Death. I remember one time when we were building Malcolm Brown's house out in Arroyo Seco, near Taos, when one of the most violent lightning storms I'd ever seen came down on us. Ed took a steel rod and walked out in the field and defied God.

It was strange. I never understood where that fixation came from. Didn't the poet Dylan Thomas write: "Go not gently into that dark night. Rage, rage against the coming of the dark"? We worshipped Thomas and once went to a reading he gave at the Cedar Bar in Greenwich Village, New York City.

Ed considered Canyonlands a place where everything stings, sticks, or bites and felt that you shouldn't go into that country without praying. He found it very terrifying. It's not a gentle country. And yeah, it's a place of great beauty, but it's also a place of terror. It can kill you in a minute.

We came very close to dying a couple of times. One time we were following a very narrow ledge with a four-hundred-foot drop near Cedar Mesa. As I started behind him, I stumbled on some hole and started slowly going off into this abyss. Ed reached down—he was a very husky guy—and he grabbed me and just hauled me over. I was on my way down. That was close.

And, you know, there were a lot of experiences like that. When you go out into remote areas, like Everett Ruess or Ed did—I mean, really go out, not on a tourist trip, but really go out and spend days and weeks out there alone—it's pretty terrifying.

ML: You mentioned Everett Ruess [1914–1934]. Who was he and what does he mean to you?

De Puy: He was our predecessor, the first white man to approach the Navajo country and love it for its own sake, instead of looking at a mesa and thinking, *Ah, maybe there are some minerals in there, how can we hack this mountain to pieces?* Ruess left California to get away from a stupid upper-middle-class life. He disappeared into those canyons and was never found. He was twenty years old. [In 1989, some bones were found in Comb Ridge that some people thought were Ruess's, but a DNA study showed that they belonged to a Native American.]

A few months after Ed died, his friends found an old cardboard box in his study that was full of poetry. Nobody knew he really took poetry seriously. Abbey's friend David Peterson, who was also the executor of his estate, put together a book of Ed's poetry with some wonderful graphics and called it *Earth Apples: The Poetry of Edward Abbey.* The poetry is beautiful, kind of short haikus. One of the most heartrending is a sonnet for Everett Ruess, which pretty much said it all:

You walked into the radiance of death through the passageways of stillness, stone and light, gold coin of cottonwoods, the spangled shade,

cascading song of canyon wren, the flight of scarlet dragonflies from
pools, the stain of water on the curve of sand, the art of roots that
crack the monolith of time.

You know the crazy lust to probe the heart of that which has no
heart we could know, toward the source, deep in the core, the maze,
the secret center of no bounds hold. Hunter, brother, companion
of our days: that blessing you hunted, hunted too. What you were
seeking is what found you. (Oracle, Arizona, 1983)

Ooh! Gives me the chills!

ML: Why do you think Abbey wanted to go back to the Maze before he
died?

De Puy: The Maze was one of the first places he went to when he
moved to the Southwest from his home in Pennsylvania. He always
found it a strange and mystical place. He wanted to see it one last time
because he knew the end was very close.

In November '88, I was living in Bluff and Ed came to my house and
said, "I don't have long to go. I want you to take me to the Maze one
last time." So we got in my old Suzuki Samurai and drove out there and
went down into the Maze and spent the night.

During one of our philosophical discussions, he became very annoyed
when I questioned certain theoretical premises. He said, "All artists
should sew their mouths shut. You're a goddamn painter, De Puy! Stop
talking about things you know nothing about!" That was the source of
many a discussion.

On the way out, he started bleeding internally and passed out. He
was dying. Luckily, he had a canteen filled not with water but laudanum. And every once in a while he'd take a sip, and it would keep him
going for a time.

What really bugged him was that for a man who loved alcohol, like
the rest of us, he couldn't drink anymore, not even a beer.

Afterward, we spent the night at our old camp in Cedar Mesa near
Muley Point. We made a camp there thirty years ago, and the fire pit

John De Puy, May 2018.
Photographer Francis Sullivan.

was still there. That night, standing round the fire, he fainted from loss of blood, and when he came to, he took another sip of laudanum to keep going. But the end was coming. He was on his way out, which was sad.

For years after Ed died, I thought much about the consciousness that came out of our years of fighting for the earth. In retrospect, I wonder if we achieved much at all. By the next century, we could all be facing extinction. If nothing is done, it's irreversible. It's as simple as that. These days when I go out to meditate, I can smell the earth dying.

But I also go back to that same cardboard box full of poetry that his friends found after Ed's death. One poem was an epitaph to me: "To John De Puy, mad man and seer, painter of the apocalyptic volcano of the world: compañero, I am with you forever in the glorious fraternity of the damned." I love that.

10 | INGRID EISENSTADTER

Biography

Ingrid Eisenstadter was one of the most elusive members of Edward Abbey's close circle of friends. She and Abbey were a couple when he was writing *The Monkey Wrench Gang*, living together in Logan and Moab, Utah, and North Rim, Grand Canyon. Ingrid was the inspiration for the character of Bonnie Abbzug.

Born in the Bronx, Eisenstadter was soon in ballet school and dancing professionally before her teenage years. She graduated from Manhattan's School of Performing Arts, which was featured in the movie *Fame* (1980). Ingrid has written articles for the *New York Times*, the science journal *Nature*, *Sierra* (Sierra Club magazine), *High Country News*, *Barron's*, and others.

Eisenstadter was longtime director of grants for the Eppley Foundation for Scientific Research in New York and continues to work in the nonprofit sector.

I interviewed Ingrid in her apartment in New York City where she is surrounded by history. I was particularly drawn to an oil painting of her great-great-great-great-grandfather. Ingrid told me, "Alas, I do not know if he was born in the 1700s or 1800s, but he lives on in my nephew who could be his twin, talking and laughing and living with that same face. The painting is one of the few family treasures that my parent's generation was able to get out of Germany in World War II, as they escaped the murderers of Jewish babies, their mommies, and unarmed men."

———

ML Lincoln: How did you and Ed Abbey get together?

Ingrid Eisenstadter: Ed and I met in the late sixties. I lived in Logan, Utah. I had just read *Desert Solitaire*, and we began to correspond. After a time, he invited me down to Organ Pipe National Monument where he worked as a park ranger. He put a dot on a map he sent to show me where he lived.

I no longer remember exactly what happened, if Ed was early or late or if I was early or late, but when my plane landed in Ajo, Arizona, he was not there. This is what happens when two irresponsible people plan to meet over a distance of hundreds of miles.

So, I hitched a ride down to Organ Pipe, knocked on his door, nobody home. I went for a stroll on the only paved road for miles around. It was dark by now, and I was skirting around the rattlers that had slithered up onto the pavement to keep warm. Eventually I see an old rust bucket heading down the road toward me, clippety-clop. It was the only car that had been on the road for half an hour. It pulled up to me and stopped. The driver rolled down the window, looked out, and said, "Ingrid?" And I looked in, and said, "Ed?"

That was how we met.

ML: Can you tell me something about your life with Ed?

Eisenstadter: We were at first glance very different. I was a Jew from the Bronx. Ed was a WASP—an Appalachian hillbilly born of Mildred Postlewaite and Paul Revere Abbey. That said, he had a very Jewish sense of humor, which is about laughing in the face of disaster. Running out of water in the desert. Getting lost in the woods. Without water. Mostly, we laughed.

Ed and I traveled a lot, often for his writing or speaking engagements. Sometimes we'd be away for weeks from whatever place we were calling home. The cars we drove were antiques, fair to call them jalopies. We were a couple before the time he was making a living at anything. I wasn't either. When one of our antiques broke down, we'd pick up another, fill the tank, and drive off.

One day when we were living in Moab just waiting for the summer season jobs to start at North Rim, I noticed a puddle under our car. I called to Ed and said, "Something's wrong with the car. Fix it." He said, "You fix it!" I said, "No, you." "You" "You." Finally I popped open the hood, and it was easy to see that it was the radiator that was leaking and that the radiator was held in place by four bolts and a clamp around the hose. That was all.

I drove to a nearby junkyard. I still remember that the new used radiator cost five dollars. I was told that I would have to bring the old used radiator back once I had replaced it or I'd have to pay six dollars. I returned to our house and replaced the radiator. I lifted out the old one, which was easy because it no longer had any water in it, dropped in the new one, screwed those bolts back in, clamped the hose, and filled it with water.

When I was done I said, "Ed, I fixed the car." He was delighted and said, "From now on, all the car maintenance falls to you," which is exactly what happened.

Another time, we broke down on a dirt road in the desert. Predictably, we had no food, we had no water, and the situation was really quite hopeless. Well, we should have been preparing to die, but instead we were laughing. I have no memory anymore of what we found so entertaining. Our only worry was that we would run out of the dehydrating wine that we found in the trunk before we died. That's how we lived. It was a good life.

ML: Tell me about living with Ed at the North Rim of the Grand Canyon.

Eisenstadter: For a couple summers Ed and I lived at North Rim, up at about eight thousand feet. Tourists routinely got dizzy, some fainted, for want of oxygen. Ed worked there as a fire lookout. Back then he would take on any work that paid him. Before then, he had worked as a

Ingrid was responsible for automotive maintenance, 1970s. Photographer unknown. Courtesy of the Collection of Ingrid Eisenstadter.

school-bus driver and a bartender, and had been in and out of the Park Service and the Forest Service with a number of job titles.

At North Rim, Ed and I lived in a house trailer, with a beautiful Civilian Conservation Corps [CCC] log cabin behind us where some of the boys on the fire crew lived. Nearby was the small entrance station to the park, also built with logs, no bricks in sight at the park. There was someone who worked out there who, when no one was looking, would hang up a sign saying, "Keep tourists out. Save parks for employees." Who could that have been? It came down a lot, but it got put back up a lot, too.

I brought the antique treadle Singer sewing machine that Ed had bought me some time before up to the trailer. One summer, not too long after we got there, the head of the Park Service on the North Rim heard I could sew. He came over one day with all these Park Service patches and uniform shirts and paid me twenty-five cents each to sew them on.

It was a fortune. I could do eight or ten of these in an hour. Easy money. I never parted with the machine; still have it today.

The lookout job was perfect for Ed because he could do his writing in the tower while he was being paid to look out for fire. At the beginning of the season he would take his typewriter up into the tower, a long climb, and leave it there for the summer, writing this and that.

No one else at North Rim could tolerate that lookout job. You have to sit all day in a little room atop the tower, looking down on treetops. On the upside, there was a 360-degree horizon visible from the lookout and nothing manmade in sight.

There's some skill to spotting a fire. At the Grand Canyon there are thunderstorms, particularly in August, every afternoon and they begin at exactly 3:00 p.m. When a snag or branch is hit by lightning, it sends up a puff of smoke. It may not send up another puff for a long time, and may or may not snuff out by itself. Big fires were rare at the Canyon. After a rain, waterdogs [insider term for *water vapor*] would rise up from the forest, looking very much like smoke. They were subtly different from smoke, however. They reacted differently to wind and had a different translucence from fire smoke, and you had to be sophisticated to see the difference. Heaven help you if you radioed the ranger station with a fire alert ["726, 650, Code 3, smoke"] when you had nothing going on but a waterdog because that night when everyone was out for a beer, the boys on the fire crew would point at you and laugh. Or call you "stupit."

Once, on my day off, I drove through the forest to the nearest supermarket, which was eighty miles away. On this occasion I went with two of the boys on the fire crew. Our boss had told us to take down a huge six-by-six-foot Park Service sign that was on National Forest grounds. To take it down, I had to stand on one of the boys' shoulders to get to the top bolts. Along comes a Forest Service truck, and the patrolman jumps out and says, "You're all under arrest. You've been stealing our signs for a long time." I climbed down from the shoulders of the smokejumper I'd been standing on and said, "No, no, really, we're Park Service, and we've been told to bring this sign back." He didn't believe us. One of the boys picked up the monkey wrench I had been using, and said, "Look, we even have Park Service tools. It says NPS right on them, National Park Service." Alas, the patrolman's reaction was: "Oh, so you stole some tools, too." Well, then along came a Highway Patrol cop, a state employee, not Forest Service. I knew him, and he recognized me, so the heat was off. We had not yet been handcuffed.

Why anyone would assume that three people in broad daylight on a highway are stealing a six-foot sign, I do not know. The relay calls began. It was a three-way radio-tower bounce in each direction, from Forest Service headquarters to Park Service headquarters and back. Our names were Stiegelmeyer, Ochterman, and Eisenstadter. The relay came back: "Stieglemeter, Ochtemeyer, and Eisenmaler are all okay."

ML: Did you and Ed do any "night work" when you were together?

Eisenstadter: No, of course Ed and I never did any monkeywrenching. That would be illegal and heaven knows we would never break the law. Maybe there were times that Ed snuck off and did some environmental preservation work in the Lincoln Continental that he would borrow from his buddy William Eastlake. And of course, Dougie [Doug Peacock] would not have gone with Ed, because Dougie would never break the law either.

Ed never advocated violence against anyone. Newspaper or website references to *The Monkey Wrench Gang* gives some people the impression, perhaps, that there's violence in the book. There's none. No one is killed, no one is threatened. Just damns and miscellaneous earth-moving machines, as it should be.

ML: Can you talk about the time Ed was writing *The Monkey Wrench Gang*?

Eisenstadter: The time that Ed and I cast our lot together is when he was writing *The Monkey Wrench Gang*. We lived a fairly isolated life. In the summer, we worked at the Grand Canyon. Autumn and winter we were alone with each other. We lived in Logan, Utah, for a time and in Kanab, a wonderful, tiny town. Then.

From time to time I'd read the stack of paper piled next to the type-writer. When I got to the last page I would ask, "What happens next?" He would respond with, "I don't know." Sometimes I would sit next to him and read the pages one at a time as they came out of the typewriter. I would say, "Hurry up! What happens next?" He would respond with, "I don't know." That went on for quite some time.

Insofar as Ed was interested in my opinion—not far at all—I expressed my objection to his stupid obscenity in the book, which served no purpose at all. I tried to convince him to bring it down, but he would stick his fingers in his ears and say, "No, no, no."

In the first draft, unbeknown to the world at large, by page 4 or 5, the Glen Canyon Dam blew up. This honor went to a certain dancer from the Bronx, who got to push down on the plunger that exploded the dam and sent it sky-high. And then crumbled down to hell. As enormous pieces of cement block rained down and huge waves of water and dust went into the air, not too far away four irresponsible people under the cover of the high-country conifer forest were dancing and singing "Hava Nagila" [Let Us Rejoice] amid the beautiful fireworks of this joyous moment. No people were hurt. And let's not forget that *The Monkey Wrench Gang* was a comedy. It was written in good spirits and, to say the least, it was a successful effort.

I was sorry to see the original first chapter go. As time passed, Ed felt that it was "too unbelievable" and he dumped it. That chapter remains to be written into history. I await that day, when the humpback chub may roam free again.

*The Monkey Wrench Gan*g was finally published in 1975. It took a while for word to get out, but then it got on a rocket ship to the moon. It was subsequently translated into many foreign languages. Ed sent me the German edition in 1987. He said, "If you can tell me what this book is about, it's yours."

ML: Did Ed model Bonnie Abbzug after you?

Eisenstadter: What does "model" mean? Bonnie came from the Bronx and she's a dancer. I am a graduate of the School of Performing Arts in

New York and was a dance major. Ed always had paper and pencil with him and not infrequently wrote down verbatim the conversations we had. When I read the manuscript and then the galleys, there they were.

Some years ago my son and his girlfriend were traveling out West and they went to Moab. My son went into a bookstore where he found a T-shirt with an illustration of Bonnie Abbzug on it. My son thought, well this is a perfect present to bring back to Mom. As he was paying, he said, "That's my mother." The woman who was at the cash register looked at him with amazement and said, "She's still alive?"

My son met Ed only once, shortly before Ed died. He was a toddler then. I tried to keep Ed's memory alive in my son, but today he no longer recalls that day, alas.

ML: Some say Ed himself was Jack Burns, the quintessential cowboy of the Old West, who appears in some of his books and in the movie *Lonely Are the Brave* [1962], based on his book *The Brave Cowboy*. Can you see Ed in the character of Jack Burns?

Eisenstadter: Yes, Ed was a cowboy, albeit of some sophistication. One day he came home with a white cowboy hat that had a very narrow brim. He explained to me that the reason for this purchase was an upcoming interview with a conservative [cowboy] politician, and narrow brims are conservative. He knew this would camouflage him when he was actually a radical, wide-brimmed cowboy.

In his earlier years, Ed rode horseback a good deal, though not so much by the time we were together. He could ride, and he enjoyed it.

ML: Did you and Ed ever go down the Colorado River?

Eisenstadter: The first time I met river runner Ken Sleight, who would eventually morph into the character Seldom Seen in *The Monkey Wrench Gang*, was when Ed and I were going to spend a week going down the Colorado River through Cataract Canyon. The run has a reputation for being dangerous, but we knew we were in good hands.

After a day or two on the river, we were nearing the notorious Big

Drop Rapids, which is named that way because that's how it is. In the middle of Big Drop's steep decline is a huge boulder, and I still remember how it threw back a big wave of water, more than enough to swamp any raft. As we approached the rapids, the water became mysteriously quiet and glassy.

To go through the approaching turbulence of the rapids, Ken decided it would be best to turn on the little three-horsepower motor that was on the back of our rubber raft. So he pulls on the starter rope, and in the silence of the approaching whitewater, the motor goes sputter, sputter. Then he pulls on the rope again and the same thing happened. After three times, we were close to the rapids, and the water was now getting very rough.

So, Ken picks up an oar, tosses another one to Ed on the other side of the raft, and announces that we would manually steer around Big Drop. Sounds like a plan. As soon as Ed put his oar in the water, however, there was a loud *crack*. The paddle had instantly broken off Ed's oar. He held it up in the air, now nothing more than a stick, and over the growing noise of the fast-approaching rapids, he yells, "Ken, I think something is wrong with my oar." Predictably, we burst into laughter, instead of preparing to die or at least swim. I no longer recall how Ken got us around that big boulder with one oar that long-ago day, but he managed, and we lived to tell the tale.

Later that day, Ken steers us onto a beach using that little outboard motor, which, of course, began to work as soon as we get past Big Drop. Ken jumps out of the raft, and suddenly I hear this strange slurping noise. I turn my head and see that Ken has instantly sunk up to his waist in quicksand. He was sinking fast. Ken leaned over and reached out to Ed saying, "Give me a hand!" Ed, without moving, looked right at Ken, and said, "Say please."

Today I don't remember if Ken actually said please or not, but Ed did grab Ken's hand and pulled him back onto the raft. Ken pushed the raft onto dry land using the little motor. That got us far enough onto the beach that we put the quicksand behind us.

ML: Were there any side canyons that you really liked or inspired you?

Eisenstadter: One night, after Ken docked the rafts for the evening, I scampered up a canyon and climbed its wall for a looksee. And, what do you know, there were people there, camping. I went over to one of them and introduced myself, "Hi, I'm so-and-so, who are you?" "Phil Hyde," he said. Well, it just so happened that Hyde was taking photographs for the very same Sierra Club book that Ed was writing at that time. And what were the chances of our meeting like that? Well, in this case 100 percent. I scampered back down that little canyon and told Ed this small-world story and he climbed up the canyon and said hello to Phil. The end product was the Sierra Club coffee table book on Utah's slickrock canyons.

SLICKROCK: THE ENDANGERED CANYONS OF THE SOUTHWEST

The words of Edward Abbey and well-known conservationist photographer Philip Hyde that eloquently portray the beauty of the endangered canyons of Southwest canyons was published as a large-format coffee table book titled *Slickrock: The Endangered Canyons of the Southwest* (1971). In the same year, a smaller version was published with a different title: *Slickrock: The Canyon Country of Southeast Utah*. A paperback version of the original large format hardcover book with the title *Slickrock* was published by Gibbs M. Smith in 1987. The books opened up readers' eyes to the threats of extractive mining and the pollution that would likely follow.

ML: I know that you and Ed went your separate ways. Can you talk about this?

Eisenstadter: After Ed and I separated, I moved to Berlin, Germany. I wanted to get away, and I knew I would not be completely lost there because I spoke some German.

Ed flew over not so long after I got there to persuade me to come

Prisoner of Park Avenue, Ingrid Eisenstadter, 2011. Photographer ML Lincoln.

home, but it was too late. He was heartbroken, and he told me this for many years, but eventually, he also told me that on his way home he stopped in London to spend some time with an old girlfriend, so in fact his recuperation period was twenty-four hours.

When spring came, I returned to my summer job at North Rim, Grand Canyon, for my third summer season, now a park ranger naturalist as opposed to law enforcement ranger. I was fired before the season ended. I no longer recall why but my boss was a jerk as I probably so informed him. I moved back to New York and started working as an editor for Sierra Club Books. From there, I started working for the New York Botanical Garden, where I eventually became the manager of their publishing program. I stayed in New York, got married, had a son, and put a few of Ed's belongings that I had not parted with in the closet.

One day I came home from work and I found my now ex-husband wearing one of Ed's ranger shirts. I said to him, "I don't think so." It came off and went back into the closet, where it has been these forty years, along with Ed's park ranger hat.

ML: It must have been a shock to learn of Ed's death?

Eisenstadter: Clarke Abbey, Ed's widow, called me early the morning that he died in March of 1989. He had obviously put me on the A List and she was so good as to honor it. I had seen him just a few months before he died. In fact, our friendship was restored a year after we separated, kindred spirits yet, and we had always stayed in touch. He spared me the knowledge that he was sick when I saw him, so it was a terrible shock.

Clarke invited me to his funeral, which would be a small and private gathering. "Come if you want." I wasn't going anywhere then. I was immobilized. Eventually Clarke invited me to the memorial service that followed some months later.

I flew out West that May to go to this "celebration of life" service at Arches National Park in southeastern Utah. I wore a black dress, black hat with a veil down over my face, and black high-heeled shoes, not aware that it would be a long hike on a dirt path through the desert to the lovely, lonely site that Clarke had chosen for this ceremony.

At the service, which a couple hundred people attended, I saw Ed's friend John De Puy. Ed always called him "Debris." He walked up behind me and said, "Is that you, Ingoo?"—which is the name Ed called me by. Ed's third wife, who was preparing to leave him behind [as his two previous wives had], died tragically of acute leukemia in her late twenties, and for a time her toddler daughter and I were friends. Ingoo was as close as she could get to saying my name, and it stuck. Debris's voice was so like Ed's. Between that and the name Ingoo, I spun around, thinking, well, perhaps he's not so dead. And there stood Debris.

I saw Ken for the first time in many years. Dougie was there, too, so many people from the ancient past.

ML: You were the whispered about mystery woman there?

Eisenstadter: Well, I don't actually know anything about any whispering, but given that I was dressed for a formal occasion and everyone else was in jeans, I suppose I was noticeable. I was upset and stayed at the very back of this huge gathering. As it broke up, Clarke walked up to me over a considerable distance and said, "Hello. I'm Clarke Abbey."

I said hello and introduced her to my friend, who had come out there with me. "Who are you?" she said. I just assumed that she knew when she came by to introduce herself.

"I'm Ingrid," I said. "Oh, you're Ingrid." That was the first time I met Clarke.

ML: When was the last time you saw Ed?

Eisenstadter: The last time I saw Ed was shortly before he died. He was in New York and took me to a party. At this party, to my considerable surprise, was the famous Russian poet Yevgeny Yevtushenko.

Both these men were of raw height of 6 feet, 2 inches, and before the evening was over, they were standing with an arm around each other's shoulder, singing some song that they knew in common, swinging beer cans in time with their music. I looked at them and I realized that these men between them had ten wives and ten children. Separated at birth.

When we left that party—Ed was going to Boston the next day—he hailed a cab and got in. It was long after dark. I stood on the sidewalk and watched the cab pull away. For no reason in particular, Ed turned around in his seat and saw me watching his departure. We didn't wave and we didn't blow kisses. We just looked at each other as his cab headed away, wondering what happened to us. That was the last time I saw him alive.

I have, however, seen him many times since. Our conversation goes on, and it's full of laughter.

11 | KIERAN SUCKLING

Biography

Feared, relentless, passionate, and confrontational are words often used to describe Kieran Suckling, the executive director of the Center for Biological Diversity, one of the most effective and powerful environmental groups in the United States. The Center primarily uses litigation against existing environmental laws to protect wildlife, ecosystems, and communities, winning favorable outcomes for 93 percent of the cases it has filed.

Suckling received a Bachelor of Arts in philosophy from College of the Holy Cross in 1987 and a Master of Arts in philosophy from the State University of New York (SUNY) Stony Brook in 1999. His intellectual interests were esoteric and diverse: phenomenology, hermeneutics, deconstruction, anthropology, and Eastern religions. But it was conservation—specifically the love of the diverse animal species that inhabit our planet—that captured his heart and became his lifelong commitment.

Suckling cofounded the Center in 1989, together with Peter Galvin, Robin Silver, and Todd Schulke, all of whom have remained active staff members and directors of key programs. The organization has more than 1.5 million members and online activists.

In addition to overseeing its conservation and financial programs, Suckling created and maintains the country's most comprehensive endangered species database. He acts as liaison between the Center and other environmental groups and negotiates with government agencies. He is a sought-after speaker who has written many scientific articles and essays on biodiversity issues.

In 2009, Suckling helped organize the Center's Climate Law Institute and helped raise more than $17 million in funding to coordinate strategies against the dangers and damages of climate disruption and to file lawsuits to advance regulations intended to address climate change. As of January 1, 2019, the Center had filed 103 lawsuits against the administration of President Trump for its climate change denials, censorship of scientists and their research on global warming, and the promotion of the killing of wildlife.

In 2012, I interviewed Kieran out in the Sonoran Desert in Tucson, and after a talk by Paul Ehrlich, which Kieran attended, that was put on by Mountainfilm Festival in Telluride, Colorado. Ehrlich is the author of *The Population Bomb* (1968). (www.biologicaldiversity.org)

———

ML Lincoln: How did your Jesuit background influence your work with the Center for Biological Diversity?

Kieran Suckling: I grew up in a very traditional Irish-Catholic family and graduated in 1987, from the College of the Holy Cross, a Jesuit school, with a degree in philosophy. Jesuits have been a defining force in my life and a big part of why I do what I do. I was really impressed with their values of social justice, social change, and integrity. That sort of Jesuit culture has been a very big influence on why I became an environmentalist and why I decided to devote my life to social change and betterment. These values were integrated into my passion for wilderness.

ML: How did you become involved in activism?

Suckling: After college, my friends and I headed West, not sure where we were going and what we were going to do. By late fall, we found ourselves in Missoula, Montana.

Kieran Suckling. Photographer Jeff Newton.

That's where I first ran into the Northern Rockies Earth First! and started doing some work with them. My friends and I were the second-generation wave. We were the academic hippies, although Earth First!ers still enjoyed calling us hippies. We would refer to Dave Foreman and Ed Abbey and others—and sympathetically so, not as a critique—as the big guys for wilderness, even though they liked to be called rednecks for wilderness.

In 1989, while still in my early twenties, I was working on my doctoral dissertation about the relationship between the extinction of languages and the extinction of species. That same year I went out West to attend the Earth First! Rendezvous in northern New Mexico, which was involved in trying to stop timber sales. At that time, Earth First! had taken on that issue, which was not in the public eye yet, and drove it into mainstream consciousness.

At one protest, I chained myself across a road in order to block access to a timber sale. A woman named Sherie and I got arrested. When we got out of jail, she helped get me a job with Peter Galvin, who was working for the Forest Service doing Mexican spotted owl surveys in New Mexico's Gila National Forest. The other member of our crew was Todd Schulke, who ran outdoor education programs. We were roaming the forests at night, imitating the call of the spotted owl, and eventually found one holed up in a ponderosa pine.

When we took the information to the Forest Service, we discovered that they had more interest in cutting the timber than saving the owls. We took the story to a local paper, which published it, and stopped that timber sale. After that, the Forest Service considered us persona non grata.

Others became involved in trying to protect the owls, such as Dr. Robin Silver, who had written a petition under the Endangered Species Act [ESA].

Our efforts to protect species matched those being taken by Earth First! to save the big trees. My work with them and the attempts to protect the owls led to a coalescing of activists who realized our manic energy, passion, and dedication could be spent working the legal system rather than doing tree sits. And those efforts led to the formation of the Center for Biological Diversity in 1989.

ML: What was the Center's first lawsuit?

Suckling: In the early nineties, no Mexican wolves existed in the wild; all were in zoos. But a study done by the US military, of all people, said that wolves could be reintroduced to the White Sands Missile Range in New Mexico.

The environmental community there formed a group called the Wolf Coalition. They had meetings with the general to convince him to say, "Yes, we want wolves." The military showed no interest. Finally, we asked, "Where is this going exactly?" We were told that the general was expected to retire in a few years and we should wait it out. We thought to ourselves, "Activism is not about waiting for your opponent to re- tire." We said, "Doesn't the Endangered Species Act say every federal agency must protect endangered species? Isn't the military a federal agency as much as the post office? Don't they have a legal requirement to follow the law? Let's sue the bastards."

When we announced the lawsuit, we didn't even have a lawyer. The next day, one calls from Santa Fe and asks, "Well, this is very interest- ing. Who's your lawyer?" We said, "You are, if you want to be." He said, "Sure, I'll take the case." We ended up re-introducing wolves into the national forests in Arizona and eventually into New Mexico forests, but not on the White Sands Missile Base. You can spend years, even decades, asking, "Pretty please, stop doing the damage." Or you can say, "It's illegal. Let's go to court."

ML: When did you meet Edward Abbey and how did he influence you?

Suckling: I first met Abbey at the Grand Canyon during the 1980s, when I wound up at the Energy Fool's Rendezvous. We were protesting uranium mining because it was having a bit of a renewed boom. And there was Abbey, seeing a threat that few people recognized, rousing people to take action against it.

Afterward, I read all of Abbey's work and was very influenced by his finding humor in subjects such as destruction of property, sabotage to stop resource extraction, and resistance to government authority and, at the same time, being very angry and driven. I loved reading about monkeywrenching, when the bulldozer is tearing down the trees, ripping the cactus, and there's nothing to do except stop that bulldozer by sending it off the cliff. Ideas like these that caused no harm to people inspired thousands to take action and helped motivate the essence of Earth First!. It was a huge contribution to the contemporary environmental movement getting off its tired ass.

Abbey was not just an activist. He was a philosopher, a keen observer of human nature, of human psychology, and of himself. This is something that some critics miss in his writing and actions. Instead, they look for contradictions. For example, some say, "Oh, this guy was a phony. He was pretending he was a redneck, but he had a master's degree in philosophy." The notion that people are consistent is a fiction. There is no human like that, and anyone who presents someone like that is probably running for president.

Much of the criticism leveled at Abbey or Earth First! came from a misperception. Ed and Dave Foreman and Howie Wolke, another Earth First! cofounder, created this persona of the redneck for wilderness. A lot of people didn't really appreciate how much of it was performance art and got very disturbed. Much of what Ed and Earth First! did basically had to do with style: it was part of a whole campaign to communicate and draw people in. We understood that everyone was sort of playing a role.

With the third wave of Earth First!ers, a growing division began, being evident between right- and left-wing people. Until then, there was a lot of camaraderie and humor. I think the hippies and the rednecks got along pretty well; better than the far lefties who were mostly folks in the Animal Liberation Front and the Earth Liberation Front who didn't get along with either the rednecks or the first two waves of people in Earth First!. In that regard, I want to say that I think that Ed and Dave also liked poking hornets' nests. So I can understand why people might be upset.

ML: Kevin Berger, in an article he wrote in *Men's Journal* [February 24, 2011], called you one of the "most feared and effective environmentalists" in the country. Many have criticized the Center from generating a political backlash and potentially getting the Endangered Species Act watered down. How do you respond to that?

Suckling: The Center has certainly generated a political backlash, but our work is not undermining the ESA. Despite the opposition spending tens of millions of dollars and generating constant wall-to-wall controversy and political pressure, they have not succeeded in being able to persuade Congress to change it. The ESA is still essentially in the same state it was when it was passed. What the opposition failed to realize is that the ESA speaks to the essence of Western culture. Look at the story of Noah and having to save all the animals on the planet, not just the charismatic ones, all of them. It's a core value of Christianity.

CURRENT STATUS OF ENDANGERED SPECIES ACT

The Endangered Species Act (ESA) of 1973, was passed by the US Congress and signed by President Richard Nixon. Its purpose is to protect plants and animals that are likely to become extinct and the habitats critical to their survival. The ESA is administered by two federal agencies, the US Fish and Wildlife Service (FWS) and the Commerce Department's National Marine Fisheries Service (NMFS). The law has been credited with rescuing such species from extinction as the bald eagle, gray wolf, grizzly bear, and humpback whale. Since its passage, the ESA has been reviled by such industries as logging, oil drilling, and mining, particularly in the West, where many extractive resources are found on public lands, many of which were designated as critical habitat. Under the directives of President Trump, the ESA itself is under threat of extinction so that extractive industries can flourish without environmental regulation.

Yes, there's been a lot of industry backlash against the Center in the form of a lot of name-calling and political attacks. If you rein in these billion-dollar corporations, you're going to have a huge economic impact. We've been lucky because others have been threatened, jailed, and even killed for effectively standing up and protecting our forests and our wildlife. Nor has the FBI targeted and acted against us, as it did with Dave Foreman, though we did have to defeat a politically motivated grand jury that was convened against us at one point. At the same time, we all have to realize that these are the risks of any important environmental work. If we are afraid, we're simply not going to be the agents of change that we need to be.

And because we do litigate so much, the Center is criticized for not compromising enough. That's really a crazy thought when you think about it. Our position is that we're enforcing laws created by Richard Nixon in front of judges appointed by Ronald Reagan. That can hardly be thought of as a radical activity or a failure to compromise. We're enforcing the compromises of the past.

We've also been called outlaws. Everything is sort of upside-down in our culture right now, in the sense that the corporations are the real outlaws. Their profits are based on violating our human rights laws, our labor laws, and our environmental laws. When the Center tries to enforce laws by litigating, the corporations say, "Well, let's compromise." Well, no! If we keep cutting the pie in half every single time industry bitches, you end up with no pie. All we'd be doing is compromising away the future.

If the industrial death machine is not pissed off at you, you probably have not been effective. The more pissed off they are, the better we know we are doing our job.

ML: What is the Center for Biological Diversity's position on the population explosion and what does it have to do with the mass extinction crisis?

Suckling: The Center is trying to combat the driving force of all environmental destruction: too many of us consuming too many things. This force is driven by an almost universal and uninterrupted propaganda message coming from the media and industry about the necessity of growth.

We need to scale back human economies so that they can work without growing. There's nothing good to be gained by adding another billion people to gobble up natural resources. Unless we deal with unlimited growth, we're not going to succeed in stopping the mass extinction crisis. If we don't, I've got very little hope for the West, for America, and for the planet.

Just take the Western United States. Anywhere you go, big cities such as Phoenix, Las Vegas, Los Angeles, and Tucson, as well as little Colorado towns like Pagosa Springs and Paonia, are booming. There's less and less place for wildlife to go, especially species that are really sensitive to human disturbance, such as bighorn sheep, wolves, and wolverines. That's why the West has become the central battleground for the tension between human overpopulation and biological diversity.

We need to also remind ourselves that its little things, like plants and insects, that are the engines that keep this entire planet working. If polar bears went extinct, it would have very huge impacts. But I'll tell you what: if ants went extinct, it would be a catastrophe. Life on earth would end in about a decade.

ML: Why is talking about the population explosion always so politically incorrect?

Suckling: In the 1970s, environmentalists used to speak about overpopulation very regularly. They don't anymore. They've become afraid of the controversy they think they will arouse. Today, many environmental groups don't want to talk about overpopulation because they don't have the confidence that it's something people believe in and people want to hear about. They tend to tie themselves in knots second-guessing what the opposition is going to do and torturing themselves with every scenario of what could go wrong and who could be angered. Consequently, they make decisions that fall behind public perceptions.

Second, when you talk about overpopulation, you're cutting through so many of the issues about land management and resource extraction, access to food and drinking water, and how we deal with industrial waste and pollution. There are certain problems that can't be solved by additional technology and better management. There's a fundamental limit on the amount of resources we can use up.

Finally, I think there's a certain right-wing conservative Christian element that feels that producing more humans, giving birth, creating new generations is part of a Divine plan that one is crossing when we say, "No. There's enough of us."

For the Center, it's really a very simple matter. If you go out on the street and say, "Hey, I think there's too many people in this world," nine out of ten people are going to say, "Yes, absolutely." We can talk about what's right and know that the public is ready to listen.

If we let the basis of all life on Earth degrade because we are afraid to speak up, then there is no way we can convince people that overpopulation matters.

ML: What is the Center's strategy and lessons learned about being an activist organization?

Suckling: The big lesson the Center learned from Earth First!, which we've kept to this day, is the importance of creativity and inspiration and the willingness to redefine the issues rather than accepting the way things are. For more than twenty-two years, we have built that lesson into our very core. We are constantly paying attention to what works and what doesn't.

Giving away Endangered Species Condoms was one of our most successful campaigns that we launched in 2009. It linked two current major crises: endangered species and population explosion. Several thousand people voluntarily are still giving free condoms away.

ENDANGERED SPECIES CONDOMS—CREATIVE OUTREACH

Two condoms are wrapped in colorful wildlife-themed artwork designed by Shawn DiCriscio, offering an entertaining way to get people talking about the link between population growth and species extinction. Each package contains an illustration of an endangered species with a rhyming slogan, such as "For the sake of the horned lizard / Slow down, love wizard." Or, "Can't refrain / Think of the whooping crane."

Inside the package is information about solutions to out-of-control population growth, such as universal access to contraception, reproductive healthcare, and education and empowerment for women and girls. Several thousand people voluntarily give these condoms to people at concerts, bars, universities, spiritual group meetings, farmers' markets, and many other types of local events. On Valentine's Day 2018, volunteers for the Center for Biological Diversity gave away forty thousand Endangered Species Condoms to people across the United States. Sarah Baillie, coordinator for the project, said, "As our population grows and urban sprawl destroys wild spaces, species we know and love pay the price. The Endangered Species Condoms help people understand how conscientious family planning can protect wildlife." The condoms are made of reduced protein latex, which is less likely to cause allergic reactions and is free of animal by-products, nitrosamine, and GMOs.

The Center doesn't avoid controversy and conflict. We don't tiptoe around difficult issues. To curry favor with politicians, with industry, with the media is incredibly self-defeating. We don't get caught up in polling and focus groups and being afraid of angering people until everything comes out bland and noncontroversial.

The environmental movement has lost some very important political battles recently, such as the failure to pass a climate bill or even to pass an energy bill, in the wake of the Gulf of Mexico oil-spill disaster. The Center then sued British Petroleum [BP] for $19 million for violating the Clean Water Act.

AFTERMATH OF BP LAWSUIT

The British Petroleum (BP) oil spill, which began with a blowout on the Deepwater Horizon rig in the Gulf of Mexico in April

2010, was the largest environmental marine disaster experienced by the United States. It killed eleven workers and spilled more than 4 million gallons of oil before the well below it could be successfully capped. It created an oil slick of more than 15,300 square miles, fouled at least 1,300 miles of shoreline, and poured some 1.84 million gallons of chemical dispersant into gulf waters. It devastated the local fishing economy, smothered corals, and killed wildlife, including more than a 100,000 sea birds, thousands of adult and juvenile sea turtles, and countless dolphins.

In December 2010, the United States filed a complaint in District Court for the spill against British Petroleum Exploration & Production, as well as several other companies. The enforcement section of the Environmental Protection Agency (EPA) led to a settlement with BP for an unprecedented $5.5 billion Clean Water Act penalty and up to $8.8 billion in natural resource damages. The court also required BP to pay criminal court– and civil court–ordered penalties of more than $20.8 billion. BP also faced private claim payments, which had grown to an estimated $14.8 billion in 2016, and are still being settled.

In 2010, BP donated $500 million for the Gulf of Mexico Research Initiative (GoMRI) to investigate the effect of oil spills on the environment and on public health.

In 2012, Congress passed the Resources and Ecosystems Sustainability, Tourist Opportunities and Revived Economies of the Gulf Coast States Act (RESTORE). The Act dedicated 80 percent of all administrative and civil penalties received from the responsible parties to ecological and economic recovery efforts in the Gulf.

Lawsuits continue to be filed, many of them from BP workers who are seeking medical benefits and from victims affected by the spill.

Simultaneously, the country has become more conservative. That's why the movement has lost a great deal of political power over the last few decades.

Edward Abbey said that we need wilderness for the human spirit. In all of our environmental battles, the human spirit is at stake. We evolved over millions of years with other species right outside our doors or huts or caves, and, deep down, they are very much part of who we are.

I believe what the Center and I are trying to do is have a respectful civil society where people don't destroy their neighbor, or the next community over, and recognize that biodiversity is part of, and necessary to, our community.

As those wild places disappear, and the wolves and birds are no longer in our backyards, we suffer—culturally and spiritually—and we end up ultimately not being who we are. The strength of our ability to move and persuade people to support environmental protection is most effective when we talk about it in these spiritual ways.

Finally, the Center takes on the really difficult issues that no one else does. For instance, we do a lot of military watchdogging at US military bases because they are bombing and destroying wildlife habitat and polluting water all over the globe.

In one case, we got a court injunction that stopped a military bombing range in some remote Pacific islands that were important wildlife habitats. The next day I get a call from a woman who wants to know where our office is. Something about her sounded suspicious so I was like, "No, we're not going to tell you where the office is. Who are you?" She says, "Well, I'm Donald Rumsfeld's secretary." I figure that this is a prank. "Give me your phone number, and I'll call you back." When she does, I Google it and find this actually is the phone number for Donald Rumsfeld's office. When I call her back, she says, "Okay. Well, Donald wants to know where you guys are." When I give her the post office box, she says, "No, he wants your physical address. He wants to know where you are physically." I refused to give it out. I don't know what this guy is going to do, maybe he's going to bomb us or something. Finally I say, "Donald Rumsfeld has the entire US military at his command. Surely he can figure out where the Center for Biological Diversity is located." Then I hung up. I think she was pretty shocked. But it was a reminder that when you shut down US military bombing, unfortunately it gets the attention of the top brass.

ML: Given the constancy of disasters, how do you maintain hope?

Suckling: Oh, man. This is the hard one. I do have hope. I think most environmentalists have hope. Is it irrational? Can we justify our hope, or is that just our psychological tic that we have in order to keep going? I don't know. I wish I had a better answer to that.

I have a quirky kind of hope that the drastic effects of global warming are probably the only way to potentially motivate people to significantly change how we live on this planet. We're already seeing rapid, mind-bending changes that can't be ignored. Many people believe that the disasters in New Orleans or Haiti were anomalies and are not going to happen again. Frankly, they believe this because of a largely unconscious racism toward so many of the people affected there.

It's ironic, and perhaps deadly ironic, to feel that when suburban white people in Miami or New York City or Boston get hit by a Category 5 hurricane, the sheer scale and devastation will motivate them to change. It's sad it has to be that way. Will it be in time? Will it be enough? We just have to pray that it is.

12 | DERRICK JENSEN

Biography

Provocative and eloquent, Derrick Jensen calls for an active and serious resistance to a human-centric world in order to fight the destructive practices of industries that are killing the planet. A deeply compassionate philosopher-poet, he has written many books, including *The Myth of Human Supremacy* (2016); the two-volume work, *Endgame* (2006); and *The Culture of Make Believe* (2004). Together with coauthors Aric McBay and Lierre Keith, Jensen wrote *Deep Green Resistance: Strategy to Save the Planet* (2011). Jensen writes for the *New York Times Magazine*, *Orion* magazine, *Audubon*, and *The Sun* magazine, among many others. In 2008, Jensen was named one of *Utne Reader*'s "50 Visionaries Who Are Changing Your World." In the same year, he won the Eric Hoffer book award. Since 2013, he has been conducting weekly audio interviews with a broad array of environmental activists and philosophers for his program, *Resistance Radio*, on the Progressive Radio Network.

The first and only time that I met Derrick was at a house outside of San Francisco, California, where a party was happening downstairs. My crew and I found a bedroom where we could conduct the interview. (www. derrickjensen.org)

———

ML Lincoln: Was your thinking in any way influenced by Edward Abbey and Earth First!?

Derrick Jensen: I was in my twenties when I read Abbey's *Desert Solitaire*. I loved it. It was revelatory. What Abbey did was to help encourage and inform people who care about the natural world, and he did that in spades. He also reinforced the idea that it isn't the culture that is crazy, we are.

When I read *The Monkey Wrench Gang* I can say that that book confirmed much of what I thought rather than influenced me. But other activists, like Dave Foreman and Terry Tempest Williams, whom I greatly respected, were very much influenced by Abbey. So I can also say that I was heavily, secondarily, indirectly influenced by him.

I don't think I would call myself an Earth First!er, but when I started subscribing to their journal back in 1990 and read Foreman's *Ecodefense: A Field Guide to Monkeywrenching*, a part of me felt as though I was coming home. It's not so much that it influenced me as it liberated me. It allowed me to breathe. It validated what I knew in my bones.

At one point, Barry Lopez said to me, "We're all holding hands through time." What this meant to me is that Ed Abbey influenced Williams and Foreman, and they influenced me, and that's how movements are built through time.

ML: What are your guiding principles?

Jensen: One of my guiding questions is, what are the largest, most pressing problems in the universe that you can help to solve using the gifts that are unique to you? I have a gift for writing and for public speaking. I don't think my gift is for huge, complex, abstract thought. I don't think anything I wrote in *Endgame* or in most of my books is intellectually challenging. I don't think it's cognitively challenging. I think it's emotionally challenging. I think that my gift is for stating the obvious. And unfortunately, most people in this culture avoid the obvious.

What this means is that I've condemned myself to a life of homework. I get off on trying to figure out a subject like the relationship

Derrick Jensen, coastal redwoods, 2009. Photographer Jim Sienkiewicz.

between perceived entitlement, atrocity, and exploitation. I mean, I literally spent two weeks just doing nothing but thinking about that question when I was writing *Culture of Make Believe*. I get off on doing that.

I don't have a gift for organization. People have said, "Why don't you quit and become an organizer?" I can't even organize my pens. My house is tremendously cluttered. I can't organize anything.

And one of the things we need is somebody to help articulate our problems.

And because I've been told I am actually influencing people to do dangerous things, I want to offer a couple of guideposts.

At the end of my book *Endgame*, I say that what I really want is for people to think for themselves. I don't want them to enter a culture of resistance because I say they should. What I want is for people to choose what is meaningful to them and come to their own conclusions.

I have a friend who used to run the battered women's program for the state of New York. I would never tell her that she should do something for the sake of salmon. One of the great things about everything being so messed up in our culture is no matter where you look, there's great work to be done. She's doing that work.

The big divide is not between those who advocate militant action and those who don't. The big divide is between those who get off their butts and those who don't.

We could do all of this nonviolently if we just had the numbers. We don't. Even during the original gatherings at the occupy movement in Oakland, California, there were only about three hundred people, whereas fifty-five thousand people went to the Oakland Raiders game. More people care about the Louisiana State University Tigers than care about real tigers.

I had a sixteen-year-old kid come up to me and say, "I want to burn a factory." I looked at him for a second and said, "Have you ever had sex?" He said, "No, I haven't." I said, "Well, think about this because if you do this and you get caught, you're going to go to prison for twenty years. You're not going to have sex until you're in your late thirties." So I effectively talked him out of doing this because I don't want a sixteen-year-old messing up his life or her life because of something they read.

I've had people write to me and say, "I'm thinking about quitting college because I read your books and I think that this society is going to collapse." I write back to them and say, "I have to tell you that I'm actually pretty conservative, and I believe in keeping my options open. So, honestly, I think if you're in college and you can stand it, you should finish because that keeps your options open."

When I wanted to quit college when I was a junior, one of the smartest things my mom ever said to me was, "Would you rather go the rest of your life saying you have three years toward a degree in physics or go the rest of your life saying you have a degree in physics?"

One reason that I could be so courageous in my twenties about wanting to be a writer and not having any money at all, being poor enough sometimes that I was collecting cans for money, is because at any point I could have quit and gotten a job starting at 35K. I had a safety net, whereas if I didn't have a college degree, my safety net would have been working at McDonald's.

ML: What is your book *Deep Green Resistance* about?

Jensen: My book *Deep Green Resistance: Strategy to Save the Planet* starts where the environmental movement leaves off: industrial civilization is incompatible with life. I've been completely befuddled by the notion that humans are fundamentally separate from and smarter than everything else in the animal kingdom. This is probably one of the central problems of this culture. People keep forgetting that the real world is what's primary. They're human supremacists, and they support capitalism.

That idea has been really foreign to me. I came to environmental work through frontline grassroots environmental activists who taught me what it meant to be doing this work "for all the critters." They recognized that capitalism is inherently unsustainable.

When I went through all the so-called solutions for global warming, I found that what many people have in common is that they take industrial capitalism as a given and feel that the natural world is one that must conform to industrial capitalism. They have an unquestioned, universal belief that humans are at the top of the food chain.

And that is insane, literally, in terms of being out of touch with physical reality.

I still remember when I was a very, very young activist sitting with one of my mentors at a restaurant. He had a napkin in front of him, put a circle on it, and said, "This is a city." Then he said, "A city can't support itself. It has to rely on a countryside. As the city grows, it will consume an ever-larger area." It is inherently unsustainable. He was mainly a forest activist, and he was saying so long as there's another frontier, it will keep expanding. But what do people do when they run over the last hill and there's no trees?

ML: What is your response to people who say you advocate murder and violence in our culture?

Jensen: Some people say I don't actually hate the culture, but instead I just hate my father and that I'm too scared to admit it so I just project my views onto the giant father of the culture. And my response to that is, well, my father could have been perfect, and salmon would still be being driven extinct, and women would still be raped, and the oceans would still be murdered. It's completely irrelevant.

What my father's abuse did is help give me a framework to understand the larger violence of the culture and to understand in my body the insatiability and stupidity of this level of sadism and violation.

Our discourse around violence is just incredibly absurd. The definition of *violence* that I really like is any act that causes harm to another. And I really like that because it demystifies violence and shows that it's ubiquitous. Most of us under most circumstances would find it not acceptable to do an act of violence to a human.

The discussion I'm really interested in is, where do we personally and socially draw those lines of where violence is acceptable and not acceptable?

For one, we have to stop ignoring structural violence—social institutions that harm people. Who is served by our discourse around violence are those who are systematically benefiting from structural violence, whether they're familial abusers or whether they're CEOs of drilling companies, which leads to this crazy rhetoric about it.

I got an e-mail from a police officer in Chicago, who said, "You know, I think you're giving police a bad rap. Our job is to protect people from sociopaths." I wrote back and said, "Great. Wonderful. I don't disagree. But why don't you protect us from rich sociopaths? Why do you only protect us from the poor ones?"

What's primary is that the planet's being murdered.

People keep forgetting what all the so-called solutions offered up for global warming have in common. All take industrial capitalism as a given. The natural world is that which must conform to industrial capitalism. Maximizing profits by any means necessary is what corporations are about. It's the definition of a corporation.

An example is how climate change has become a lobbying arm of the solar and wind movement and how important it is for the government to give them subsidies. The solution doesn't touch the substantive issue that the world is getting killed.

ML: So how do you help people understand the correlation between environmental harm and personal harm. How do you persuade the masses to wake up?

Jensen: It's a big divide. I don't think you can wake up the masses. When you have hundreds of people rushing to a store to buy tennis shoes, they're not going to think about saving the frogs or salmon. My work isn't for sleepwalkers, it's for people who have woken up and feel afraid.

Part of the problem is that many people have forgotten what's real. We perceive this culture as what's real. After the earthquake and nuclear disaster at Fukushima in 2011, many lost electricity and water. Even so, Japanese ministers said that the reason they have to keep going with nuclear is because no one can imagine continuing to live without electricity. Didn't they know that right now there are two billion people on the planet who are living without electricity? And frankly, humans lived up until about a hundred years ago very well without electricity, and you'd better imagine living without electricity because the industrial generation of electricity is not sustainable.

What people who are alive in one hundred years will care about is whether they can drink the water and breathe the air. They're not going to care what form our resistance took, not going to care how we voted, not going to care if we made really great films or if we wrote really big books. What they're going to care about is physical reality. And that's what's most important to me.

Even environmentalists don't generally talk about the fact that the way to stop this culture is by destroying the industrial infrastructure, which supports what seem like good ideas to avert climate change. Even somebody as smart as Peter Montague [cofounder of Environmental Research Foundation], who wrote the great *Rachel's News*—I just love his work—said that the reason that carbon sequestration [CO_2 storage] is a bad idea is because if all of the carbon leaked out at once it could "disrupt civilization as we know it." It's like: "No, Peter. It could end life on Earth, which is a little bit more important."

It's the same in a personal family. Within an abusive family you can talk about anything you want in the world except for the abuse you have to pretend isn't happening.

The Scottish psychiatrist R. D. Laing talked about the three rules of a dysfunctional family, which are also the three rules of a dysfunctional culture. Rule A is: Don't [talk about it]. Rule A$_1$ is: Rule A does not exist. Rule A$_2$ is: Never discuss the existence of nonexistence.

ML: Some people say voluntary transformation can change the social system that is aligned with resource exploitation. What do you think?

Jensen: It became clear to me a long time ago that this culture would not undergo any sort of voluntary transformation, not only because I've asked thousands of people but also it's just very clear when you look around that unquestioned beliefs are the real authority.

One of the best examples I can think of is the response by those in power to the melting of the icecaps. They're not responding with horror and with attempts to stop the destruction. Instead, they're responding with what I can only perceive as lust at the increased access to resources. They're seeing this as an opportunity.

Another way we can understand this is that 25 percent of all women in this culture are raped in their lifetimes. More than 19 percent fend off rape attempts. And most of those rapes are not committed by burly strangers breaking in through doors, but by those who profess to love these women—by dad, by older brother, by babysitter, or boyfriend. And if those sorts of atrocities are being committed against those that they purport to love, what chance is there that they could voluntarily act to save the salmon?

Still another way to talk about all this is that the anthropologist Ruth Benedict [1887–1948] found one simple rule that divides the good from the bad cultures: the good ones recognize that humans are both social creatures and selfish creatures. What they do is destroy the selfishness-altruism split by socially rewarding behavior that benefits the group as a whole and by disallowing behavior that benefits the individual at the expense of the group. Bad cultures, on the other hand, reward behavior that benefits the individual at the expense of the group. And it's basically Behavior Mod 101: what you reward is what you're going to get.

Basically, where I go with my book *The Culture of Make Believe* is that an economic system that is based on competition is going to lead inevitably to atrocity as people compete for resources as they compete for everything. There will be no voluntary transformation in a culture that systematically and socially rewards behavior that benefits the individual at the expense of the group. That's what getting rich is all about, and that's a really powerful motivator.

Another reason I don't believe we're going to have a voluntary transformation is similar to the somewhat true cliché that drug and alcohol addicts don't generally change until they hit bottom. But not abusers. Lundy Bancroft wrote an interesting book called *Why Does He Do That? Inside the Minds of Angry and Controlling Men*. He's talking about the psychology of abusers. He says one of the reasons that abusers so rarely change is because they're addicted to power. They don't hit bottom; everybody else does.

That's what we see with the dominant culture, is that while the salmon are hitting bottom and the oceans are hitting bottom, those in power, who are responsible, are socially rewarded. In fact, those of us who live in this culture are socially rewarded. Many people live fairly toasty here. The elites, the global elites, continue to be rewarded for their exploitation of those living less well. It's extremely addictive.

Once you socially commit yourself to overshooting the carrying capacity of the planet and to nonsustainability, your way of life must be based on conquest. If you overpopulate an area and then you don't want to have a reduction in size, you don't want to allow a die-off, then what you need to do is conquer more territory.

This culture has been on that path of overshoot for the last six- to ten thousand years. Once you start down that path, you either have to accept a correction or die off. And this culture has set itself onto this path of gross overshoot for so long that it perceives it as the only way to be. It perceives the behavior as normal. How you perceive the world affects how you behave in the world. And if you perceive the world as consisting of resources to be exploited, that's how you'll treat the world. There's a great line by a Canadian lumberman: "When I look at trees, I see dollar bills."

And I saw an example of this having to do with crabs just last year.

There was an article in the paper about why crabbers work so hard during the crab season. And the harbormaster said, something like, "Just imagine all these envelopes, each one filled with $1.50, because that's how much they get per crab. Then imagine all these envelopes flying all over the ground. You're going to run around picking them up as fast as you can."

The problem is that a crab is not $1.50. A crab is a crab, with a life just as valuable to it as yours is to you and mine is to me.

The hypocrisy, all the way around, is just stunning.

When people perceive the world as consisting of resources to be exploited as opposed to entering into a relationship with the natural world, there's not going to be a voluntary transformation.

We have to act in alignment with the earth. I used to think that only people can fight back. But the earth is fighting back, with its hurricanes and tornadoes. For me, the earth is more important than the social systems that spawned it.

ML: So what do we do?

Jensen: Because I don't believe that the perpetrators of these atrocities will change voluntarily, my primary goal is to reduce their reach. If you can't destroy the oil economy, you can at least make it so they can't get to the center of the ocean and they can't bomb the moon.

So the strategy is, first off, start thinking about who is the enemy. Who is killing the planet? You know, so many indigenous people have said to me that the first and most important thing that we have to do is to decolonize our hearts. We're not killing the planet. The capitalists are killing the planet, those who are running it. We need to separate ourselves from the enemy. That's a good thing about the occupy movement. They're separating themselves. That's the first step.

The next step is to ask what we want. Most people, even when some of them say they are environmentalists, don't know what they want. I'm very clear on what I want. I want to live in a world that has more wild salmon every year than the year before. I want to live in a world with more migratory songbirds this year than the year before. I want to live in a world with living oceans.

Since I don't believe that most people, especially those in power, are reachable, what is important to me is to attempt to destroy the capacity of the rich to steal from the poor and the capacity of the powerful to destroy the planet.

Basically, this is a war. It's been a war for a long time. And we as environmentalists don't often think in terms of strategy, frankly. Any military historian, any military strategist, understands that wars are not usually won on the battlefield. Wars are won with industrial capacity. The way you win this war is by destroying the enemy's industrial capacity. You take out their infrastructure.

When people ask, "How can we save the salmon?" that's not what they're really asking. What they're really asking is, "How can we save the salmon without doing any of those things?" When people say, "How can we stop global warming?" they don't mean, "How can we stop global warming?" They mean, "How can we stop global warming without stopping the burning of oil and gas?" You can't.

Another way to look at this is, what would we do if space aliens came down and they were systematically deforesting the planet, and they were changing the climate, and they were vacuuming the oceans, and they were putting poison in every mother's breast milk? We would know exactly what to do, which is we would destroy the alien infrastructure.

But when destruction is being done by those to whom we have pledged allegiance, we suddenly get really, really stupid. And it's long past time to stop being stupid.

To put it simply: what do salmon need to survive? They need five things. They need for dams to be removed. They need for industrial logging to stop, industrial fishing to stop. They need for the oceans not to be murdered. And they need for global warming to stop. My loyalty is with the salmon and with the delta smelt and with migratory songbirds. What I want to do is to destroy the material conditions that make it possible for those in power to kill them off.

If you destroy a planet and the other critters that live there, people can't live on it either. You can't have an expansionist economy on a finite planet. It's obvious. Any way of living based on the use of non-renewable resources won't last. It doesn't take a rocket scientist to figure that out. In fact, it takes anybody but a rocket scientist to figure that out.

So what are the steps necessary to get there? How do you stop global warming? Ask any eight-year-old and they'll tell you: stop burning oil and gas. Ask a thirty-five-year-old and they'll tell you some fancy scheme involving solar technology and rare earth mining in China. That'll help high-tech companies, but it won't help the earth. Technology isn't going to fix our planet. It's going to help kill it.

We need to take action to do everything possible to make sure the dominant culture doesn't drive creatures like the coho salmon extinct.

As I said in "Beyond Hope," my article in *Orion* magazine, "Frankly, I don't have much hope. But I think that's a good thing. Hope is what keeps us chained to the system, the conglomerate of people and ideas and ideals that is causing the destruction of the earth. . . . When we stop hoping the situation will resolve itself and somehow not get worse, then we will finally be free—truly free—to honestly start working to thoroughly resolve it . . . A wonderful thing happens when you give up on hope, which is that you realize you never needed it in the first place. You realize that giving up on hope doesn't kill you, nor did it make you less effective. In fact it made you more effective, because you ceased relying on someone or something else to solve your problems . . . I would say when hope dies, action begins."

13 | BOB LIPPMAN

Biography

A rafting trip through the Grand Canyon sponsored by a Tulane University geology class in 1970 (and subsequently becoming a Colorado River guide) connected Bob Lippman with environmental issues related to the Colorado River; in particular, the Glen Canyon Dam impacts and the lawsuits filed by Ken Sleight and Friends of the Earth (FOE) to protect Rainbow Bridge from reservoir encroachment.

Lippman finished law school in 1980 and interned with David Brower and FOE in San Francisco. His specialty is environmental law. He moved to Flagstaff, Arizona, and organized the Grand Canyon/Colorado Plateau chapter of Friends of the River. For more than two decades, Lippman fought to protect and enhance Colorado River integrity, and he assisted indigenous communities living near the Grand Canyon that were threatened by energy development (uranium and coal) and civil rights violations. He also taught courses in indigenous studies and political science, including environmental law, as adjunct faculty at Northern Arizona University. When he retired in 2001, Lippman and his wife moved to Castle Valley, Utah, built a solar home, and volunteered time to program public affairs news and music shows for KZMU, a noncommercial, community-funded radio station in Moab, Utah.

I interviewed Bob on the rooftop of his off-the-grid home in Utah.

———

ML Lincoln: How did you meet Ed Abbey?

Bob Lippman: I first met Abbey in Moab, Utah, in 1977. I was ranting at a public hearing on another crackpot project boosted by the Grand County Commission Cabal. I think it involved paving a road to the overlook of the confluence of the Green and Colorado Rivers in Canyonlands National Park.

Abbey approached me after the proceedings, when I was fleeing from the pitchforks and torches, introduced himself, and thanked me for what I had to say. In my overwhelmed state, I managed to thank him for all of his books because they affected thousands of lives and launched thousands of brave deeds. It was a reference to Abbey himself who said, "One brave deed is worth a hundred books, a thousand theories, a million words."

Ed then invited me to a gathering up at Pack Creek Ranch that night where I got to hang with him, "Seldom Seen" Ken Sleight, and other local activists. [Ken and his wife Jane bought the ranch in 1986.] Ed and I became collaborators and friends. In a memorial piece I wrote for Ed in 1989, I characterized Abbey as an auspicious appearance of "Coyote—the fool, trickster, mud head, Kokopelli—the curmudgeon or avatar who unmasks our individual and collective follies and our petty, destructive pursuits, calling us musically back to the beauty and bounty of the land, the desert, the great Web of Life, the Mother that births and sustains all life."

After my 1980 flight from law school graduation, I moved back to Moab and Flagstaff, and even prior to establishing any so-called law practice, I organized the Grand Canyon/Colorado Plateau chapter of Friends of the River. Ed would come out and do benefits for us and make speeches—what he called agitprop—to help us publicize, in only ways that he could, the impact of some of the activities we were speaking out against, the main ones being the dam(n)ing of the Colorado River, and the despoliation of the Grand Canyon by Glen Canyon Dam, uranium mining, and industrial tourism.

ML: You were at the dam when Earth First! threw the fake plastic crack over it. Can you give us your description of the experience?

Bob Lippman. Dory "Sunshine Daydream," Grand Canyon Dory Run, 2006.
Courtesy of Pam Hackley.

Lippman: It was literally a watershed day in the environmental movement. Dave Foreman, one of the cofounders of Earth First!, made it very clear that direct action and a symbolic event, such as placing a crack in Glen Canyon Dam, were needed to wake up not only the government, the regulators, and the developers but the environmental movement itself, which had atrophied.

Apparently the movement had forgotten the exhortation of David Brower, who led the last-minute fight against Glen Canyon Dam—but unfortunately when it was too late—who said, "Polite conservationists leave no mark, save for the scars on the land that could have been prevented had they stood their ground."

I believe this was the premise of Earth First!, which morphed into "No Compromise in Defense of Mother Earth." Foreman articulated the need for an environmental movement that was not centrally or hierarchically organized, to push beyond the movement's envelope into direct action, and to act pursuant to the much broader truths of interconnected ecological processes on this planet.

ML: Weren't you part of a research team that dealt with the trial of Dave Foreman and the Prescott Four?

Lippman: I was peripherally involved as a research assistant. Part of what that trial was about was, that the government wanted to send a clear message to Earth First!ers and other environmentalists that civil disobedience would not be tolerated and that activists were to be treated as eco-terrorists. The trial, which began in 1991, was held in Prescott, Arizona.

During the discovery process, which constitutionally mandates that the government has to allow examination of the evidence against the defendants prior to trial, tape recordings were obtained that showed how FBI infiltrators—indeed, *agent provocateurs* had been placed inside Earth First! events and particularly the activities of environmental activists in Arizona. These agents were looking for and even creating evidence to entrap the activists and to stifle dissent and environmental organizing and activism in general. These were the types of antidemocratic activities used in older COINTELPRO programs [a counterintelligence program conducted by the FBI from 1956 to 1971 to discredit and divide various forms of political and social movements, such as the civil rights and antiwar movements].

One of the surveillance tapes disclosed that one informant that had infiltrated into the Earth First! circles said, "What we're really trying to do is get Dave Foreman and send a message." Had it not been for that disclosure, the Prescott trial—which the prosecution had framed as involving "eco-terrorism"—in my opinion, could have gone to completion, likely with full prosecutions and sentences for all defendants. But the damning disclosure allowed for some sort of negotiated plea bargaining and settlement of the case, unfortunately without resolving any of the substantive issues or defenses.

ML: Isn't monkeywrenching a form of civil disobedience?

Lippman: The idea of monkeywrenching, as put out by Abbey, has been manipulated and distorted by fearful corporations, politicians, government agencies, and the media into some sort of boogeyman of "eco-terrorism." This is Orwellian doublespeak in the post-1984 world.

Monkeywrenching is a legitimate form of nonviolent civil disobedience, motivated by a practical and legal basis of absolute necessity in the tradition of Gandhi and Martin Luther King, involving no violence or harm to life. In fact, Abbey stated that the number one rule for monkeywrenching is that all life is sacred. Do no harm.

In looking at the Orwellian aspect, the real eco-terrorists are unmasked as those responsible for releasing toxins into the environment; the corporations that are tearing up the planet and disrupting and unraveling Earth's life-support ecosystems, putting all life at risk of extinction, and thwarting humans' ability to maintain a livable planet upon which to otherwise thrive.

ML: What did you think about Tim DeChristopher's legal defense during the 2009 trial that eventually convicted him for disrupting a Bureau of Land Management [BLM] sale by bidding on oil and gas leases in Salt Lake City, Utah?

Lippman: Tim went to prison for merely paper-monkeywrenching the BLM oil and gas leasing auctions in December 2008, despite attempting to articulate a legally recognized, legitimate defense of necessity.

The standard legal and political protocol for the environmental response on the oil leases was exhausted and ineffective. And even if the courts were to hold that there were flaws in the leasing system, they would have simply sent the BLM back to the drawing board for a more legally sufficient impact analysis and the agency would have then re-auctioned the leases pursuant to that process.

OBAMA CANCELS OIL AND GAS LEASES BID ON BY TIM DeCHRISTOPHER

The George W. Bush administration rushed to sell oil and gas leases during the final weeks of the 2008 administration without requiring any environmental impact analyses. In early January 2009, a lawsuit filed by Earth Justice won a temporary restraining order that blocked the BLM from finalizing the leases. In February 2009, Ken Salazar, the US Bureau of Interior secretary appointed by President Barack Obama, canceled the oil and gas leases around national parks and monuments in Utah, the very leases that DeChristopher bid on. Salazar asked for environmental impact statements on the others before they could go up again for auction. None of this part of the story was allowed during the jury trial.

Tim's legal team, which ironically included attorney Patrick Shea, former director of the BLM, and consultant Dr. James Hansen, the preeminent international climate scientist with NASA, sought to establish that the defendant was acting out of a pure intent to prevent a greater harm—in this case the production and emission of climate-altering greenhouse emissions from oil and gas development in America and elsewhere—after exhausting all other legal remedies. This is what is known as the common law "necessity defense."

THE NECESSITY DEFENSE

The necessity defense is beginning to be more commonly used on behalf of direct action environmental activists, according to Dean Kuipers' article "Pipeline Vandals are Reinventing Climate Activism" (*Wired*, November 8, 2018). A jury would have to prove the following: (1) The harm that would have resulted from obeying the law would have significantly exceeded the harm actually caused by breaking the law. (2) No legal alternative to breaking the law was available. (3) The defendant was in danger of imminent physical harm. (4) A direct causal connection existed between breaking the law and preventing the harm.

In early 2018, Tim DeChristopher and thirteen other activists did win a necessity case, although it was not by jury trial. The thirteen activists included Karenna Gore, daughter of Al Gore and director of the Center for Earth Ethics at Union Theological Seminary in New York. According to Kuipers, the activists "were charged with civil infractions after disrupting construction of a high-pressure gas pipeline being built through the Boston suburb of West Roxbury. At the hearing Judge Mary Ann Driscoll found them 'not responsible' by reason of necessity." It is interesting that in one of the earlier necessity cases in the modern environmental age, the defense was successfully advanced by another political family member, when Amy Carter, daughter of President Jimmy Carter, along with Abbie Hoffman and thirteen others, were acquitted by a jury in 1987 on charges of trespass and disorderly conduct, in protesting CIA activities.

Relating Tim's trial back to Abbey, Ed was going to feature the use of the necessity defense in the last chapters of *Hayduke Lives!*, his sequel to *The Monkey Wrench Gang*. I had been consulting with Abbey on a grand trial ending for *Hayduke Lives!*, as Abbey had intended a very different ending in that book than was ultimately published posthumously. He was going to have the entire "monkey wrench gang" prosecuted and tried. But the legal team was going to turn the tables at the trial and put the government on the defensive. They would creatively use the common-law tools that are presently established in the legal system to have the jury acquit the defendants by finding that even though they may have violated the law that they were acting out of an intent to prevent a greater harm to the general welfare. Taking it even further, Abbey would have had the judge slap contempt orders against the government for conspiracy along with the corporations they were ostensibly charged with regulating, for failing to follow its own laws and regulatory procedures. This would have been a tremendous coup at the end of the book, and a poignant and powerful message socially and legally for what is possible. And it would have opened up a whole new response to the present constraints of the political and environmental law systems.

Unfortunately, Ed had become quite ill and had very little time left, and his family and editors had to patch together an ending pretty quickly, as he didn't have time to work out the details of his intended ending.

Meanwhile, DeChristopher, pursuant to a pretrial ruling that was arguably arbitrary and capricious, was barred from presenting this defense by the judge, whose "logic" was that the defense was not relevant, that it was insufficient to show the dire necessity, the last resort of action, and that there were other options available to Tim. The case moved to trial, apparently without any interlocutory appeal of the ruling, and Tim was convicted by a jury who was not permitted to hear arguments and experts on the defense of and grounds for necessity. Tim's response was, again, that both environmental law and legal justice have reached a point where they are not effective or viable; legal avenues were simply ineffective to prevent the planetary catastrophes that are looming and unfolding with climate change.

Tim was courageously on the right track, and I applaud his efforts. The legal system needs to be confronted with the fact that it is not responsive to modern needs and is failing to apply present facts and science to the law to compel a correct and just result. Tim's case attempted to bring these substantive issues to the legal and political forum. If I were on the jury, I certainly would have wanted to know what the motive of the defendant was, for knowingly and intentionally violating a regulation or law, before I weighed in with a verdict that would put him behind bars.

When Tim was in Moab speaking at a rally regarding the local oil leasing situation in February 2009, I presented him with a copy of *The Monkey Wrench Gang*, signed by the author, which I knew I had been holding onto for a good reason. Tim was the reason! I think Tim is a real fulfillment of many of Abbey's philosophies and vectors. And he is one of the few individuals who understands the urgency of our environmental and social problems today and the need for direct action.

I would like to think that we will be seeing a lot more Tim DeChristophers in every community. He is not just a leader to be followed. He is someone to be imitated. In many ways he was acting out of a long history of nonviolent civil disobedience.

If I had to characterize the political and environmental situation in just a couple of words, I would say *dysfunctional insanity*. Before acting, humans need to step back and find their sanity—their true nature—then commensurately act upon that. All of us have the inherent power and right to stand up, speak our truth, be heard, and to organize in our communities for life and a livable planet and future.

ML: What do you find are the flaws in the way environmental law is practiced?

Lippman: There's a huge conceptual flaw in the entire idea of environmental law. Our current political and legal systems are unwilling and unable to properly deal with the environmental and ecological problems we have and the ecological catastrophes we are imminently facing.

Michael Moore, in his 2009 film *Capitalism: A Love Story*, talked about the banking industry and unfettered capitalism. He said you can't regulate evil. And in a sense, that's the problem with environmental law. The licensing of "acceptable levels" of pollution or harm, and making decisions that are often arbitrary or speculative as to what the technical standards would be in finding those levels, is a flawed approach. What are acceptable levels when you find increased number of cancers or deaths in a population due to a chemical that is released into the environment? Further, what is the impact of corporate influence and money on those determinations?

Nor is there anything meaningful in the law—other than petitioning for an injunction based on "irrefutable proof of impending harm," or the necessity defense—that proactively and preventatively involves regulating or eliminating harm before it's done. In other words, there's very little room for being able to prove that something that has not been released into the biosphere yet might be harmful, let alone acting on that proof or knowledge. The burden of proof always tends to be on the public, not on the corporation or the persons responsible for releasing that pollutant nor on an independent body of scientific experts. This points to the failure of the political and legal systems to think scientifically and ethically, seven generations ahead, and why the entire system needs to be transformed.

In his book *Beyond the Wall*, Abbey said, "The domination of nature leads to the domination of human beings." That's what's currently happening globally. People don't control the government, and the government does not truly regulate these corporations. The regulators are the very same people in this revolving door of government that come from and go back to these very same corporations that are ostensibly regulated under environmental law and administration. And both sectors attempt to dominate both nature and human beings.

ML: What are the flaws as you see them in the environmental movement?

Lippman: The environmental movement has become professionalized and is playing by the rules of a system that was essentially designed by corporate lobbyists to allow polluting and impactful corporate activities to continue, albeit somewhat "regulated" and "orderly."

It is compelling that money has not only corrupted the political process, resulting in environmental harm; it has also to a great degree tainted the environmental movement in a similar way. And just like the government has been infiltrating social and environmental groups on a local level and disrupting them, the moneyed interests have been infiltrating the boards of directors of environmental organizations from within and slowly—and sometimes radically—tempering and shifting their priorities, policies, and levels of commitment.

And unfortunately, to raise a discourse about this often brings on a very negative and hostile response. Jim Stiles, for example, editor of the newspaper *Canyon Country Zephyr*, tried to raise these issues for years about funding of environmental organizations. Stiles made a compelling case that particular people on the boards of these large organizations, as well as organizational endowments, often earn their money from coal development, fossil fuels, nuclear development, and from the very evils that these organizations are ostensibly set up to confront and transform. However, Stiles's allegations were met with a great measure of hostility from the institutionalized environmental organizations. How can they do any kind of meaningful environmental work when influenced and hobbled by that kind of funding and policy constraint?

Another institutional impediment within large environmental organizations has been the perceived need for "credibility" and for "maintaining a seat at the table" in the environmental administration process. This psychological impediment, the fear of "rocking the boat," by its nature compromises the effectiveness of both the message and the work. And grassroots environmental groups have often found themselves in conflict with the big organizations, on top of their local struggles.

Today, however, new grassroots environmental movements are sprouting up on a watershed basis all over the country and the world. Groups such as Peaceful Uprising, which Tim DeChristopher organized in Salt Lake City, or 350 Climate Action, are beginning to involve local movements, taking to the streets and lobbies in their local communities to act and, if necessary, to engage in civil disobedience.

ML: What do you mean by "watershed basis?" Are you talking about local bioregional movements?

Lippman: Over 150 years ago, explorer, scientist, and ethnographer John Wesley Powell offered a stern caution to politicians and business boomers about development of the American West, declaring that we need to inhabit and govern the West on a watershed basis. As one of the original bioregionalists in Western civilization, he was way ahead of his time. And he worked extensively with Native Americans, studying cultural adaptations to landscapes and resources and establishing the Bureau of Ethnography. Powell noted how indigenous communities were localized and adapted to their watersheds, natural drainage basins, and microclimates, and he foresaw that if the West were to be settled, and exploited or colonized, on a basis other than localized watersheds, that we would be piling up what Powell called a "heritage of conflict."

And sure enough, that heritage is fully and tragically realized and with us right now. Rivers are dammed, water has been diverted across watershed divides, overallocated and universally polluted, air pollution has destroyed visibility and human health, landscapes and habitat have been devastated, and sprawl—including Abbey's pet bugbear of industrial tourism—is universal. Industrial activity is everywhere, and we can't even regulate it on a "traditional" environmental law basis because of arbitrary boundaries and a morass of jurisdictional conflicts.

The disgruntled founders of Earth First! saw the flaws in that system and wanted to push far beyond the limits and political constraints of environmental policy and the regulatory process. More importantly, the founders wanted to build a movement from the ground up, not from the top down, so that people could take back their watersheds, and communities could take back decision making within those watersheds. They did not want water barons, logging, grazing, and mining companies, and other multinational corporations to exploit resources of a colonialized watershed, leaving with the so-called profits and paying for none of the externalities, such as pollution, the appropriation and destruction of public lands for development and extraction, and a legacy of ecological, social and public health impacts.

We need to relocalize our communities to intelligently and appropriately inhabit their watersheds based upon bioregional carrying capacities, resources, and ecological processes, and not impose upon them out-of-scale, colonialized exportation of natural resources, such as diverting Colorado River water to Phoenix, Denver, or Las Vegas.

All this brings us back to grassroots democracy whereby an ostensibly *informed* majority will be able to determine what is acceptable and appropriate on an ecological and scientific basis within the watershed.

ML: Is living off the grid one of your personal solutions?

Lippman: Personal responsibility means both self-reliance and interdependence, and collectively transforming the way we live into a new, bioregional paradigm of clean energy and transportation. It's not the end; it's a transition. We need to understand and radically change the system that keeps us physically and mentally dependent and enslaved, and truly embody the change we wish to see in the world, with a truer, more Earth-centered and nature-embedded lifestyle. To borrow from Einstein, we can't fix the broken system or solve our environmental problems with the same consciousness or mindset that started the problems.

When my wife and I moved to Castle Valley, Utah, in 2000 [Y2K], we built a compact, off-grid, passive solar home. We used natural adobe bricks and recycled Rastra foam block to create a more energy efficient and ecologically appropriate habitation.

We're producing our own power from a 2.5-kilowatt solar and wind system here, which is plenty for the two of us, using power very conservatively to run a few, basic high-efficiency appliances.

The local utility doesn't extend their power lines as far as where we live. Had there been a grid, we'd be hypothetically selling the surplus back to the power company—good clean energy, apart from the manufacturing impacts, of course—that isn't derived from coal, nuclear power, or hydropower. This is the kind of decentralized system that small communities like Castle Valley and larger ones like Moab can encourage by setting up rural electrical-solar cooperatives and finding ways to finance them through bonds and creative pay-back funding that will put solar panels on every rooftop.

Our garden, watered by a deep well, produces much of the food we eat, and our community has placed certain protections over our watershed, as the community is fully dependent upon its clean aquifer.

Living this way really keeps us more fully conscious of, and connected with, Nature and the natural forces—the cycles of sun, stars, plants and animals, weather, season and climate—and we are most grateful for the opportunity.

Many community visionaries are also transforming urban environments through similar methods and alternatives.

KAYENTA SOLAR FACILITY

In 2017, 120,000 photovoltaic solar panels at the Kayenta Solar Plant went operational, becoming the first utility-scale solar plant on the Navajo Nation, according to an article in the *Arizona Daily Sun* by Emery Cowan (July 21, 2018). The 27.3-megawatt plant, which went online last summer, now generates enough power for 18,000 homes on Navajo lands. According to Milton Tso, president of the Cameron Chapter, the tribe is facing the closure of the Navajo Generating Station. "The way I see it is coal is dying, and we need to look into more clean energy, and we have the weather for it."

The bottom line is that humans need to think and live differently, based on an awakened and expanded perception of reality. This is consistent with everything the mystics, shamans, physicists, and scientists are saying. We must stop arguing about strategies, see what is really happening on this planet, grieve compassionately, love unconditionally, and come up with new systems and solutions.

As I get older, I'm driven more toward the spiritual, sacred side of political activism. We need to adopt spirituality into human thought and action on a day-to-day basis, recognizing that interdependence and cooperation, and *not* separateness, competition, and conflict, is the true ecological reality. We need to connect with the divine genius that keeps us

alive and thinking every day. If humans did that, it would change everything about the choices we make in a culture that still believes in materi-
alistic growth for the sake of growth—Abbey's definition of cancer.

ML: How does Abbey influence you now?

Lippman: In many ways, Abbey was both a nineteenth-century person
and twenty-first-century person, although he would probably never
admit to it. There are contradictions within all of us. Abbey is an example for us, not only on how to act, but perhaps how not to act. In my
1989 memorial piece on Abbey, borrowing from the author's warning
in the foreword of *Hayduke Lives!*, I wrote: "WARNING: The reading
of Edward Abbey's works may incite a compelling case of personal
re-evaluation and a call to action. Those who take him seriously may
be arrested. Those who do not will be buried by a Mitsubishi bulldozer,
and worse."

The ability to act has been beaten out of us. We need to stand up
with a true uprising in this eleventh hour-plus of the planet as we know
it, as ecosystems are unraveling, and restore not only the natural balance but reclaim our dignity and power while we still can. Dr. King's
admonition that the civil rights movement was not merely a political
struggle but a spiritual *movement* would be a well-taken analogy at this
moment in history.

Abbey even gave us, or expounded on, anarchist rules of conduct.
And I know that sounds like a contradiction in terms, but the first is
that all life is sacred, and the second is that you have to act responsibly.

It goes back to understanding that we're all one interest group, and
until humanity makes that leap into that consciousness, politics won't
overcome the horrific degradation, the perfect storm of disconnected-
ness that keeps harming us and prevents us from making what Tim De-
Christopher referred to as a "livable future."

I think finding sanity could be a metaphor for what Abbey was point-
ing to. All of us know inherently, as sacred anarchists and thinking and
feeling human beings, our connections to Nature and each other, what's
right and what's wrong, and what is *necessary*.

14 | KEN SANDERS

Biography

Ken Sanders's deep commitment to community forms a bridge between environmental activists and people who love Western Americana books, maps, and artifacts. He opened Ken Sanders Rare Books in 1990, an antiquarian bookstore, and moved to its current location in 1997 in Salt Lake City. Its inventory of more than 100,000 books specializes in Utah, Mormon history, and Western Americana. The bookstore has one of the largest collections of Edward Abbey books and Robert Crumb comics, t-shirts, and other paraphernalia in the United States. The store has hosted hundreds of book signings and art exhibitions, including the state of Utah's largest ever poetry reading, a fiftieth anniversary performance of Allen Ginsburg's *Howl*, by Utah sonosopher Alex Caldiero.

Ken was an avid reader and a serious collector of books from age fourteen. While in high school, he ran a mail-order business for underground comics and for science fiction, monster, and fantasy books. He co-owned the Cosmic Aeroplane Bookstore, which opened in 1967, one of the first hippie counterculture shops in Salt Lake City.

In 1980, Sanders founded Dream Garden Press to publish books about Utah and the intermountain West. Among the dozens of books the press issued were the Robert Crumb illustrated edition of *The Monkey Wrench Gang* (1985), *The Last Refuge of the Illiterate* (2005) by Charles Bowden, and *Ghosts of Dandy Crossing* (2014) by environmental activist Katie Lee.

In 1982, Ken was a founding member of the Fund for Wild Nature (then the Earth First! Foundation), which provides grants for the protection of biodiversity and wilderness.

Sanders is a member of the Antiquarian Booksellers' Association of America and served on its Board of Governors for six years. As the Association's security chair, Sanders was responsible for bringing numerous book thieves to justice. He often appears as an Americana specialist for PBS's *Antiques Roadshow* and was honored by the Salt Lake City Mayor's Award for Contributions to the Arts in 2005.

I interviewed Ken twice at his bookstore, as well as filming the presentation he held in honor of the twentieth anniversary of Ed Abbey's death. (www.kensandersbooks.com)

———

ML Lincoln: Ken, how did you meet Dave Foreman?

Ken Sanders: I'd been bugging Ed Abbey about doing a calendar based on his works. And from earlier experiences I had learned that it was best not to call him on the telephone because Ed hated telephones. Basically, you'd better have something to say because otherwise you're going to have this Zen phone conversation—you're going to be talking and he doesn't say anything.

One day, Ed calls me up out of the blue and says, "Ken, if you want to talk about that silly calendar come down to Lone Rock Campground off Lake Powell for some spring rites." That's all he told me.

THE EDWARD ABBEY WESTERN WILDERNESS CALENDAR

The calendar Abbey referred to was a literary calendar to be published by Dream Garden devoted to Abbey's works. The project evolved into a lavish, full-color photographic calendar with Abbey quotations called *The Edward Abbey Western Wilderness Calendar*. It was first published in the fall of 1981 and included such photographers as Philip Hyde, Eliot Porter, and David Muench. Each year Sanders updated the calendar, and it stayed in publication for ten years.

Then a few years before the tenth anniversary of the first publication of *The Monkey Wrench Gang* (1975), Sanders got a very clear vision of Robert Crumb caricatures of the book's characters in his mind's eye. Abbey's over-the-top prose, the exaggerated situations, and the characters in that novel seemed absolutely perfect for the bizarre one-of-a-kind cartoon style that Crumb had. Ed was dubious about the project and had never met Crumb. It took two or three years for Sanders to pull off that project. The special edition was published in 1985.

Crumb and Abbey finally met for the first time at Courthouse Towers in Arches National Park, on March 24, 1985. This was just before Sanders held a promotional party in Moab to celebrate the new edition. According to Sanders, "Oddly enough, the two of them—as Mutt and Jeff as they are—really got along well together, were very much interested in one another, and stayed in touch. And, yes, my special edition did invigorate interest in the book."

I was planning a backpack into the Maze about that time, so I took off four or five days early and drove down to Lake Fowl. I leave in my flat-black Chev pickup and drive three hundred miles. I'm driving out this bumpy road when I see this Volkswagen bus covered in enormous black plastic. It's leaking off both sides of it, both ends of it.

There's these hard-looking cowboy-type guys in cowboy boots and hats standing and blocking the road, staring at me. It's like they want to know: "Who the hell are you? What the hell are you doing here?" So these guys stop me in the middle of the road. I didn't care for their bedside manner and their attitude. The last thing I was going to tell them was that Ed Abbey sent me. I was thinking, "Who the hell are they? What are these guys doing here?"

So I backed up the truck and drove around 'em. We had a pretty tense standoff until a few hours later that evening, when Abbey shows up. Once they found out that I was a pal of his, it was like: "Guess what we're going to do tomorrow morning?" Gleefully they tell me their plans. "It's a three-hundred-foot plastic crack. It's twenty feet wide and tapers down to nothing. And we're going to drop it off Glen Canyon Dam tomorrow morning." "Hmm, that sounds good," I say. "Count me in!"

So early the next morning, we drove down to the dam. And I was still a little like, "Well, I'm not quite sure about these five guys and one woman." So I trailed them. One fellow drove the getaway truck that carried the enormous "crack."

In those days, you could actually drive to the dam. Thanks to us, you can't do that anymore. They don't let you walk out on it or anything else.

We took the crack down there and the five of them shouldered it. And as they walked out on the dam with it, I followed. Thanks for Louisa, the one female in the group, who had the ropes and knots abilities to get that crack tied down and engineered to be able to drop it off the face of the dam. And then the crack unfurled. It stopped about halfway, and we're kind of, "Oh, no!" It unkinked itself and rolled the rest of the way, revealing a 300-foot-by-20-foot piece of plastic that was cut to simulate a big crack that tapers off to nothing at the end.

We'd parked my pickup in the visitor's center parking lot beforehand and that became the stage that Ed used. Behind him are what Jack Loeffler called the "Hopi Kachinas" [power lines] striding off through the desert. Ed's up there saying, "And these alien things, I feel no kinship with." Afterward, there's this park ranger, and instead of arresting us, he's trying to get Ed Abbey's autograph.

Then, fifteen, twenty minutes later, all hell broke loose. Law enforcement from Utah and Arizona, sheriff's departments, highway patrols, and even the Coast Guard and the Park Service law enforcement showed up.

By then, they were pissed. They wanted to arrest us. But, hell, we were just having a demonstration in a parking lot. And this was before 9/11 so we were still allowed to do things like that without being thrown in prison in Guantanamo. You probably never could get away with that kind of shit nowadays.

That's the story of how I met Dave Foreman and the rest of the Earth First! founders. It was March 24, 1981, John Wesley Powell's birthday, the first man to run the Colorado River back in 1869.

I helped organize many Earth First! protests throughout the eighties. One was in 1983, against a nuclear waste dump that was proposed for Lavender and Davis Canyons in Canyonlands National Park. A public hearing was being held in the Joseph Smith Memorial Building—the old historic Hotel Utah—in Salt Lake City. All the mucky mucks were there—DOE officials, county people, state people—holding this big, serious, daylong hearing. Many well-meaning environmentalists signed up to get their five-minute turn at the podium.

I had my band dressed in white-paper radiation suits with giant beehive hairdos with little bees in them invade the event. I dressed one friend like a shaman in century-old royal-purple-and-gold Masonic robes with lots of glittery sequins. He took over the microphone and delivered a speech I wrote about how you can take your nuclear waste and shove it down a deep, dark hole. The rest of us went down the aisles dumping bags of vermiculite on all of the officials' heads, which we imagined might look like nuclear waste. I had gone to a gardening store and bought big bags of vermiculite, which is a really weird substance they use in gardening, and later found out it's made from contaminated vermiculite from Montana that has asbestos in it.

But like Bush in Iraq, we had no exit plan. I fully expected we would be arrested. So we look around. Nothing's happening. Everybody's kind of in shock. So, exit stage left and make like an O. J. Simpson slow-speed getaway to Mexico, get in our cars and drive away.

What did the media pick up on the 6:00 p.m. TV news? Did they show hour after hour of boring testimony? No. They showed a bunch of really weird-looking people in beehive hairdos and white radiation suits sprinkling fake nuclear waste on the people that wanted to bring us the dump. It was a very effective protest.

ML: In your opinion, when did the FBI start monitoring Earth First! activities?

Sanders: I started noticing a heavy FBI presence in 1983 when James

Mike Roselle, Ken Sanders (foreground), and Bart Koehler, down the Lower Canyons of the Rio Grande, Big Bend National Park, Texas. Earth First! trip Christmas to New Years, 1983 or 1984. Photographer unknown. Courtesy of the Collection of Ken Sanders.

Watt, secretary of the interior, was invited to a twentieth anniversary birthday party for Lake Powell. Earth First! staged a funeral. It turned into a huge elaborate event that started exposing the dark side of protesting. The FBI had SWAT teams surrounding the dam and the Navajo Generating Station. They had sharpshooters with high-powered rifles following and videotaping us constantly. It got really, really creepy.

From then on, the stakes in the environmental battle increasingly kept getting higher and more serious. More activists began to be involved in virtually every Western state and large cities like Portland and Seattle.

By the mideighties, the Earth First! road shows had gotten larger and larger. There were so many dirty tricks being played by the Feds, and it was getting really ugly. And I could just see the handwriting on the wall. The movement changed from focusing on saving wilderness and splintered into groups that had different agendas, from veganism to animal rights. I'm not saying that any of those causes are bad things, but some involved a lunatic fringe on the left or the right that began to take things too far. I didn't like where it was going. I tried to talk to Dave Foreman and others: "Look, we need to have a yippie-like funeral for Earth First!. We need to kill this movement now, because we've lost control of it." Dave wouldn't have it.

Ed Abbey became seriously convinced that he would be assassinated—and I mean that in all seriousness—by all the people that didn't like him, which were legion. He told me this during a series of autograph parties that I held in Salt Lake and Moab to celebrate my publication of the Robert Crumb illustrated edition of *The Monkey Wrench Gang* in 1985. Ed had come down from doing classes at the University of Montana in Missoula. Before the parties, he was sitting in the rocks and hoodoos of the Fiery Furnace at Arches National Park to write a speech that he would give at Missoula a couple of days later. He called it "Sacred Horses and Dead Cows."

Just before the event, he borrowed a gun from a friend. He strode up to the podium—he's a very big, imposing man—wearing a cowboy hat and swinging this six-shooter over his head. He slams it down on the podium and announces: "There'll be a question-and-answer period after my remarks *IF* there are any questions." In the speech he called the

ranching community a bunch of welfare bums and a cowboy someone
who spent his entire life contemplating the ass of a cow, or words to
that effect.

ML: When did the Feds start arresting environmental activists in Earth
First!?

Sanders: Within a year of Abbey's death in 1989, the FBI came swoop-
ing in on a bunch of trumped-up charges against Dave Foreman. In
1990, they arrested him and four others for allegedly being part of a
made-up nuclear sabotage conspiracy.

In the same year, the FBI arrested Judi Bari and Darryl Cherney, who
were protesting logging of old growth redwoods in California, on the
suspicion of transporting illegal explosives. They accused Bari of allegedly being the "mad bomber" that planted a pipe bomb between the
seats of her car, which "accidentally" blew up and permanently screwed
up her pelvis and injured her companion Darryl Cherney. Who did it? It
wasn't Judi or the environmentalists, at least that much was proven.

JUDI BARI AND DARRYL CHERNEY

After almost two months of investigation, prosecutors announced
they had insufficient evidence to charge the pair with a crime. In
2002, a federal jury found the FBI had violated Bari and Cherney's
civil rights in the case, and the pair was awarded a $4.4 million pay-
out. Bari wasn't around to see it because she died of breast cancer
in 1997. In 2015, a new criminal investigation was reopened to find
out who planted the bomb.

I think it was absolutely not coincidental that the FBI decided to tar-
get environmental leaders and throw the movement into utter emotional
turmoil and chaos following Abbey's death. They were classic tactics:
take out the leaders.

ML: Is that what happened to Tim DeChristopher? Was his arrest a gesture by the government to try to silence activism?

Sanders: Yes. In 2009, Tim DeChristopher was indicted, and in 2011 he was convicted of two nonviolent federal felonies: (1) violating the Federal Onshore Oil and Gas Leasing Reform Act and (2) making a false representation to the federal government.

Despite decades of deadbeat bidders at the Bureau of Land Management [BLM] oil and gas lease auctions, Tim DeChristopher is the only person that was criminally charged and prosecuted under this act. He was sentenced to a federal penitentiary for two years and given three years parole.

Like me, most of the world had never heard of Tim DeChristopher before that fateful BLM auction in Salt Lake City in December 2008, when he posed as a bidder for oil and gas leases. He pushed up auction prices and then bought several leases in and around Arches and Canyonlands National Park in Southern Utah. When the BLM discovered that he was an environmental activist, they stopped the auction.

From day one when Tim was arrested, there was never any hope of him ever coming out unscathed. He got railroaded by our justice system. The government wanted him punished and was going to do so, no matter what it took. During the trial, Tim was not allowed to tell the jury why he did what he did, a gross betrayal it seemed to me, of the American justice system. There's something horribly wrong when one of the most talented and brightest of our young people is incarcerated in a federal prison for two years over the type of activity that he did.

Only after Tim was convicted was he allowed to make a statement in court. Here is part of his statement after his sentencing hearing: "This is a case about the rights of citizens to challenge the government. The US Attorney's Office makes clear that their interest is not only to punish me for doing so, but to discourage others, even when the government is acting inappropriately. . . . Those who are inspired to follow my actions are those who understand that we are on a path toward catastrophic climate change. They know their future is on the line. And they know we're running out of time. The closer we get to that point where it's too late, the less people have to lose by fighting back."

Eventually, the auction itself was determined to be illegal, but that wasn't enough to overturn Tim's conviction.

ML: Would you call what Tim did monkeywrenching?

Sanders: Yes. Even though Tim's tactics did not fit the traditional definition, Tim DeChristopher monkeywrenched those BLMers and the oilmen and threw the auction into utter chaos. It's one of the most creative acts of civil disobedience that I've witnessed.

Before that fateful auction, Tim was just another student at a university here in Salt Lake City, like tens of thousands of young people all over the country. Now he's internationally famous. I don't know what to call him, maybe a political prisoner for exercising his rights and thoughts for social justice.

To me, Tim was a new type of American patriot.

ML: Do you see what Tim did as a continuation of the philosophical positions put forward by Ed Abbey?

Sanders: I think Ed would have been one of Tim's biggest supporters. As different as are their methods, philosophically, they're brothers. I think that Tim DeChristopher perceived an inequality and an injustice that was going to affect a whole new younger generation that lives on the planet. Like Ed, he was watching the rape of the last vestiges of natural resources. Tim's actions were acts of courage and defiance.

What I'd say to Ed Abbey if he were still around is, "You know, Ed, I don't know if the old-school monkeywrenching is going to get anything done anymore. I think the stakes are higher. I think the problem is nearer. And, like Tim DeChristopher, we've got to take more direct action."

Abbey accomplished what he set out to do: to become a moral leader for his beliefs. And, though Tim DeChristopher took a different tack, he too showed himself to be one of the leaders for social justice.

ML: How did you get to know DeChristopher?

Sanders: I got to know Tim right after his arrest, when I started fund-raising for him and eventually for his whole Peaceful Uprising group that had sprung up around his actions. I got to know him even better after he was paroled.

During the last six months of Tim's prison sentence, Tim was transferred to a halfway house in Salt Lake City. A condition of his transfer as a parolee was for Tim to have a forty-hour-a-week, full-time job, which he lined up with the Reverend Tom Goldsmith of the Unitarian Church. When Tim attempted to go to work, the Department of Justice [DOJ] declared that the Unitarian Church backed social justice issues and forbade Tim from working in a place that had the same convictions that Tim was sent to jail for.

The next thing I know, one of his supporters calls me and said, "Look, the job's fallen through at the Unitarian Church. Is there any way Tim could come to work for you?" It took me under five seconds to say, "Yes. I'd be happy to hire Tim DeChristopher at the bookstore." The idea went through his attorneys, and then the halfway-house people came down to interview me. In their infinite wisdom, the DOJ determined that Tim's working at my bookstore would be more appropriate than the Unitarian Church. I'm not saying it makes any sense; I'm just trying to explain to you what I was told. Apparently bookstores are safer than churches.

Twenty-four hours later he was working here full-time. For the duration of Tim's parole, I became a sort of warden. As part of the sentencing to the half-way house, Tim was forbidden to do interviews with the media or put statements on social media, such as Facebook. If he starts doing what they consider to be social-justice activities, I was told that any violation of these restrictions would land him right back in prison. He was effectively denied being able to speak out about his case or anything at all to the public or the media.

ML: Do you feel what Tim did was the beginning of a resurgence of direct action against climate change?

Sanders: Tim DeChristopher was a breath of fresh air. I had come to be sort of jaded from the environmental wars and government repression and, frankly, I'd kind of retreated.

While still attending the university, Tim inspired thirty-two students from the University of Utah to attend the mining protest in Washington, DC, with Wendell Berry, Bill McKibben, Terry Tempest Williams, our former mayor Rocky Anderson, and many other luminaries. It was the students' first experience with civil disobedience. My generation screwed the planet up as well as any for the future. But I think Tim DeChristopher and a new generation of kids are coming up with new ways of defining what the problems are. Tim is a great example of someone who decided to take direct action for a cause that he believed in. And I think the real question to be asking here is: In the two years subsequent to his actions, why aren't more of us in prison? Why aren't more of us doing this? We all should be in prison if he's going to prison.

Tim will be a huge force for change. And I think that is because the federal government made a living martyr out of this young man. His actions and the Peaceful Uprising social justice movement that he's cofounded are going to have global repercussions. He's an articulate spokesman for saving what's left of the future of the planet.

ML: What do you say when people say protesting won't work against the government or big business?

Sanders: Then they win. And the Draconian nature of the win is it poisons the planet and dooms all of us. It's a bad tradeoff to take every square mile of wilderness and suck the oil or the gas and water out of it and use harmful chemicals and processes that are going to pollute the earth, the sky, and the planet just so people can drive their cars for another week.

It's always seemed such a dichotomy to me that the very people that are closest to the land—ranchers and farmers and people that live in small communities surrounded by lots of wilderness and desert—would be natural allies of the land that they need, and that they would be able

to see the necessity of the sustainability to keep all parts of the ecosystem alive. But for some reason, they don't. These ideas are often derailed
by short-term profits, short-term thinking.

If the original generation sold mineral rights, their children and
grandchildren are still living on that land. What do they think of the
poisoning of their lands and the aquifers beneath their feet?

When you lose a river going somewhere to a dam or clean air to a
coal plant, that's a forever loss. They don't tend to go away. There's no
penalty for the long-term ramifications.

Edward Abbey once called Alaska "America's last pork chop," meaning it's the last unspoiled spot of America that we can eat and satisfy
our hunger.

ML: Is Ed Abbey's writing still relevant today?

Sanders: I believe so, based on my experience in the bookstore. We can't
keep used Edward Abbey books in stock and we sell hundreds of new
books every single year. *Desert Solitaire* and *The Monkey Wrench Gang*
have now each sold in excess of millions of copies each. Not bad, when
you realize that the first printings of most of his books were only five
thousand copies. Every one of the twenty-one books that Ed Abbey ever
wrote in his fifty-year-plus career is still in print, with the exception
of *Jonathan Troy*, his first novel. Ed was embarrassed by it and never
would allow it to be republished. Abbey is selling more books dead than
he ever did alive.

A new generation of college-age kids that were born since Ed Abbey
died are reading his works for the first time and finding relevance. I did
a talk at Westminster College in Salt Lake, and four hundred people
showed up. I was talking mainly to an incoming crop of college fresh-
men who weren't yet on the planet when Ed Abbey died. They weren't
there to listen to me. They were there to listen to me try and reanimate
Edward Abbey, trying to keep his words alive, his thoughts alive. Why?
Because he was such an eloquent writer, and there's such a deep philosophical underpinning in even his most cavalier tales of personal adventure and is important to remind folks about.

Bob Lippman, Bart Koehler, Ken Sanders, Howie Wolk, Katie Lee, John Nichols,
Dave Foreman at Pack Creek Ranch, Utah. Photographer Meredith Ogilby.

ML: What is the single most important piece of advice you would give to young environmentalists?

Sanders: They need to act locally, even when solutions to problems seem to have impossible odds. No issue is regional anymore; every local cause is going to profoundly affect the planet. If people in our communities don't act, and do nothing, then the forces against them win automatically.

Whatever they do, however they do it, they have to do it first and foremost for themselves. Every single person makes a difference.

So much is about education and exposure. If these young people don't know what's been lost, or what's being lost, or what's at stake to be lost in the future, how can they feel deeply about an issue that they're unaware exists? They have to read Edward Abbey, Rachel Carson, and Aldo Leopold. They have to read contemporaries like Bill McKibben and Michael Pollan.

There are as many ways to save the environment as there are to destroy it. Everybody isn't the same. Everybody's not wired the same. We're not all created equal.

I think every individual has got to find a way to participate that works for them. We've all got to find our own way to be Tim DeChristophers, Rachel Carsons, and Edward Abbeys.

15 | TIM DeCHRISTOPHER

Biography

Tim DeChristopher came to the public's attention as a climate activist when he protested a December 2008 Bureau of Land Management (BLM) oil and gas auction held in Salt Lake City, Utah, by bidding on the leases. He was arrested and, two years later, convicted of two nonviolent federal felonies: violating the Federal Onshore Oil and Gas Leasing Reform Act and making a false representation to the federal government. He served fifteen months in prison and six months on parole. He was a member of the First Unitarian Church in Salt Lake; while waiting for trial, he cofounded the organization Peaceful Uprising.

After serving his prison sentence, DeChristopher attended Harvard Divinity School and earned a master of divinity.

DeChristopher, Maria Marcum (a United Methodist), and Jay O'Hara (a Quaker from Cape Cod) cofounded the Climate Disobedience Center in 2015. The organization provides legal and spiritual resources to help nurture resistance and moral imagination among people and groups that are willing to take risks on behalf of climate change.

In 2016, DeChristopher was among thirteen people—including the daughter of Al Gore—arrested for protesting a new natural gas pipeline in Boston, Massachusetts. In 2017, Judge Mary Ann Driscoll listened to the defendants plead their case at the Boston Municipal Courthouse and dismissed them. She reasoned that the harm that would have resulted from their obeying the law would have significantly exceeded the harm actually caused when they allegedly broke the law—a major tenet of what is commonly known as the "necessity defense."

In 2018, on behalf of Rhode Island Interfaith Power and Light, De-Christopher issued a public statement condemning the incarceration of children and families on the southern border. He called the practice of separating families from children "deeply immoral and a terrifying harbinger of our social response to a future of climate disruption."

DeChristopher's deep commitment to balancing spirituality with activism could be likened to that of the Jesuit Daniel Berrigan's antiwar pacifism and radical spirituality for social and political justice in the 1960s.

I interviewed Tim in Salt Lake City and at Ken Sander's Rare Book Store for the twentieth anniversary of Ed Abbey's death. It was a talk where people gathered to hear "Ken Sleight—Mr. Old School" and "Tim DeChristopher—Mr. New School." (www.timdechristopher.org; www.peacefuluprising.org)

———

ML Lincoln: How did Edward Abbey influence you?

Tim DeChristopher: I never met Edward Abbey. I was born a few years before Abbey died. I only met him through his books. When I was eighteen, right after I graduated from high school, I read *The Monkey Wrench Gang*. I guess it was kind of a weird age to be reading it: I was old enough to understand it, but not quite old enough to realize that it wasn't a manual.

It did give me the perspective that environmentalists didn't always have to play by the rules and that there were ways to work outside of the system.

In that same year, I also read his book *Beyond the Wall*. The biggest thing that I learned came from his introduction, where he wrote, "Sentiment without action is the ruin of the soul." Although I haven't picked up that book since then, I always knew that this was true. My sentiment grew stronger and stronger when I was in college, because I saw how much action we need to really protect ourselves, how threatened my future really was, and how most of what we're doing isn't enough to stand up to that threat.

ML: Is that the sentiment that compelled you to protest the auction of 116 parcels of Utah public lands for potential oil and gas development in December of 2008?

DeChristopher: Yes. When I got to the auction, protesters were walking back and forth with their signs looking resigned and hopeless. It made me think about other protests I'd been to, how I've done all the things environmentalists are supposed to do, but how we still see exploitation wins.

Two minutes later, I found myself inside the door. A BLM official asked, "Hi. Are you here for the auction?" I said, "Yes, I am." She said, "Are you here to be a bidder?" I said, "Yes, I am." All it took was showing my driver's license and filling out a form. I didn't even have to pretend to be anybody that I wasn't. On the form it asked, "Who do you represent?" I wrote, "Tim DeChristopher. I represent myself." There was no question at all whether I had millions of dollars to be bidding on a bunch of land in southern Utah. In the BLM's rush to get the leases sold before former president Bush was out of office, they skipped making sure bidders had the ability to pay.

While I sat there, I thought about how I was feeling that I was still torn by the ruin of the soul that Abbey wrote about. For so long, I had seen so much injustice going on as our land kept being stolen and our climate threatened.

I felt a moral imperative to stand against this auction and *saw* that I had this opportunity do something. The first time I bid for one of the oil leases, I drove up the price by $75,000. I thought to myself that it was the most effective thing I had ever done in my whole life!

As I kept bidding and driving up the prices for the leases being sold to all oil companies, I felt better than I had in a while. In a half-hour, I probably cost the oil companies about three-quarters of a million dollars. And in those moments, what was really interesting was that when my action matched my sentiment, it healed my soul.

I think that the measure of an effective action is that it costs the opposition money. But even though I drove up the prices, I knew that more big chunks of red-rock desert were going to get destroyed by the oil companies. So I knew that I could be doing more, that I could actually be winning those bids and potentially protecting those lands so that they didn't get developed at all.

Finally, I knew that I had to jump completely in and start winning the bids. Once I made that decision, this amazing sense of calm came over me. I won thirteen parcels in a row—about 22,500 acres for a total of about $1.8 million, all of them adjacent to national parks and monuments, like Canyonlands. And as I started winning, I thought to myself, "Well, I'm probably going to go to prison." They were probably some of the most peaceful moments in my life.

After winning the bid on the thirteenth parcel, the BLM stopped the auction, and an agent came over and said, "We need to talk outside." The BLM announced a break. Afterward, BLM officials came back in and tried to explain what was going on: "There was this guy who just won all these parcels and had no intention of paying for them. Apparently there was some false bidding. And we're going to try to figure out what to do."

The room erupted into chaos. The oil companies got really upset and started yelling at the officials and asking what was going to be done and making all these demands. Some activists started arguing with the oil companies, while others went outside to tell protesters what had happened. They also went to news media crews. "You guys have got to get in there. Something important is going on." The media started looking for me and ended up sticking around for several hours after the auction to talk to me.

ML: Would you call what you did monkeywrenching or an act of civil disobedience?

DeChristopher: Maybe it's a little bit of both.

A lot of the newspapers and other media called what I did monkeywrenching. Ken Sanders, Ken Sleight, and some of the others from back in the day told me there were some very specific guidelines for it—that it was something done at night, usually done alone, and that you never talked about it afterward. Monkeywrenching didn't seem like something where you're supposed to follow the rules. You should just go out and break 'em! Maybe I ended up stretching the definition a little bit.

But when I was in a back room with the federal agents, I told them I was there to disrupt this auction and that I was committing an act of civil disobedience against laws that I felt were unjust and that I considered myself a patriot—someone who is willing to stand up and defend my country. Public property that belonged to all Americans was being threatened and stolen by corporations who had inside access and were allowed to write the rules.

That was the really powerful thing that I learned from Edward Abbey—it really does take action to make us whole again, to put us in that right place, and to fix our soul. So I really feel like I owe Abbey a debt of gratitude. He planted seeds in my head a long time ago, and my thoughts grew and grew until finally I couldn't hold them in anymore. So, in a large way, bidding at that auction started with him.

Since the auction, there's been a lot of hard stuff to deal with and a lot of tough times. And in those moments, I've always taken a lot of comfort in knowing that somewhere Henry David Thoreau is smiling down on me, and somewhere Edward Abbey is smiling up at me.

BIDDER 70

Bidder 70, a compelling documentary film by Beth and George Gage, tells the story of Tim DeChristopher's patriotism and willingness to face prison when he derailed the BLM oil and gas auction. According to the Gages, "Climate change is upon us and there is nothing more important to work for than what Tim called a 'livable future.' His commitment to future generations, his evolution as a leader, and his willingness to courageously accept the consequences of his action make this a story we hope will inspire and motivate a new generation of activists." *Bidder 70* won twenty major film festival awards.

ML: What do you think of other Abbey novels?

Tim DeChristopher. Photographer Daphne Hougard.

DeChristopher: I was never very happy when I finished reading an Edward Abbey book; it never really made me feel good. When I finished *The Monkey Wrench Gang*, I felt pretty terrible about where we had come from. But it's a really funny book, too. It expresses a lot of people's attitudes about wilderness preservation and their powerlessness to stop it.

When I finished *Good News*, I felt even more terrible about where we were headed. After reading *The Fool's Progress*, I felt pretty awful about where I might be headed myself.

Hayduke Lives! may be the darkest book Abbey ever published, and it disturbed me because it was a nightmarish vision of the future. The book takes protests to a very logical conclusion, where the stakes are more elevated, where there's more at risk and the consequences are even greater, both for the fate of the planet but also for the fate of those who choose to defend it.

Although I never really sought to follow in Edward Abbey's footsteps—and still don't and don't think that I have—his writings kind of lit a fire in me. I didn't just feel bad; the productive part was that it sparked my anger and struck something really personal and really deep. Anger is what often drives us to action. We can only hold onto anger for so long before we have to do something. It's certainly what motivated me to start bidding for oil leases. I hope it will motivate members of my generation to become activists.

ML: How do you feel about the activism of your generation?

DeChristopher: I wouldn't call my generation activists. I was born the year that Ronald Reagan took office and so we've always been taught that we're powerless to change things in a big way in our country. We've always been taught that big corporations make the decisions and that they're the ones with power. No wonder our generation feels somewhat hopeless.

My generation was affected by the social upheaval of the sixties and seventies and saw it as a failure. We saw that people who stood up and tried to fight were basically beaten back. The victories in the antiwar movement didn't take power away from the military-industrial complex. A generation later, and we seem to be back in the next Vietnam, marching to wars without end.

I think that's why so few young people are involved with defending their own future from climate change. We see how big this threat is. We're reading the science. We're listening to people saying, you know, we need to make drastic revolutionary changes in our whole economy and our whole industrial system in order to defend our civilization.

I'm not quite sure how people my age cannot be angry against the political and business leaders of this country that are at war against them. How can we not be angry when we hear many big green environmental groups tell us, "Here are ten easy things you can do to save the world—go change your light bulbs." We know that it's nonsense. We see that what we're being asked to do is not nearly enough to win this battle.

We aren't looking for something to just make ourselves feel better. Nor are we looking to relieve a lifetime of guilt for our overconsumption, like our older generation. We're looking for something that will be effective to put us on a path for a livable future.

ML: What would you say to the statement made by Kathleen Sgamma of the Independent Petroleum Association of Mountain States: "When we take public lands and put them off-limits to national gas development, we're denying ourselves a resource we need."

DeChristopher: To the petroleum industry that says we should just have all of our lands open for any kind of resource exploitation, I'd say that there's got to be some kind of balance. But we do need to make sure that the decisions about where we drill and what lands are destroyed for that oil should be made in an open and democratic process, not behind the closed doors of the administration. It shouldn't just be that everything should be available for exploitation.

There needs to be a line drawn for lands that need to be protected; we need to know about the areas that we're not going to sacrifice, and understand that we're not going to burn all the furniture to heat the house, that we're going to keep something worth saving.

ML: What do you say when Bob Bennett, an eminent senator from Utah, charges that Utah would be hurting for revenues from oil leases if lands weren't available for production?

DeChristopher: What Bob Bennett is referring to are potential revenues from the severance taxes that the oil companies pay when they extract oil. In Utah, those are actually very low, and there are enough loopholes so that most of them don't actually end up paying any taxes. So that's a pretty small amount of revenue that Utah is missing out on.

I also think that what the state receives is outweighed by all the external costs for allowing oil development in our state. It doesn't take into account the taxpayer dollars that help build the roads for the oil companies to go and drill. It doesn't include the healthcare costs for the pollution created. We have hundreds of people who suffer from poor air quality every year in the Salt Lake City valley.

Probably the biggest unaccounted cost will be the mitigation costs for global warming. It's really unimaginable, incalculable of how huge those costs will be. Nor do we seem to understand that those costs will eventually come out of our taxes. Transitioning to a clean energy economy and using alternative energy rather than relying on oil will eventually save our economy a lot of money.

ML: Do you think conservancy groups or individuals will be permitted to buy up leases and not develop the resources?

DeChristopher: Something that's still undecided by our legal system is whether or not individuals or environmental groups can bid on these leases, win them, and not develop them. There's some precedent with grazing rights: when people bid on grazing permits, they actually don't have to graze the land. But it's undecided as to how or whether this would apply to oil. It's a very fuzzy issue. It's been tried for decades and it's never panned out to anything worthwhile.

TEMPEST EXPLORATION COMPANY

In early 2016, Terry Tempest Williams and her husband, Brooke, formed Tempest Exploration Company, and submitted noncompetitive bids on two oil and gas parcels on 1,120 acres close to where they lived in Grand County, Utah. On March 29, 2016, Williams published an essay titled "Keeping My Fossil Fuel in the Ground" in the Opinion Pages of the *New York Times*. She explained why she and her husband would keep the oil and gas resources in the ground. "Our purchase was more or less spontaneous, done with a coyote's grin, to shine a light on the auctioning away of America's public lands to extract the very fossil fuels that are warming our planet and pushing us toward climate disaster."

A primary requirement of the Mineral Leasing Act is that the lessee of an oil and gas lease be reasonably diligent in developing its lease. This was the basis on which Edwin Roberson, BLM Utah state director, rejected the Williams's lease offers. In the formal appellate brief (October 18, 2016), Roberson explained: "Viewed objectively and in their totality, your express statements to date show intent to not diligently explore for and produce the oil and gas resources underlying the two lease parcels for which you have submitted noncompetitive lease offers. Therefore, since you have stated publicly that you intend to keep the oil and gas resources in the ground and, therefore, not comply with the diligent development requirement plainly set forth in your noncompetitive lease offers, the lease offers are hereby rejected."

The case was the first to formally challenge BLM policies regarding oil and gas leases, including the agency's willingness to extend ten-year leases in perpetuity even though they are not being developed.

ML: What kind of protests will work? What is effective action?

DeChristopher: Here's a story about this. While I was attending the University of Utah, all these environmental events were being held by some of us who felt strongly about climate change. We'd show a film and say, "Come and discuss climate change." Maybe ten people would show up.

Then we changed tactics. We said, "Hey, we want you to come to Washington, DC, with us. Miss a week of class, pay a couple hundred bucks, and risk arrest outside of a coal-fired power plant." We got tons of responses to that, and we ended up with thirty people going to Washington and standing in the cold at a coal plant, linking arms against arrest, because it was something big enough to make us feel like it might have a chance to work.

When Ken Salazar, former president Obama's secretary of the interior, decided to cancel seventy-seven oil leases near pristine federal lands, I felt like what I did at the auction is an example of how the movement should be working. There are groups on the inside, like the Southern Utah Wilderness Alliance [SUWA] and the National Resources Defense Council [NRDC], that are doing whatever they can do, with lawsuits and other forms of legal advocacy. There are people on the outside like me that are doing the more controversial stuff that really pushes the boundaries and brings a lot more attention to the issue. When both of us are working together toward the same goal in our own ways, we're able to be far more effective than either one of us could have been on our own.

There has been far too much acceptance of the idea that if you are an environmentalist, you should just sign the internet petitions and send in donations so that the big groups can hire a lawyer or lobbyist to fight your battles.

What we need right now is an uprising. We need more people willing to sacrifice and be on the streets than we've had so far.

Perhaps the only reason that I was able to sit there in an auction room and say, yeah, I'm willing to go to prison for a few years, was that I took the protest very personally. I don't want to be an individual who twenty, thirty years down the road is trying to figure out what we were going to do about a few hundred million refugees whose homes are underwater or who are starving because our agricultural system has collapsed. I don't want to say to some young person, "Well, yeah, there was something we could have done. But that would have required me to go to prison for a few years, and I wasn't willing to do that to protect your future." If we're going to have a future, that's what a lot of people are going to have to start feeling. They're going to have to think about what it personally means to stand up and defend the things that we care about.

Whatever action we take it's got to be effective. We have to believe we are taking actions strong enough to make changes. We want to win. I think the only way that young people are going to get involved with the environmental movement is to start asking a lot more of them. Don't ask them to do something easy. Ask them to do something that's going to make a difference.

As a man of the desert, Edward Abbey felt like people were at war with him and at war against his home and that they were making war against the West. It's still happening. Those same corporations are making war against our future. I think a lot of answers can be found by reading Abbey. Not that we should be following exactly what he did, but that we should feel as passionately as he did, that we should take it as personally as he did, and that we should get as angry as he did.

16 | TERRY TEMPEST WILLIAMS

Biography

Terry Tempest Williams is distinguished for her eloquent writing on the moral, political, and spiritual relationships between wilderness and humans. Whether writing about the loss of pelicans in the Great Salt Lake, Utah, the cancer caused to her family during atomic bomb tests in Nevada, or the effects of genocide in Rwanda, she is a crucial voice combining ecological consciousness and ethical social change.

She has written fifteen books, including *Refuge: An Unnatural History of Family and Place* (1991), *The Open Space of Democracy* (2004), *The Hour of Land: A Personal Topography of America's National Parks* (2015), and most recently *Erosion: Essays of Undoing* (2016). Her articles have been published in the *New Yorker*, the *New York Times*, *Orion* magazine, and in numerous anthologies worldwide.

Williams has received numerous awards for her leadership in the American conservation movement, including the Robert Marshall Award from the Wilderness Society (2006) and the David R. Brower Conservation Award for activism (2010). On the fiftieth anniversary of the Wilderness Act, Williams received the prestigious Sierra Club's John Muir Award (2014) at a ceremony in San Francisco. She was inducted into the American Academy of Arts and Letters in 2019.

Williams joined the Harvard Divinity School as a writer-in-residence in the 2017–2018 academic year and continued in 2018–2019. During her residency, she spent time "contemplating and writing about the spiritual implications of climate change" and leading seminars with students.

I interviewed Terry on my birthday at her home in the high desert in southeast Utah, a quiet oasis among the breathtaking red-rock buttes, mesas, and spires. The second interview was held in Salt Lake City outside the US District Courthouse surrounded by people who were protesting on behalf of Tim DeChristopher at his trial.

She and her husband Brooke divide their time living in Castle Valley, Utah, and Cambridge, Massachusetts. (www.coyoteclan.com)

———

ML Lincoln: How do you reconcile polarized opinions in Utah?

Terry Tempest Williams: In 1976, I was teaching at the Carden School in Salt Lake City. One day, I had all of the first-graders swimming on the floor imagining that they were whales, the door flew open, the needle jumped off the turntable playing humpback whale songs, and Mrs. Jeffs, the headmaster, said, "What on Earth is going on?" One of the children stood up and said, "Why, we're searching for our mates." I was yanked out of the room. Before I was fired, Mrs. Jeffs—with her husband, Mr. Jeffs—looked at me very seriously and said, "We have a question for you, and you'd better think hard about how you are going to answer. Are you an environmentalist?"

I remember saying, "I am." Then she said, "Are you aware that the devil is an environmentalist?" I said, "I am not."

So how do you—how do we—be conservationists in the state of Utah, where many people hold those points of view? Consistency. I think we consistently show that we are not devils, nor are we angels, but rather we are human beings living with other human beings on the planet.

ML: When did you meet Ed Abbey and how did he influence you?

Williams: I met Ed Abbey in Salt Lake City in 1975 at a benefit for the Utah Wilderness Association. He and Barry Lopez were speaking at the

Terry Tempest Williams. Photographer Meredith Ogilby.

University of Utah. It was the same year that Abbey's novel *The Monkey Wrench Gang* was published. After the talk, Brooke proposed to me. On one hand he had my emerald engagement ring, and on the other, a copy of Abbey's novel. So our marriage has always been intertwined with that. The book changed my life.

Ed was a mentor. He was a friend. I knew Ed in Moab when I was a young writer. He was very supportive—not without his edge. He said things to me early on that I've never forgotten. For example, *Refuge*—a book that I had written about the rise of Great Salt Lake and the death of my mother from ovarian cancer—received a scathing review in the *New York Times*. I was at Ed's house, and he said, "Congratulations." I said, "Excuse me?" He said, "You know, if we are pushing the boundaries, then we shouldn't be getting all good reviews." I've held onto that, and I think he's right. If we really want to stretch culture, if we really want to take down the machine, so to speak, then we're not going to make people comfortable. Ed surely didn't.

I love Ed Abbey. My relationship with him was respectful. Personally, I did not find him a misogynist. I never saw him treat his wife Clarke with anything but affection and love. That's my sense, yes, but Ed was a man of his generation, no question.

ML: Does your family hold differing political points of view?

Williams: My family and I do not see eye to eye politically. I'm not sure we ever voted for the same president; in fact, I'm quite sure that we did not.

Then in college at the University of Utah, I became a fan of Edward Abbey's books, especially *The Monkey Wrench Gang*. Monkeywrenching became something close to my heart, not because I believed it, but because I come from a family of pipeline contractors. The tool of choice in my family was a shovel, not a monkey wrench, though my father had one in his toolbox. It wasn't until much later that a monkey wrench became a tool of anarchy or, as Ken Sleight taught me, a metaphor for one's own creativity.

When Ed Abbey was talking about monkeywrenching, Dave

Foreman [cofounder of Earth First!] and others were out doing it. My family were among the beneficiaries: the engines of the Tempest Company's trucks, bulldozers, caterpillars, and backhoes in my family's construction business were sugared. So Ed Abbey's name was, I would say, on the edge of profanity and blasphemy in my family.

This did not prevent me from asking my father—who is the Marlboro Man without the cigarette—"Dad, will you come with me to hear Ed Abbey?" "Over my dead body," he said. And I said, "Really?" He said, "Where is he speaking?" I said, "East High School here in Salt Lake City."

He was dubious. Then he said, "I'll go on one condition: you come with me and see what happens when those machines won't start when my men are ready to work, and I'll go see who this guy is who's been sugaring my trucks." We struck a deal.

Ed gave one of his wonderful, meandering river-trip narratives. When he talked about politics and immigration, I thought, "I'm doomed. This is it." But I saw my father sit upright. He was listening. He was laughing. He was paying attention. When it was over, he was the first one to stand after Ed sat down. Then everybody stood and gave him a standing ovation.

My father was also the first person that went up and said, "Mr. Abbey, I don't agree with your politics, but I agree with you. Let me be the first one to contribute to your campaign as governor of Arizona." And he handed Abbey a crisp dollar bill.

Why? What was it? I think Ed spoke from an authentic place. What my father recognized in him was not only a tall man with boots who spoke his mind, but someone who touched his sense of wildness in the great outdoors and of the essential nature of the American spirit. I think Ed's great carrying capacity and testament to his charisma and to those truths that he embodied was how he charmed my own father.

I love that because what it says is wilderness is not a political issue, it's a spiritual one. And my father, who has been in the pipeline business his whole life, loves wilderness as much as anybody.

A monkey wrench was also the last gift that my brother Steve gave to me. [Steve Tempest died in 2005 of lymphoma.] What I can tell you about Steve is that he ran Tempest Enterprises, which laid thousands of miles of pipe in the American West in eight Western states, part of the infrastructure that allows us to heat our homes and have water run from our taps. Steve said, "I may not understand completely what you're doing, but I am right there with you." I think that's what we're talking about—a solidarity of action.

That's how Abbey and his book wove circles around family and community, around marriage, about marriage to the land, fidelity—to me, it's all intrinsically connected.

ML: Why are we forgetting our connection to wildness and what is that doing to us?

Williams: My greatest concern as an environmentalist in the state of Utah is we are forgetting our source. We are forgetting what wildness even is and what it means. It's no longer a common, shared experience. It used to be that it was our only experience of what it meant to be human. We had to know what wildness meant because it was our survival. I would argue it still is our survival.

Even the most urban of people have a sense of bird song or a sense of ocean or a sense of the moon. I think it's just that we've forgotten the context in which we are held by them. And certainly, author Richard Louv talks about how important it is to reconnect children with nature. Rachel Carson speaks of those things. I think we all have an understanding of wildness at our core. I think we just don't know how to articulate it. It's based in experience and our experiences in nature can be as diverse and varied as we are.

RICHARD LOUV'S THEORY, NATURE-DEFICIT DISORDER

Richard Louv speaks internationally on nature-deficit disorder, a concept he first introduced in his bestselling book *Last Child in the Woods: Saving Our Children from Nature-Deficit Disorder* (2005), on the importance of children's and adults' exposure to nature for their health, and on the need for environmental protection and preservation for greater access to nature and the health of Earth. According to Louv, "Nature-deficit disorder is not meant to be a medical diagnosis but rather to serve as a description of the human costs of alienation from the natural world." He is a journalist and author of nine books, including *The Nature Principle: Reconnecting with Life in a Virtual Age* and *Vitamin N* (2002). His books have helped launch an international movement to connect children, families, and communities to nature. He is cofounder and chairman emeritus of the Children and Nature Network, an organization helping build the movement (www.childrenandnature.org).

I've been a naturalist since I was eighteen years old and taught at the Teton Science School in Kelly, Wyoming, on the edge of Grand Teton National Park. What I saw is that it became harder and harder for students to connect to the core of wildness, but when they did connect to wild nature it was profound. I've never had anyone who didn't go out into a wild place who didn't feel restored or overturned. How can you be reminded about who you really are if you don't experience wildness? I think this is one of the reasons it is important to protect open spaces. If you don't leave some wilderness alone, how can you experience it?

But as our consciousness is expanding, so is our view of wilderness. Especially now, with climate change upon us, we're beginning to understand wilderness is no longer a single-issue, irrelevant cause mired in nostalgia as critics have said. Actually, wilderness is speaking to us from the future in terms of what the land holds—water, biodiversity, and that it can act as a carbon sink.

ML: What does compromise mean to you?

Williams: Compromise is not a word that I carry in my medicine bundle. What is compromise? We've all been compromised. The way in which we live our lives is to be compromised. The planet has been compromised.

We're all complicit. For me it becomes a question of choices. What choices are we given? How do we keep asking for more options when they are being closed—whether it's developing oil and gas on our public lands, or mining coal, or atomic bomb testing in the desert, or even whether it's politicians that have forgotten what it means to listen? My own family was compromised when the atom bomb was tested in Utah in the 1950s.

ML: What do you mean by that? What happened?

Williams: I belong to a Clan of One-breasted Women. Nine women in my family have had mastectomies, and seven are dead.

A year after my mother passed from ovarian cancer, I kept having these reoccurring nightmares—this flash of light in the night in the desert illuminating buttes and mesas—over and over and over again. Sometime afterward, my father and I met for dinner. He said, "How are you?" I said, "Actually, I keep having this nightmare." I explained this flash of light in the night in the desert. He said, "Well, you saw that." And I said, "Saw what?" He said, "I thought you knew. It was a common occurrence in the 1950s. I actually remember the day. It was September 7th. We were coming home from California, an hour or so before dawn. You were sitting on Diane's lap. It was the day before your birthday. She was pregnant with Steve. We were driving toward Las Vegas when this explosion lit up. I thought the oil tanker in front of us had exploded. We pulled over. And suddenly, rising from the desert floor, was this golden-stemmed cloud, this mushroom. And within a few moments, a light ash was raining down on the car."

At that moment, I realized the deceit we had been living with—children growing up in the American Southwest drinking contaminated milk from contaminated cows, even from the breasts of our mothers, who became years later members of the Clan of One-breasted Women of the atomic West in that moment in time. The atomic bomb was always tested when the winds were blowing toward Utah, because in the government's minds, Utah was largely the home of God-fearing people, Mormons, who would not question their government.

What do you do with that? In 1988—the year after my mother had passed—I went down to the Nevada Test Site after reading Henry David Thoreau's *Civil Disobedience*, Gandhi's book on noncooperation, and Martin Luther King's "Letter from Birmingham Jail." What mattered to me was to physically cross the line and say no to nuclear testing and yes to a collective resistance. I was with a group of nine women from Utah, alongside a group of Shivwits (Paiute) and Shoshoni people, Jesuits, and members from Kazakhstan—a community of resisters, if you will—and we crossed that line at the Nevada Test Site.

I'll never forget being met by a female officer who cinched handcuffs around my wrists. She frisked my body. When she reached down to my ankles, she felt a bulge in my boots. She lifted up my pant leg, retrieved a pad of paper and a pen, looked at me, and said, "And these?" I remember our eyes meeting, and I said, "Weapons." Our eyes met again. She put them back in my boots, put my pant leg over them, and we continued.

There are many different kinds of monkey wrenches—a pencil, a pen, among them. I think about Camus, when he says that at some point we have to begin to understand that words are more powerful than munitions.

How do we take our anger and turn it into sacred rage? For one, I began writing *The Clan of One-Breasted Women* [published in 1991]. For another, I sought a community of people that understood what that meant.

ML: What is community?

Williams: *The Monkey Wrench Gang* to me is a novel about community. That's the enduring legacy of Edward Abbey. He created a different kind of community—one that honored a sovereignty of spirit. He took the word *radical* and brought it into the notion of conservative, to conserve, to protect, to love.

When I committed civil disobedience at the Nevada Test Site over and over again, I was in community. When we chose to be arrested on the eve of the Iraq War in front of the White House, and I stood with fellow writers Alice Walker, Maxine Hong Kingston, and Susan Griffon, I was in community. Code Pink: Women for Peace is a community.

The real radical question becomes, "What about other?" What is other? Is it a man, is it a woman, a child? Or is it a community of prairie dogs? And what might a different kind of power look like, feel like? How might we redefine power to include rocks, rivers, plants, animals, and human beings? It's not only about other beings, but about other possibilities, a different way of living on Earth.

ML: I get to a place of silence in these deserts. Silence is a philosophy for me, a real way of life. I need silence. How does silence affect your life?

Williams: When we moved to Utah's red rock desert from Salt Lake City, what was so striking was the silence, the stillness, and to be able to expand large enough to hold that, to be present with it, to not fear it, but let it envelop us.

I also realized that silence is time. Here in the desert, rocks tell time differently. Silence is everything to me, in terms of what it nourishes, what it feeds, and what it inspires in terms of a creative life. If I don't have silence in my life, if I don't have stillness, if I don't have open space, then I am left standing on the edge of madness.

Silence is also paradoxical because it has a shadow side that is familiar. In the dominant, patriarchal culture and religion that I come from, it was very easy to be silenced, to be self-silent, to have self-censorship.

So when I think about silence, I ask, am I moving toward the silence that nourishes me or am I moving toward a silence that censors me? I think that also has everything to do with the heart of anarchy because it is at the heart of anarchy.

When we are silent, when we allow ourselves to be quiet, then I think that's where we realize both what we love and what we are losing. And I think it inspires action. Again, it's that paradox. If we're still, then we're preparing to act. When we act, we're preparing to return to stillness. So it's this dance. In terms of being silenced, the first step we take to shatter that silence is direct action. We are seeing this now with Black

Lives Matter, with climate activists—from Standing Rock to the Maldives.

ML: Direct action was what Tim DeChristopher did when he bought up oil and gas leases. I was sickened when he was arrested for that. How did you get to know him?

Williams: I first met Tim at Sugar House coffee shop in Salt Lake City. And the first question I asked him was: "Tell me about your family. How do your parents feel about this?" Because the bottom line is it's not easy, and you pay a price personally.

Although we can all be supporting Tim, ultimately he's in this alone. When I watched him walking to that courthouse, he was alone. And all the singing in the world, all the marching, and all the letters don't change that. Tim made a sacrifice. I think what singles him out in my mind is that he committed an act of civil disobedience alone. As a result, a community was created around him.

I was at Tim's trial and the thing that was so horrifying, that absolutely shook, once again, my belief in a democratic society, was that Tim was never allowed to fully tell his story. If he'd been allowed to do so, he would not be in prison. And that was the justice's intent, that the trial would be based on technicalities, on laws that had no physical standing, and a narrative that was bloodless.

And when Tim did tell even the limited story of why he did what he did, why he bid up the oil and gas leases, it was when he turned around and saw the radical feminist Krista Bowers in tears that he then said, "Now." When that happened, the shift in the courtroom was palpable. They took a break, adjourned, and then the trial returned with the same kind of bloodless legalese that moves no one. And it gave the jury no place to move, no place to speak. It was another form of silence.

I kept thinking if the jury had received proper instructions and knew that it was possible to say no, that it was possible to say yes, that it was possible to vote, as Thoreau says, not just with a piece of paper, but with your whole influence—then I know that there would have been members of that jury that did not believe Tim DeChristopher should go to prison. They had the power to shift that beyond any of the instructions that the judge gave them. But they did not use that power out of ignorance or fear or both.

Anarchy is something that we have to be trained in. But the jury didn't have that education. That's why I think a film like yours is so important, because to hold a monkey wrench, to have a voice, to move forward with sacred rage, is our right as Americans and as citizens on this planet, especially at this moment in time. We have to be encouraged to be activists because it goes against our good nature to rock the boat, to disturb, to make people uncomfortable.

Do you know what it's like to be in my hometown, Salt Lake City, and see hundreds of people show up on behalf of public lands? It was deeply moving to me when they walked from Pioneer Park to Exchange Place, across from the courthouse, to support Tim DeChristopher, a college student in economics, who followed his gut and raised the paddle number 70 in an auction. In so doing, he exposed the bogus nature of these oil and gas leases that are ravaging our public lands in America's red rock wilderness. There were helicopters flying around in Salt Lake City that day, and I thought, what are they afraid of? They have a right to fear us. And they have no idea of our numbers.

I love Tim. He's a friend. I've watched him grow. That trial was a trial for our future. As a friend said, "I think we're going to look back on this trial as we do through the lens of history to the Scopes Trial." The fate of the planet is in question. What are we going to do about that? And that's where I wonder about justice.

What Tim has represented and asked us to consider is: What are we willing to do for a livable future? How am I personally accountable for that future? In many ways, Tim is the next generation of direct action. For that, I am grateful. His is a leadership of great courage and great heart. That's what I see in my students—they are taking their anger and turning it into sacred rage. They are taking the mirror of culture and turning it back on us. None of us are immune. Each of us must become accountable. Can we love the world enough to change.

Ed Abbey says, "Sentiment without action is the ruin of the soul." There are a lot of souls in this country that are raising their fists and opening their hearts and saying, "Give me the monkey wrench," which originally meant: "Keep these lands wild." But today it goes deeper, broader—with more urgency: "Climate change is affecting all of us. We must change or face a devastating future."

ML: Well, isn't part of that future the out-of-control population growth? For some people, it's a politically incorrect subject, a threat.

Williams: If we are honest, there's just too many of us. People bristle at that statement. The nature of each generation is to pass something on to the next, and it's not always positive. But it's just not our generation that's passed on nuclear waste and consumption and the residue of fossil fuel consumption. This has been going on for a long time, decades, centuries, beginning with the Industrial Revolution. It is in our nature to expand and consume. Can we change? That is the question I keep asking myself. Do we have it within us to act with restraint in the name of those who will come after us?

Brooke and I have been married four decades, childless by choice. The only thing I've been completely responsible about in my life is birth control and keeping a journal. Birth control gave me my voice as a woman early on. It was important that I did have control of my body, that it did belong to me, and that a man in Washington or in the Utah legislature did not have control over my reproductive rights.

That is uncertain now. If a man knew what a woman never forgets, he would love her differently—because every day a woman is thinking: Am I pregnant? Am I now responsible for one life, two lives, three? It's in our own sovereignty of souls as women that we can continue to practice personal conservation. Whether it's population or whether it's populating the landscape, it's the same issue. It's about empathy and respect and choice.

I can also add we adopted a son from Rwanda. We don't have to give birth to children in order to have children in our lives.

ML: What keeps you from giving in to pessimism?

Williams: It's really important to note joy. When there's so much pessimism in the world, sometimes you wonder if you can even get up in the morning. What I love about the Coyote Clan, or monkeywrenching, or coming to appreciate wildlife, from grizzly bears to wolves to great horned owls, is there's so much joy, unpredictable, unmediated, spontaneous joy.

And I think you can't know joy without having suffered the losses— whether it's loss of family, or loss of these wildlands, or losses of freedom and justice.

What is so important is that we make note that alongside loss is joy. When you see someone like Tim DeChristopher, who's facing prison time—there's still this incredible, incorruptible seedbed of joy. We see that all the way through the American conservation movement, which is now being recognized as not only preserving the sacred nature of wildlands but is aligning itself with social movements and environmental justice.

I can tell you that how we recognize each other in the Coyote Clan is simple. We're connected by joy and love. What we're really talking about on every level is very simple. It's love. When I think about Rachel Carson's work, it was tied to what she loved. When I think about Doug Peacock, it's love. When I think about Ed Abbey, it's love. When I think about Dave Foreman and Earth First!, it's love. When I think about the monkey wrench that my brother Steve gave me, it was about love.

COYOTE CLAN

The Coyote Clan is associated with Terry Tempest Williams's website, coyoteclan.com, as well as with people who are fighting to prevent the loss of wilderness. They want to heal the damage that has already been caused, not only to the lands themselves but also their deeply felt emotional losses. In her book *An Unspoken Hunger: Stories From the Field* (1995) Williams writes: "Members of the Clan are not easily identified, but there are clues. You can see it in their eyes. They are joyful and they are fierce. They can cry louder and laugh harder than anyone on the planet. And they have an enormous range" (78).

Wendell Berry, Terry Tempest Williams, Bill McKibben, and Jim Hansen at
Power Shift 2009, Washington, DC. Photographer Sallie Dean Shatz.

ML: You also talk about death eyes? Isn't that related to compassion?

Williams: I often think that if we are asking the world to change, then
we should also be asking ourselves to change as well. We've had our
civil war; perhaps we're in the midst of another. People are weary of
not being heard. Many Americans feel invisible at best and targeted at
worst. I would also say as a critique of ourselves: Are we listening? Are
we aware of our privilege—as white people?

What will it take for us to have cultural death eyes? And that means
that your gaze is met with another in need. And it's friendship. We
don't have a lock on death eyes. We just know what that feels like. As a
community-seeking people, we are being jolted right now as a country.
If you go to the Gulf Coast, where I was in 2010 with the British Petroleum [BP] oil spill, those people have death eyes. New Orleans has death
eyes. People in Vermont after Hurricane Irene, they understand death
eyes. They've got silt eye-high in their basements and in their living

rooms. So I don't believe that this country doesn't understand what grief or sorrow is. Go to any Native American community and you will find death eyes.

On a personal level, *death eyes* is defined as turning my eyes inward—my eyes locked with my mother's as she's dying of cancer, with my dying brother, with prairie dogs, with Rwandan genocide survivors, my own eyes.

How can we make things better? What's needed is conversation—to connect the dots, to say, "Something isn't right in the world. I'm sad. Are you? My heart is breaking. Is yours?" How can we resist together? In solidarity? To me, that's what *The Monkey Wrench Gang* is about. It is alive and well, here, now, everywhere.

I think about Ed's first line in *Desert Solitaire*: "This is the most beautiful place on earth." And I think about his last, which is: "Will it be the same when I return?"

We are all wrenched—heartbroken, wrenched, wrenched, wrenched.

And, again, it comes down to some really tough choices. How shall we live? What does that look like? And those choices require sacrifice.

The world is so beautiful. How can we not respond?

The questions that I keep asking myself are: How serious am I? How serious are we? It strikes me that there is going to be a moment, and we will be watching for it, when we will find each other and we will say, "Now. Now. Now we will lay our bodies down."

So I'm waiting. I'm watching with revolutionary patience for that time when we say, "Now."

Acknowledgments

When I produced my documentaries *Drowning River* and *Wrenched*, I had some filmmaking experience, but I had little knowledge of putting together a book. This would need a team with different skills. I often saw it as ironic, as most people write books first and film adaptations follow.

I asked my friend of thirty-eight years, Diane Sward Rapaport, to help. She contributed her fifty-year experience in writing, editing, book production, and publishing. Her knowledge and skill set were invaluable. Over the two and a half years in the making of the book, our deep friendship and respect for each other's work ethic contributed to the enthusiasm for the project. Diane's patience and humor made her a joy to work with.

Diane was the structural editor for the interviews and likened it to film editing: "Many people think of editing as grammar and spelling. My concern was preserving the integrity of concepts and stories presented and making sure they flowed smoothly and easily for the reader."

The backbone of this project was Vicki Day, my book production coordinator and administrative assistant. We began working together ten years ago during the production of *Wrenched*. She has an incredible ability to track details that build with surprising speed. She kept the two Geminis organized through all the compilation of intricate layers of drafts and redrafts. Quite a task!

I particularly want to thank Bill McKibben for writing the foreword. He was in the middle of a nationwide promotion for his new book, *Falter: Has the Human Game Begun to Play Itself Out?*, yet he responded quickly. I have admired Bill's books and followed his activism for many years.

I could not have done this project without the love and support of Rand Bellows, my husband. As I read aloud the countless evolutions of this manuscript, his constructive feedback over morning coffee was a time I looked forward to. He knew this was important work. I was very grateful for his perceptive comments and questions. During the production of the film *Drowning River*, Rand earned the nickname "Wagon Master." Our film crew often camped, and Rand plied the crew with food and coffee. His good humor and stories were always appreciated when the crew would be flagging after a day's work.

Clarke Abbey's support during the making of *Wrenched* and this book is deeply appreciated. Thank you.

I am deeply indebted to the sixteen people whose interviews are published in this book. Their contributions did not end with the interviews. They were gracious with their time and were meticulous in going through the drafts, making sure their stories and thoughts were accurately represented, adding detail and clarification where necessary.

I particularly want to thank Ken Sleight and his wife, Jane, who were very encouraging during the making of the film and this book. He was the first person I interviewed for *Wrenched* and from then on we were buddies.

My deepest thanks to my amigo Jack Loeffler whose knowledge of historical detail and intellectual breadth was particularly helpful in the making of *Wrenched* and in writing this book.

A special thanks to Ken Sanders for coming up with the title *Wrenched from the Land* and Terry Tempest Williams for her thoughtful input.

Every book needs readers to make sure what we presented was as interesting as we thought. Kari Nielson read many chapters and sent back thoughtful suggestions. Two friends were very helpful in reading my introduction: Terry Morse, who wrote *The Aspen Kid*, and Ted Bright, attorney. Their careful reading of the introduction and their comments were invaluable to me. I am also appreciative of the two peer reviewers that the University of New Mexico Press assigned to review the manuscript, including Sean Prentiss who wrote *Finding Abbey*. What was helpful was that they *got* what the book was about, gave it high praise, and made us feel we were on the right track.

I am indebted for the professional help of Mark Mitchell, CPA extraordinaire, and to Kathleen Williamson, long-time friend and Tucson attorney.

I can't thank enough all the photographers and individuals whose images I had the pleasure of reviewing for this book. They include Julian Cardona, Merrick Chase, David J. Cross, Isabel Ferreira-De Puy, John De Puy, Jack Dykinga, Ingrid Eisenstadter, Dave Foreman, Pam Hackley, Daphne Hougard, Mark Klett, Katherine Loeffler, Jo-Anne McArthur, Milo McCowan, James Q Martin, Terrence Moore, Nancy Morton, Jeff Newton, NAU Cline Library, Meredith Ogilby, Andrea Peacock, Doug Peacock, Rick Ridgeway, Ken Sanders, Sallie Dean Shatz, Jim Sienkiewicz, Ken Sleight, Francis Sullivan, Serena Supplee, Eric Temple, Hulleah Tsinhnahjinnie, and PK Weis.

Isabel Ferreira-De Puy was most helpful in preparing the selections of John De Puy's vast collection of paintings for the cover of this book. The one I finally chose is called *The Needles*, which is in Canyonlands.

Randall Bellows III, my stepson, a professional photographer in New York City, was enormously helpful with preparing the photographs for submission to the publisher.

My heartfelt thanks to Ryann Savino for photo research and for reading to me the chapter drafts while we ate chocolates.

I want to thank all the people that I interviewed for my film *Wrenched*: Ilse Asplund, Shonto Begay, Andy Bessler, Charles Bowden, Ernie Bulow, Rose Chilcoat, Kim Crumbo, Dennis Cunningham, Tim DeChristopher, John De Puy, Veronica Egan, Ingrid Eisenstadter, Richard Engebretsen, Dave Foreman, Catherine Hardwicke, Derrick Jensen, James Kay, Lierre Keith, Katie Lee, Bob Lippman, Martin Litton, Jack Loeffler, John Macrae, Annette McGivney, Peg Millett, Doug Peacock, Karen Pickett, Bucky Preston, Robert Redford, Ben Rosenfeld, Craig Rosebraugh, Ken Sanders, Jane Sleight, Ken Sleight, Gerry Spence, Jim Stiles, Kieran Suckling, Paul Watson, and Terry Tempest Williams.

I am equally indebted to the extraordinary team that was integral to the production of *Wrenched*. I was incredibly fortunate to have worked with Kristi Frazier, who was my producer, and Patrick Gambuti, my editor. Other team members were Kurt Engfehr, Bryan Reinhart, Ariana Garfinkel, Parker Dixon, James Frazier, Jeremy Hawkes, the late cinematographer Ed

George, Marisa Kapust, Esq., Mathew Gross, Karen Mackenzie, Noel Fray, Peter Broderick, Skywalker Sound (Marin County, California), Post Factory (New York City), Andrew Gross, Lori Silverstone, transcriber, and all the others whose production and technical skills helped to make this film-making process a success.

I want to thank all those at the University of New Mexico Press who were involved in the publication of this book: Clark Whitehorn (former acquisitions editor), Stephen Hull (director), Alexandra Hoff (senior editor), Sonia Dickey (acquisitions coordinator), Felicia Cedillos (senior book designer), Katherine White (sales and marketing manager), James Ayers (editorial, design, and production manager), and Denise Edwards (freelance copy editor for UNM Press).

So many friends and colleagues have sustained me throughout this journey, including Marty Gwinn, Wendy Miller and Tim Turner, Vanda Pollard, Hanna Flagg, Darcey Brown, Barbara Browning, Lynn Anderson, Andy Nettell, Connie and Larry Whit, Jessie Magleby, Peggy Hodgkins, Serena Supplee, Miso Tunks, Jeff Mattsen, Jim Hook, Kitchel Family Foundation, E. J. Gore, Moab Physical Therapy, Tim Fuller, Cheryl Whitbread, Moab Landscape Maintenance, Martha Ham, Anne Vitte Morse, Sharifeh Robinson, Susie DeConcini, Aunt Molly Cook, Marly Brinkerhoff, Majic, the late Kate Cunningham, Pam Gibson, Fiona Raison, Linda Gallagher, Richard Martin, the late Paul Nonnast, Jacqueline Rickard, Monica Pfister Sohn, Christian Woodard, Margot Bradley, and Francie Rubin.

Winona LaDuke of the White Earth Reservation is an inspiration to me through her writing and activism.

Finally, I am thankful for the support of my husband's family, his sister Lisa, half-sisters Anne and Cynthia, half-brother Whit, and Rand's mother, Mary Lou, and his father Ran and wife Jeff.

And I am deeply grateful for the love and encouragement of my family—my sisters, Tisha and Carolyn; my brother, Ridge; and my loving nieces and nephews, Carrie, Cindy, Catherine, Holly, George, Tommy D., Daphne, and Tom. You all truly are what family means.

Editor's Note

ML had an uncanny knack for drawing out the stories and views of the people she interviewed. She was meticulous in her research and respectful in her communications with them. "Getting it right"—making sure their ideas were presented with integrity—was her primary goal throughout the process of putting this book together. She was particularly thorough in choosing the photos for this book. She has a great sense of humor and an essential ethical nature. Her passion is to do whatever she can to mitigate what more and more seems like global catastrophe. As is mine. I loved working with her and with Vicki Day because we contributed such different skills.

It was a great pleasure for me to work with the transcripts. I read many of the books these activists have written. Their interviews made me feel as though I was personally meeting them. They were so very different in personality. I thought of the causes that they championed as spokes in a wheel—all focused on one interactive circle, the preservation of our earth and the creatures that inhabit it, including ourselves. Namaste.

Diane Sward Rapaport

About the Editors

ML Lincoln is a director, producer, author, teacher, and activist. Her award-winning documentary films, *Wrenched* and *Drowning River*, feature conservationists who were outraged at the loss and degradation of lands and rivers in the American Southwest. As the author of *Wrenched From the Land: Activists Inspired by Edward Abbey*, she captures how these uncompromising individuals lit the flame of environmental activism and gave the movement its soul.

Wrenched (2014) was accepted into twenty-eight national film festivals and, to date, has been showcased in ninety-four community screenings across the United States. Numerous awards include Best Editing of a Documentary at the Santa Fe (New Mexico) Film Festival 2014 and People's Choice Award at the Flagstaff (Arizona) Mountain Film Festival 2014. The film also screened internationally at the Planet-in-Focus Film Festival in Toronto, Canada, 2015; the Environmental Film Festival in Melbourne, Australia, 2014; and the South African Eco Film Festival in Cape Town, South Africa, 2015.

Drowning River (2007) received the LeAnn Lucero Award and an Honorable Mention at the Taos Film Festival. Many festival screenings included the Big Easy International Film Festival in New Orleans (Louisiana), Sedona International Film Festival (Arizona) and Aspen Shorts Film Festival (Colorado). The film received recognition as Best Picture and Best Director at the Sedona Film School Shorts Film Festival (Arizona).

ML began her storytelling in her teens with a Super 8 camera. She took part in the Vietnam antiwar protests in New York City, where she participated in street theater and worked with underprivileged children during the Harlem riots of the mid-1960s. While living in Tucson in the 1990s–2000, she received recognition for developing the successful More Exposure Project, photography workshops for Tucson's kids at risk, including pregnant teenagers.

ML's photographs have been included in such magazines as *Utne Reader* (cover photo), 1994; *The Photo Review*, 1992; *ArtSpace Magazine*, 1988; and appeared in such anthologies as the second edition of *Exploring Color Photography* by Robert Hirsch (1992) and in *America's Historic Places: An Illustrated Guide to Our Country's Past* (1988). In 1992, she was given the Arizona Governor's Art/Purchase Award for her mural photograph of Tajikistan.

Numerous galleries and universities have featured her photographs, including San Diego Art Institute, National Juried Exhibition, San Diego, California; University of Arizona, Union Gallery, Tucson, Arizona; Arizona 1980–90: A Decade in Perspective, Arizona State University, Kerr Cultural Center, Tempe, Arizona; Tucson Museum of Art, Tucson, Arizona; and Metro Art International Competition (winner of Certificate of Excellence), New York City.

In the late 1970s, ML attended film school in Los Angeles and worked on productions at the American Film Institute. In 1990, she received her bachelor of fine arts degree from Prescott College, in Prescott, Arizona. In 2007, she received an advanced filmmaking degree from the Sedona Film School in Sedona, Arizona.

ML lives in southeast Utah and Arizona. She supports such grassroots organizations as Great Old Broads for Wilderness, Southern Utah Wilderness Alliance, Center for Biological Diversity, and the Rewilding Institute.

———

Diane Sward Rapaport, founder and president of Jerome Headlands Press, is a writer, editor, and publisher.

In the late 1960s, Rapaport was the first woman to be hired as an artist manager by Bill Graham's Fillmore Management. She turned down the job of managing the Pointer Sisters in 1974 with a new goal: to teach musicians business and help them control their own careers and avoid predatory business practices.

Rapaport is considered a pioneer of music business education in colleges and universities, writing and copublishing some of its first textbooks. She was among the first people to argue that university graduates with music degrees be given classes in copyright and business.

How to Make and Sell Your Own Recording catalyzed the independent recording industry and has sold more than 250,000 copies since its publication in 1979. *The Musician's Business and Legal Guide*, edited by attorney Mark Halloran, has sold more than 150,000 copies since its publication in 1992.

Her book *Home Sweet Jerome* (2014) is a history of Arizona's richest copper mining mecca, famous ghost city, and notorious hippie redoubt.

Rapaport edited activist Katie Lee's books about Glen Canyon. She has edited many books for Taoist Lineage Master Bruce Frantzis, including *Dragon and Tiger Medical Qigong* (2010), Taoist *Sexual Meditation: Connecting Love, Energy and Spirit* (2012), and *Tai Chi: Health for Life* (2006).

Rapaport graduated magna cum laude from Connecticut College in New London with a double major in English and history and earned a master's degree in renaissance literature from Cornell University in Ithaca, New York. She was an honorary Woodrow Wilson Scholar.

She lives in Hines, Oregon, where she works with a community water-planning collaborative to help slow the decline of water levels in a closed-basin aquifer due to overallocation of groundwater irrigation certificates and illegal wells.